LIVING WITH WISDOM

A Life of Thomas Merton

LIVING WITH WISDOM

A Life of Thomas Merton

JIM FOREST

ORBIS BOOKS
Maryknoll, New York 10545

Founded in 1970, Orbis Books endeavors to publish works that enlighten the mind, nourish the spirit, and challenge the conscience. The publishing arm of the Maryknoll Fathers and Brothers, Orbis seeks to explore the global dimensions of the Christian faith and mission, to invite dialogue with diverse cultures and religious traditions, and to serve the cause of reconciliation and peace. The books published reflect the views of their authors and do not represent the official position of the Maryknoll Society. To learn more about Maryknoll and Orbis Books, please visit our website at www.maryknollsociety.org.

Manufactured in the United States of America

Designed by Roberta Savage

Photo on p. ii:
Merton writing in a tool shed on the Abbey grounds.
(Photograph courtesy of Columbia University, Butler Library)

Library of Congress Cataloging-in-Publication Data

Forest, Jim.
  Living with wisdom : a life of Thomas Merton / by Jim Forest.
    p. cm.
  Includes bibliographical references and index.
  ISBN-13: 978-1-57075-754-9
1. Merton, Thomas, 1915-1968. 2. Trappists—United States—Biography.
3. Monks—United States—Biography. I. Title.
  BX4705.M542F665 2008
  271'.12502--dc22

                          2008012650

to
Tom Hassler-Forest

We have what we seek.
We don't have to rush after it.
It was there all the time,
and if we give it time
it will make itself known to us.

THOMAS MERTON

What more do I seek than this silence,
this simplicity,
this "living together with wisdom"?

THOMAS MERTON
Dancing in the Water of Life

If you want to identify me,
ask me not where I live,
or what I like to eat,
or how I comb my hair,
but ask me
what I am living for,
in detail,
and ask me what I think
is keeping me
from living fully
for the thing
I want to live for.

THOMAS MERTON
My Argument with the Gestapo

Contents

Preface: Meeting Merton   ix

A Few Words of Thanks   **xvii**

A Chronology of the Life of Thomas Merton   **xix**

Pax Intrantibus   **1**

Childhood   **5**

England   **17**

The Christ of the Icons   **25**

Cambridge   **32**

New York City   **38**

Gilson, Huxley, Blake, and Maritain   **49**

Conversion   **56**

Brother John   **61**

Saint Bonaventure's   **72**

The Court of the Queen of Heaven   **78**

Brother Louis   **85**

Thomas Merton versus Brother Louis   **92**

Father Louis   **100**

Abbey Forester   **111**

Containing the Divided Worlds   **120**

Waking from a Dream   **131**

A Hermitage on Mount Olivet   **140**

Hagia Sophia   **144**

Silencing   **155**

Pastor to Peacemakers   **167**

Monk in the Rain   **176**

Father Louis, Hermit   **184**

A Proverb Named Margie   **193**

A Member of the Family   **204**

Asia on My Mind   **213**

Everything Is Compassion   **222**

Jonas Overshadowed   **234**

Afterword   **241**

List of web links   **246**

Notes   **247**

Index   **255**

Permissions   **262**

Preface: Meeting Merton

As he did with so many others, Thomas Merton entered my life through the pages of his autobiography. In 1959, I was on Christmas leave from the Navy, waiting in the New York City Port Authority Bus Terminal, when I noticed a paperback copy of *The Seven Storey Mountain* for sale at the newsstand. The story of a young man who had become a monk seized my interest immediately. I bought the book and started reading.

In the bus going up the Hudson Valley, I would occasionally look up from the text to gaze out the window at the heavy snow that was falling that night. Merton's book has ever since been linked in my mind with the silent ballet that snow makes during its brief, swirling passage through street lights.

It was thanks to Dorothy Day, founder of the Catholic Worker movement, that I came into personal contact with Merton. Just a year after reading *The Seven Storey Mountain,* I was on leave from my Navy job at the weather bureau in Washington, DC, and had decided to spend my break with the Catholic Worker community in New York. My first few days were spent at Saint Joseph's House in Manhattan, but one day I was sent to the Catholic Worker's rural outpost on the southern tip of Staten Island, the Peter Maurin Farm. In the large, faded dining room of an old farmhouse, I found half a dozen people gathered around a pot of tea and a pile of mail at one end of a large table. Dorothy Day began reading letters aloud, pausing to comment and tell stories, as was so often her custom.

The only letter I still recall from that day's reading was one from Thomas Merton. It amazed me that Dorothy Day was among his correspondents. The Merton I had envisioned through reading *The Seven Storey Mountain* had withdrawn from "the world" with a slam of the door that had reverberated around the world. Dorothy Day, on the other hand, was as much in the world as the mayor of New York.

Merton told Dorothy that he was deeply touched by her witness for peace, which had several times resulted in arrest and imprisonment. "You are right going along the lines of *satyagraha* [Gandhi's term for nonviolent action; literally, the power of truth]," he wrote. "I see no other way. . . . Nowadays it is no longer a question of who is right but who is at least not criminal. . . . It has never been more true than now that the world is lost in its own falsity and cannot see true values."

Partly thanks to the influence of Merton and Dorothy Day, I applied for and received an early discharge from the Navy and, in the early summer of 1961, joined the Catholic Worker community in New York City. At the time, I thought it might be a stopping point on the way to a monastery.

Dorothy knew of my interest in Merton's book and the attraction I felt for monastic life. She began to share with me the letters she received from Merton. Then one day she gave me a letter of his to answer. He had sent her a poem about Auschwitz and the Holocaust that he had written during the Eichmann trial in Jerusalem, "Chant to Be Used around a Site for Furnaces." In his letter to Dorothy, Merton described it as a "gruesome" work. I wrote to tell Merton of our appreciation of the poem and our plans to publish it in the next issue. It would serve, I commented, as *The Catholic Worker*'s response to the Eichmann trial.

Not many days later I had a response from Merton in which he noted that we live in a time of war and the need "to shut up and be humble and stay put and trust in God and hope for a peace that we can use for the good of our souls." A letter to me from Thomas Merton! I could not have felt more elated had I received the map revealing the location of pirate gold.

Though I didn't realize it at the time, that single sentence revealed a great deal about the long-term struggles in which Merton was engaged. I thought what he said was aimed at me (how apt the advice was!), but, as was so often the case in his letters, he was addressing himself as well. He had enormous difficulty shutting up, feared he was lacking in humility, and often resisted staying put.

In December 1961, Merton suggested that perhaps I would like to come to the monastery for a visit. There was never any question in my mind about accepting, but first there was an issue of *The Catholic Worker* to get ready for publication — I had recently become the paper's managing editor — and also a night class in English literature at Hunter College to complete. I put off the trip to Kentucky until the beginning of February 1962.

I had no money for such a journey. Volunteers at the Catholic Worker received room and board plus small change for minor expenses, subway rides, and the like. I never dared ask even for a penny, preferring to sell *The Catholic Worker* on street corners in Greenwich Village, keeping a small portion of the proceeds for my incidental expenses (mainly bread, cheese, orange juice, beer and an occasional book), giving the rest to the community.

Confronted with a nearly empty wallet, I opted to travel by thumb. A companion on the Catholic Worker staff, Bob Kaye, joined me. Before sunrise one cold winter morning, we loaded up on Italian bread still warm from the oven of the Spring Street bakery and set off.

The going was slow. I recall standing in nighttime sleet at the side of a highway somewhere in Pennsylvania watching cars and trucks rush past, many of them with colorful plastic statues of an open-armed Jesus of the Sacred Heart on the dashboard. Sadly, this image of divine hospitality seemed to have little influence on those at the wheel behind the statue. It took us two and a half exhausting days to travel the eight hundred miles to the Abbey of Gethsemani.

Finally, we reached the monastery. After the guest master, Father Francis, showed us our rooms, my first stop was the monastery church. There was a balcony in the church that was connected to the guest house. Surviving such a trip, I found thanksgiving came easily, but my prayer was cut short by the sound of distant laughter so intense and pervasive that I couldn't resist looking for its source. I hadn't expected laughter at a penitential Trappist monastery.

The origin, I discovered, was Bob Kaye's room. As I opened the door the laughter was still going on, a kind of gale of joy. The major source was the red-faced man lying on the floor, wearing black and white robes and a broad leather belt, his knees in the air, hands clutching his belly. Though the monk was more well-fed than the broomstick thin, fast-chastened Trappist monk I had imagined, I realized instantly that the man on the floor laughing with such abandon must be Thomas Merton. His face reminded me of David Duncan's photos of Pablo Picasso — a face similarly unfettered in its expressiveness, the eyes bright and quick and sure, suggesting some strange balance between wisdom and mischief. (Merton once remarked that he had the face of a "hillbilly who knows where the still is.") And the inspiration for the laughter? It proved to be the intensely strong smell of feet that had been kept in shoes all the way from the Lower East Side to Gethsemani and were now out in the open air. If the Catholic Worker had manufactured a perfume, this would have been it.

After that weeklong stay at Gethsemani, *The Seven Storey Mountain* became a new and different book. No wonder that Merton had twice mentioned the films of Charlie Chaplin in its pages. Not only did I become aware that Merton was someone capable of hurricanes of laughter, but I learned that he was far from the only Trappist who knew how to laugh, though no other monk seemed to exhibit this trait quite so readily and explosively as Merton.

The abbot, Dom James, though a most hospitable man, was not initially quite so positive about a visitation of ragged Catholic Workers. In those days most American men were tidily trimmed, thanks to frequent haircuts, but, as far as Bob and I were concerned, haircuts were a massive waste of money. Merton apologetically explained that our shaggy hair did not please the abbot. If we were to stay on at the abbey, Dom James insisted we have haircuts. Merton hoped we wouldn't object. No problem, we replied. On our second morning at the abbey, we took turns sitting in a chair in the basement room where the novices changed into their work clothes. (Merton in denims could have been taken for a New York City taxi driver.) The room also served as a barber shop. While the novices stood in a circle laughing, a good deal of hair fell to the concrete floor. Going from one extreme to the other, Bob and I were suddenly nearly as bald as Yul Brynner.

After the haircut Merton took me to the abbot's office. I can no longer recall what the abbot and I talked about—perhaps about my conversion, or community life at the Catholic Worker—but I will never forget the solemn blessing Dom James gave me at the end of our conversation. I knelt on the floor near his desk while he gripped my skull with intensity and prayed over me. He had a steel grip. There was no doubt in my mind I had been seriously blessed. I have ever since had a warm spot in my heart for Dom James, a man who has occasionally been maligned by Merton biographers.

I recall another monk at the monastery who had much less sympathy for me and still less, it seemed, for Merton—or Father Louis, as Merton was known within the community. This was the abbey's other noted author, Father Raymond Flanagan, whose books were well known to Catholics at the time, though they had never reached the broad audience Merton's books had.

Merton and I were walking down a basement corridor that linked the guest house kitchen to the basement of the main monastery building. There was a point in the corridor where it made a leftward turn, and standing there, next to a large garbage container, was an older monk who was not so much reading as glaring at the latest *Catholic Worker,* which he held open at arm's length as if the paper had an unpleasant smell. There was an article of Merton's in it, one of his essays about the urgency of taking steps to prevent nuclear war. Father Raymond looked up, saw us coming his way, balled the paper up in his fist, hurled it into the garbage container, and strode away without a word, leaving a trail of smoke.

Once again, Merton's response was laughter. Then he explained that Father Raymond had never had a high opinion of Merton's writings and often denounced him at the community's chapter meetings. "In the early days Father Raymond said I was too detached from the world, and now he thinks I'm not detached enough." The tension between the two never abated. Even ten months before his death, Merton recorded in his journal a verbal attack by his brother monk, who was furious about Merton's opposition to the Vietnam War. (See *The Other Side of the Mountain: The Journals of Thomas Merton, 1967-68.*)

During that first visit I had my initial glimpse of Merton's openness to non-Catholics and, more strikingly, non-Christians. It happened the first evening I was there. There was a hurried knock on the door of my room in the guest house. Merton was standing there, but in a rush as he was late for Vespers. He wanted me to have the pile of papers in his hands, a collection of Jewish Hasidic stories that a rabbi had left with him a few days before. "Read these—these are great!" And off he hurried to Vespers without further explanation, leaving me with a collection of amazing tales of mystical rabbis in Poland generations before the Holocaust.

I recall another evening a day or two later when Merton was not in a hurry. He was in good time for Vespers and already had on the white woolen choir robe the monks wore during winter months while in church. It was an impressive garment, all the more so at close range. I reached out to feel it thickness and density. In a flash Merton slid out of it and placed it over my head. I was astonished at how heavy it was! Once again, Merton laughed. The robe met a practical need, he explained, as it was hardly warmer in the church than it was outside. Without it, the monks would freeze to death.

The guest master knew I was at the monastery at Merton's invitation and thought I might be able to answer a question which puzzled him, and no doubt many of the monks. "How did Father Louis write all those books?"

I had no idea, no more than he, but I got a glimpse of an answer before my stay was over. A friend at the Catholic Worker had sent a letter to Merton in my care. He urged Merton to leave the monastery and do something "more relevant," such as join a Catholic Worker community. (Over the years Merton received quite a few letters telling him that he was in the wrong place.) I was a little embarrassed to be delivering such a message.

What is most memorable to me about this particular letter was the experience of watching Merton the writer at work. He had a small office just outside the classroom where he taught the novices. On his desk was a large gray typewriter. He inserted a piece of monastery stationery and wrote a reply that seemed to issue from the typewriter at the speed of light. I had never seen anyone write so quickly, and with just four fingers. You will often see a stenographer type at such speed when copying a text, but even in a city newsroom one rarely sees actual writing at a similar pace.

I wish I had made a copy of his response. I recall Merton admitted that there was much to reform in monasteries and that monastic life was not a vocation to which God called many people, yet he gave an explanation of why he thought the monastic life was nonetheless an authentic Christian vocation and how crucial it was for him to remain faithful to what God had called him to. It was a very solid, carefully reasoned letter, filling one side of a sheet of paper, and was written in just a few minutes.

When I first met Merton, more than two years had passed since the Vatican's denial of his request to move to another monastery where he might live in greater solitude. By the time of my visit, he was able to spend part of his time in a newly built cinderblock building that stood on the edge of the woods about a mile north of the monastery. It had initially been intended as a conference center where Merton could meet with non-Catholic visitors, but he saw it primarily as his hermitage. Merton had lit the first fire in the fireplace several months before, on December 2. There was a small bedroom behind the main room. Merton occasionally had permission to stay overnight, but it would not be until the summer of 1965, three years later, that it became his full-time home. At that point he became the first Trappist hermit in modern times.

When I came to visit, the hermitage already had a lived-in look. It was winter, so there was no sitting on the porch. We sat inside, regularly adding wood to the blaze in the fireplace. There was a Japanese calendar on the wall with a Zen brush drawing for every month of the year and a black-on-black painting of the cross by Merton's friend Ad Reinhart. There was a bookcase and, next to it, a long table that served as a desk placed on the inside of the hermitage's one large window, which offered a view of fields and hills. A large timber cross had been built on the lawn. On the table was a portable Swiss-made Hermes typewriter. Off to one side of the hermitage was an outhouse which Merton shared with a black snake, a harmless but impressive creature.

What Merton took the most pleasure in when he showed me the hermitage was a sheet of parchment-like paper tacked to the inside of the closet door in his bedroom—a colorful baroque document such as one finds in shops near the Vatican: a portrait of the pope at the top in an oval with a Latin text below and many decorative swirls. In this case it was made out to "the Hermit Thomas Merton" and was signed by Paul VI.

During that visit, the latest copy of *Jubilee* arrived. *Jubilee* was a monthly journal edited by Ed Rice, Merton's godfather, with the collaboration of a small, committed staff of talented, underpaid colleagues, one of whom was Bob Lax. Merton was among the magazine's advisers, cheerleaders, and notable writers. In the years it existed, 1953 to 1967, *Jubilee* was unparalleled among religious magazines. There wasn't a single issue that failed to be arresting—impressive photo features plus some of the most striking typography of the time. The content was wide-ranging, with vivid glimpses of church life, portraits of houses of hospitality, profiles and interviews with remarkable people, and well-illustrated articles on liturgy, art, and architecture. In that particular issue was a set of photos of life in an Orthodox monastery. One of the photos showed a heavily bearded Athonite monk who looked older than Abraham. He was standing behind a long battered table in the refectory, while in the background was a huge fresco of the Last Judgment. The monk's head was bowed slightly. His eyes seemed to contain the cosmos. There was a remarkable vulnerability in his face. "Look at him," Merton said. "This guy has been kissed by God!"

My visit ended abruptly. A telegram came from New York with the news that President Kennedy had announced the resumption of atmospheric testing of nuclear weapons, thus another escalation of the Cold War and yet another indication that nuclear war might occur in the coming years. Anticipating such a decision, I was part of a group of New Yorkers who had planned to take part in an act of civil disobedience, a sit-in at the entrance of the Manhattan office of the Atomic Energy Commission, the federal agency responsible for making and testing nuclear weapons. The abbey provided money for our return to New York by bus rather than thumb. Not many days later, now with a slight stubble of hair, I was in a New York City jail known locally as "The Tombs."

Merton had played a part even in that event. I recall a letter from him, sent care of the Catholic Worker, hand-delivered to me during the hour or two that we sat on the frigid pavement awaiting arrest. (My monastic haircut made me interesting enough to be featured on the front page of *The New York Daily News* the following morning.)

There was to be another visit to the abbey two years later, in November 1964. By then I was working for a New York City newspaper while in my spare time helping lay the foundations of the Catholic Peace Fellowship, of which Merton had already become one of the advisers. A good deal of our correspondence during the last seven years of his life had to do with our shared concern with the issue of war and peace. Some extracts from Merton's letters appear later in this book.

It would be impossible for any author to write a book about Merton without giving attention to his extraordinary efforts to prevent another world war and to challenge Christians to a renewed appreciation of the example Christ has given us of a life free of violence. Yet one of the dangers of having known Merton through a common preoccupation is the temptation to overstress that interest while ignoring or slighting others. I hope this biography comes reasonably close to getting the balance right.

Whatever other labels one might apply to him—essayist, social critic, ecumenical explorer, poet, photographer, artist, correspondent—Merton was primarily a Christian monk. He spent far more time at Mass, in prayer, and in meditation than in writing books and letters or doing anything else likely to bring him to public attention. For much of his life as a monk, he carried various time-consuming responsibilities within the community, not least his years as master of novices. There was also the customary physical labor of the community in which he participated along with everyone else. The ordinary substance of life is what is inevitably most neglected in a biography; the stress is put on events rather than "non-events." But Merton was mainly interested in the latter.

There is a story of a nun who once received communion from Merton's hands. Rather than swallow the host, she placed it in a clear glass jar and afterward regarded it as a relic. It was not merely the Body of Christ, but had been touched by Thomas Merton! One hopes the story is apocryphal, but it does suggest a familiar problem—our human tendency to idealize, even idolize, those whom we admire. It is not the purpose of this biography to iron out the wrinkles in Merton or to imply that he was a flawless man. He would find the idea laughable. As he noted in a letter to a fellow monk who was in Rome at the time, "Anyone who imitates me does so at his own risk. I can promise him some fine moments of naked despair." Merton's inner contradictions and shortcomings are a major theme of his journals, substantial parts of which were included in books Merton edited for publication. As anyone familiar with his journals will know, what might be a major enthusiasm one day could well be the target of severe criticism a few days later. Merton never held an opinion half-heartedly. Neither did he always make good choices or act wisely. As he said in a letter to a friend in England, "The most difficult kind of ethic is the kind that impels you to follow what seems to be your own inner truth. And of course you always make plenty of mistakes that way." Like every monk, he confessed his sins at least once a week and found what he had to confess far from minor. He fell time and again. What is impressive in Merton's life was the determination he exhibited after each fall to get up and make a fresh start.

Inevitably a book of this size neglects much that was important in his life and writing. Nothing will please me more than to know that this book helped open the door to Merton's own writing and to some of the other books about him.

—Jim Forest

A Few Words of Thanks

This present work had its beginning in 1979 with a much smaller book—*Thomas Merton: A Pictorial Biography*—written at Don Brophy's suggestion for the Paulist Press.

Twelve years later, at the suggestion of Robert Ellsberg of Orbis Books, that abbreviated biography was rewritten and greatly expanded, becoming *Living with Wisdom*. Now, seventeen years later, it seemed to Robert that it would be a good moment to take a fresh look at the book and reissue it in a revised third revision, to be published in the year of the fortieth anniversary of Merton's death. My thanks to Robert, not only for publishing both editions of *Living with Wisdom,* but for all the time and care he invested in both manuscripts.

There are a great many other people who have in various ways participated in this project.

I have a special debt to Michael Mott, whose Bible-sized biography, *The Seven Mountains of Thomas Merton,* remains the most complete and detailed Merton biography, as well as a fine example of the writer's craft.

Thanks also to:

the late Bob Lax, Merton's dearest friend, for his advice, encouragement, and gentle presence;

Robert Giroux, James Laughlin, and Naomi Burton Stone for various Merton books they have sent me over the years;

Monsignor William Shannon not only for advice and encouragement over the years but for the insights in his book on Merton's spirituality, *Thomas Merton's Dark Path*;

Dom John Eudes Bamberger for his essay on Merton and Eastern Orthodoxy;

Sister Donna Kristoff for her essay on Merton and icons;

Brother Patrick Hart for many years of friendship and helpful responses to questions about Merton;

the late Robert Daggy, former director of the Merton Center in Louisville;

Paul Pearson, who now directs the Thomas Merton Center and patiently assisted me time and again as this book was being revised;

Robert O'Neill at Boston College and Kenneth Lohf at Columbia University for help with photos;

and to Bob Grip, who helped find errors in the manuscript of the previous edition.

Finally I bow to my wife, Nancy, beloved companion in prayer, reading, writing, parenthood, and pilgrimage.

— JF

A Chronology of the Life of Thomas Merton

1911   Merton's parents, Owen Merton (an artist who grew up in New Zealand) and Ruth Jenkins (an artist whose home was in the United States), met as art students in Paris.

1914   Owen and Ruth were married in London on April 7.

1915   Thomas Merton was born January 31 in Prades, France.

1916   Due to the First World War, in the summer Owen, Ruth and Tom moved from France to the USA, living at first with Ruth's parents, Sam and Martha Jenkins, in Douglaston, Long Island. That fall Owen and Ruth rented a four-room house in nearby Flushing, Queens.

1918   John Paul Merton was born November 2.

1921   Ruth Merton died from cancer October 3.

1922   Thomas Merton accompanied his father on a painting trip in Bermuda. Owen began an affair with the novelist Evelyn Scott.

1923   While Owen traveled in France and North Africa, Thomas stayed with his grandparents in Douglaston.

1925   Tom moved with his father to Saint Antonin-Noble-

Val, forty miles above Toulouse in the south of France. John Paul remained with his grandparents.

1926   Tom became a student at the Lycée Ingres in Montauban, France.

1927   Recovering from tuberculosis, Tom spent the summer with the Privat family.

1928   Tom moved with his father to the home of Maud Grierson Pearce, sister of Owen's mother, in Ealing, West London, England. In September he became a student at Ripley Court, a prep school in Surrey.

1929   Tom began his studies at Oakham Public School, seventy miles northwest of London. While with his father on holiday that summer, Owen was suddenly taken ill. Doctors diagnosed a malignant brain tumor.

1930   In light of Owen Merton's illness, Sam Jenkins made financial arrangements for his grandsons.

1931   Owen Merton died January 8 in London of a brain tumor. Thomas Bennett, a London physician and a close friend of Owen, was appointed Tom's guardian.

1932   During a hike along the Rhine Valley in Germany, Merton suffered a toe injury after being run off the road by young Nazis. Back at school in England, he nearly died of blood poisoning.

1933   Having graduated from Oakham in February, Tom visited Italy in the spring, with a long stay in Rome, then spent the summer in the U.S.A. before starting his studies at Clare College, Cambridge, in October. His concentration was on modern languages (French and Italian).

1934   After a difficult year at Cambridge, Merton left for the

U.S.A., living with his grandparents on Long Island. As he wasn't a U.S. citizen, he had to return to London to obtain a U.S. visa. This was his last visit to Europe. He sailed back to New York on November 29.

1935   In January Merton began his studies at Columbia University.

1936   Sam Jenkins, Merton's grandfather, died October 27.

1937   Martha Jenkins died August 16. Merton was appointed editor of Columbia's *1937 Yearbook* and art editor of the Columbia journal, *The Jester*.

1938   In February Merton received his Bachelor of Arts diploma in February, then entered Columbia's Graduate School of English where he began work on a thesis about William Blake. On November 16 he was received into the Catholic Church at Corpus Christi Church in Manhattan.

1939   In February Merton received a Master of Arts degree from Columbia for his study of "Nature and Art in William Blake." Merton was confirmed at Corpus Christi Church on May 25, taking the confirmation name "James."

1940   Merton took a job teaching English at St. Bonaventure University in Olean, New York. He began doing part-time volunteer work in Harlem at Friendship House. In April he went on an Easter trip to Cuba.

1941   In April Merton went to the Abbey of Our Lady of Gethsemani in Kentucky for an Easter retreat. On December 10, two days after resigning from his teaching position at St. Bonaventure's, Merton returned to Gethsemani. Three days later the abbot, Dom Frederic, accepted him as a postulant choir monk.

1942   On February 21, Merton was vested in the white robes of a novice and was given the monastic name Frater Maria Ludovicus (Brother Mary Louis). In July, his brother John Paul was baptized while visiting Gethsemani.

1943   In April John Paul Merton died of wounds sustained while fighting in World War II.

1944   On March 19, Merton took simple vows.

1947   On March 19, Merton took solemn vows, a lifetime commitment to remain a monk at the Abbey of Gethsemani. In June he was given a cell of his own for sleeping.

1948   Merton's autobiography, *The Seven Storey Mountain,* was published in October and quickly became a best-selling book.

1949   On May 26, Merton was ordained a priest. In December, Dom James assigned Merton to give orientation and introductory theology classes to the novices. *Seeds of Contemplation* was published the same year.

1951   Merton was appointed Master of Scholastics. In June he became a U.S. citizen. In October he was given the post of Abbey Forester. Publication of *The Ascent to Truth* and *No Man Is an Island.*

1952   As a place for writing and greater solitude, Dom James gave Merton use of a former toolshed. Merton called it St. Anne's.

1953   Publication of *The Sign of Jonas,* a book based on Merton's monastic journals.

1954   Publication of *Bread in the Wilderness.*

1955   Dom James offered Merton the possibility of becoming a full-time hermit living in a watchtower near the abbey. Instead Merton accepted appointment as Master of Novices.

1956   In July Merton traveled to Saint John's University in Minnesota to take part in a two-week seminar on psychiatry and its applications to religious life. *The Living Bread* was published.

1957   This was the year that marked the beginning of Merton's immersion in Russian literature and religious writing. *The Silent Life* was published.

1958   On March 18 what is sometimes called "Merton's epiphany at Fourth and Walnut" occurred in Louisville. In August Merton began his correspondence with Boris Pasternak. Publication of *Thoughts in Solitude.*

1960   In March Merton was given use of a more private cell within the abbey. The following month Merton received a priestly stole sent to him by Pope John XXIII. Also in April Merton proposed to Dom James the creation of a small house out of sight of the monastery that could function both as a center for ecumenical gatherings and also serve as a place of part-time seclusion for Merton. Permission having been given, construction began in October. Publication of *Disputed Questions* and *The Wisdom of the Desert.*

1961   "The Root of War Is Fear," an expanded essay based on a chapter from his new book, *New Seeds of Contemplation,* was published in *The Catholic Worker.* In the months that followed, essays highly critical of militarization and preparations for nuclear war appeared in various journals. Merton found himself being fiercely criticized. Publication of *The New Man.*

1962   In April Merton received a letter from Dom Gabriel
        Sortais in Rome, the Trappists' Abbot General, forbid-
        ding him to publish books or further essays on war and
        peace. However Dom James, Merton's abbot, gave
        Merton permission to publish both *Peace in the Post-
        Christian Era* and *Cold War Letters* in mimeographed
        editions that were widely circulated from hand to hand.
        Merton's "love affair" with photography began with the
        photos he took while visiting the Shaker community of
        Pleasant Hill in Kentucky.

1963   Late in the year, due to pain in his left arm and the base
        of his neck, Merton was a patient at Saint Joseph's
        Infirmary in Louisville. Publication of *Emblems of a
        Season of Fury.*

1964   Publication restrictions that had been imposed on
        Merton in 1962 were eased by the new Abbot General,
        Dom Ignace Gillet. In June Merton was given permis-
        sion to make a trip to New York to meet D.T. Suzuki,
        the Japanese Zen Buddhist scholar, with whom Merton
        had corresponded. In November Merton hosted a small
        retreat at Gethsemani for friends active in peace work.
        On December 15-16 Merton was permitted his first full
        day and night at the hermitage. Publication of *Seeds of
        Destruction.*

1965   On August 20 the Council of the monastic community
        formally decided that Merton was relieved of his
        responsibilities as Master of Novices and was now free
        to begin living full-time at the hermitage. Publication of
        Gandhi on Non-Violence, The Way of Chuang Tzu and
        Seasons of Celebration.

1966   Due to persistent back pain, on March 23 Merton
        entered Saint Joseph's Hospital in Louisville for spinal
        surgery. While recovering, he met and fell in love with
        a nurse. They managed to correspond and to meet

each other from time to time after Merton's return to the monastery. By October the relationship had ended. Publication of *Raids on the Unspeakable* and *Conjectures of a Guilty Bystander.*

1967   In May the Vietnamese monk and poet, Thich Nhat Hanh, spent two days at the abbey as Merton's guest. On July 16, Merton said his first Mass at the hermitage. In September Dom James announced his retirement as abbot, though he remained in office until January. In December Merton published the first of four issues of *Monks Pond,* a literary journal. *Mystics and Zen Masters* was published.

1968   In January Dom Flavian Burns was elected as Gethsemani's new abbot. In April a small chapel was added to Merton's hermitage. On September 11 Merton began what would prove to be his final journey. His route took him first to Christ of the Desert Monastery in New Mexico and then to Alaska. Before departing for Asia he had stops in Santa Barbara, Our Lady of the Redwoods, and San Francisco, all in California. On October 15 he flew to Asia, where his travels took him to India, Sri Lanka, and Thailand. He had three meetings with the Dalai Lama in early November. On December 3 he visited Polonnaruwa, Sri Lanka, where he saw the carving made in living rock of the sleeping Buddha. On December 10, while at a conference center near Bangkok, Merton died after giving a lecture at a meeting of Asian Benedictines and Cistercians. It was the 27th anniversary of his arrival at the Abbey of Gethsemani as an applicant monk. Three books were published that year: *Cables to the Ace, Zen and the Birds of Appetite* and *Faith and Violence.*

* * *

Pax Intrantibus

Hidden away in the farm country of Kentucky, in a region best known for sour-mash whisky and purebred horses, is a Trappist monastery set, in Thomas Merton's words, in a "very wide valley—full and rolling and dipping land, woods, cedars, [and] dark green fields."

Unlike the monumental ancient abbeys in Europe, no one visits the Abbey of Our Lady of Gethsemani to admire the stonework or gaze at the architecture. The collection of stone, brick, and wooden buildings could hardly be plainer. The inhabitants, once you adjust to their black and white robes, are similarly plain. It is the life the Trappists lead that is astonishing.

The Trappists are a branch of Benedictine monasticism, following the Rule of Saint Benedict written in the sixth century. In the eleventh century, at the time of the Cistercian reform movement, Benedict's rule had been more strictly interpreted, and then still more rigorously applied by the abbot of La Trappe in France, Abbé Armand-Jean de Rancé, founder of the order of Cistercians of the Strict Observance. Opting for plainness, the Cistercians were wary of the decorative arts. Our Lady of Gethsemani in Kentucky had been founded by monks sent over from France in 1848. It wasn't until 1935, with the election of Dom Frederic Dunne, that the monastery had its first American-born abbot.

In the days of Latin liturgy, there were two Latin

Opposite:
The gateway to the Abbey of Gethsemani as it was in 1940. (Photograph courtesy of the Abbey of Gethsemani Archives)

1

words painted over the monastery gateway: *Pax intrantibus*—Peace to all who enter. The words were well established in that location on December 10, 1941, when an inconspicuous man with a bland face, blue eyes, and thinning, sandy hair arrived from New York.

Thomas Merton must have read the words over the gateway with a fine sense of irony. Gleeful man that he could be on solemn occasions, perhaps he laughed. It was only three days since the Japanese attack on America's Pacific fleet at Pearl Harbor and only two days since America's entry into World War II. Lines of young men were waiting their turn at thousands of draft and recruiting offices, over the doors of which another Latin motto could appropriately have been painted: *Bellum intrantibus*. War to all who enter.

Here he was, marching off like so many others, but by himself, out of step, and in the wrong direction.

Many of his compatriots would have found his approach to such a gateway a scandalous sight. A coward, obviously. A man indifferent to Nazi armies and exploding homes. But an unlined face can be misleading, and a monastery is rarely an escape hatch. The young Merton was not unaware or on the run. He was well acquainted with the streets of London, now full of demolished buildings and pitted with bomb craters. For years, awareness of the war in Europe and its horrors had eaten away at his soul as acid rain chews limestone.

The peace he sought in the monastery wasn't safe seclusion. He had come to the Abbey of Gethsemani partly because he was convinced that the places where prayer is the main business of life are not at the edge of history but at the center, and that he could do more for peace from here than on any battlefield. He was at the monastery gate for the same reason others were signing up as soldiers: to put his life on the line.

But there were other aspects to his motives. Unlike many who were marching off to battle, he believed that there was little the world treasures that was worthwhile.

From volunteer work in Harlem, he knew about slums and the human face of racism. After years of being an outsider in France, England, and America, he felt little connection with flags and the idolatries they represent. The world's clamor had made many deaf to conscience. Merton longed to leave the noise behind, even the noise of his own typewriter with which he had previously sought to tap out an identity. He wanted to leave behind his name and every claim to a place in the world.

Much that he came for, he found: a silent and austere life; a life of prayer and worship; a community trying to live for God. But not anonymity. In less than a decade, Merton's writings would be talked about from soup kitchens to the papal apartments in the Vatican. His autobiography and a parade of other books, translated into many languages, would be read not only by Catholics and other Christians, but also by Jews, Buddhists, Hindus, Muslims, and many with no religious labels. His writing would occasion conversion for many thousands of readers.

Exactly twenty-seven years later he would die, on the other side of the planet but still a monk of this abbey, by then not only famous but also controversial. His essays on war and racism would have brought accusations that he was a Communist disguised in monastic robes. For a time his monastic superiors would have silenced him, though vindications followed, among them gifts from two popes and publication by one of them, John XXIII, of an encyclical that could have been written by Merton: *Pacem in Terris (Peace on Earth)*. In that decade of assassinations, some would say his death wasn't an accident but murder, and blame it on the CIA.

Pax intrantibus.

The young Merton rang the bell and waited. An old monk showed his face. "I want to be a monk," said the visitor from New York.

Above:
Thomas Merton with "Aunt Kit," his father's sister, during a surprise visit to Gethsemani in 1961. (Photograph courtesy of Boston College, Burns Library)

Thomas Merton in his infancy at Prades in the French Pyrenees. (Photograph courtesy of the Thomas Merton Center)

"On the last day of January 1915, under the sign of the Water Bearer, in a year of a great war, and down in the shadow of some French mountains on the borders of Spain, I came into the world. Free by nature, in the image of God, I was nevertheless a prisoner of my own violence and my own selfishness, in the image of the world into which I was born."

(The Seven Storey Mountain)

Childhood

Mother wanted me to be independent, and not to run with the herd.

THOMAS MERTON
The Seven Storey Mountain

Thomas Merton was born during a snowstorm late on the last day of January 1915 in Prades, an ancient town in the French Pyrenees not far from the Spanish border. The First World War had begun just a few months earlier. "Not many hundreds of miles away from the house where I was born," Merton wrote in his autobiography, "they were picking up the men who rotted in the rainy ditches among the dead horses and the ruined seventy-fives, in a forest of trees without branches along the river Marne."[1]

Prades was and remains a place of beauty. The house in

Church of St. Pierre in the main square of Prades. (Photograph by Jim Forest)

Merton's parents, Ruth and Owen.
(Photograph courtesy of the Thomas
Merton Center)

which Merton was born was just two blocks from the town's main square, with a church dedicated to Saint Peter on one side. Behind the house was a narrow, deep garden. Merton's father, Owen, had his art studio on the top floor.

Not far to the south of Prades, along a road climbing the south side of Mount Canigou, were the ruins of a large Benedictine monastery, Saint Michel de Cuxa, that had been founded about 878 and lasted until 1791, the time of the French Revolution. Later in life, Merton would wonder if being born near such an abbey was a factor in his later becoming a monk.

Merton's parents had met in 1911 as art students in Paris. Both in their mid-twenties, Ruth Jenkins had grown up in Ohio in the American Midwest, Owen Merton in New Zealand. They married in London in April 1914, two months before their move to Prades.

It was an artist's attraction to southern light, inexpensive living, and the presence of friends nearby that had brought the Mertons to Prades, but in the summer of 1916 the war chased them to America to take shelter in the home of Ruth's parents, Sam and Martha Jenkins. The house was in Douglaston, Long Island, a commuter ride from Sam's editorial offices at Grosset & Dunlap in Manhattan. That fall Owen and Ruth rented a dilapidated four-room house in Flushing, Queens, five miles from Douglaston. Two of the rooms were "barely larger than closets."[2]

Owen was an artist of considerable talent. His paintings, his son later observed, expressed a vision of the world that was "sane, full of balance, full of veneration for structure, for the relations of masses and for all the circumstances that impress an individual identity on each created thing." His vision "was religious and clean."[3] But Owen's sales were rare, and the family lived close to destitution. Ruth's father was well-off and eager to help, but Ruth and Owen's pride allowed no familial philanthropy. Owen worked as a gardener, was the organist at a nearby church, and played the piano at a local movie theater in the days before sound tracks.

Tom's parents held radical convictions, among them dedication to simple living and pacifism. Owen had no intention of getting fitted for a uniform and learning how to use a bayonet. Immune to the recruiting posters, military songs, and rhetoric about the "war to end all wars," he continued to paint, but found America did little to bring his brushes to life. Ruth had been drawn to the Quakers. On Sundays she went to the Friends Meeting House, where she was certain not to hear any words in praise of war.

Though Ruth had given up painting, her artist's eye is apparent in photos she took of Tom. In one of them her son is sitting in a child's chair, using the seat of an adult chair as a desk. The photo has an icon quality: life haloed in light.

What appealed to her most about Tom was what she

Thomas Merton, age four, as photographed by his mother. (Photograph courtesy of Boston College, Burns Library)

"I was nobody's dream child. I have seen a diary Mother was keeping in the time of my infancy and first childhood, and it reflects some astonishment at the stubborn and seemingly spontaneous development of completely unpredictable features in my character, things she had never bargained for: for example, a deep and serious urge to adore the gas-light in the kitchen, with no little ritualistic veneration, when I was about four. Churches and formal religion were things to which Mother attached not too much importance in the training of a modern child. . . ."

(The Seven Storey Mountain)

recorded in such photos—an early reader capable of intense concentration. But often she found him a difficult, stubborn child who, it seemed to Merton as he looked back on his childhood, failed to meet her expectations.

Merton remembered Ruth as a "slight, thin, sober little person with a serious and somewhat anxious and very sensitive face . . . worried, precise, quick, critical," a mother of "insatiable dreams and of great ambition for perfection,"[4] which he couldn't, or wouldn't, live up to. "Mother wanted me to be independent, and not to run with the herd. I was to be original, individual, I was to have a definite character and ideals of my own. I was not to be an article thrown together, on the common bourgeois pattern, on everybody else's assembly line."[5]

At age five, his mother sent him to bed early for refusing to spell *which* with the first *h*. "In the natural order, perhaps solitaries are made by severe mothers," he noted later in life.[6]

Tom's younger brother, John Paul, born November 2, 1918, was more placid. "Everyone was impressed by his constant and unruffled happiness," Merton remembered, without his older brother's "obscure drives and impulses."[7]

Merton recalls his father as being more serene. "He was a man of exceptional intellectual honesty and sincerity and purity of understanding," wrote Merton from the monastery, "a man with a wonderful mind and a great talent and a great heart." He took no interest in spelling. In common with Ruth, he wanted to keep Tom's mind "uncontaminated by error and mediocrity and ugliness and sham."[8]

Then the first great tragedy in Tom's life occurred. In the summer of 1921 doctors discovered that Ruth had cancer of the stomach. In October, on her deathbed in a

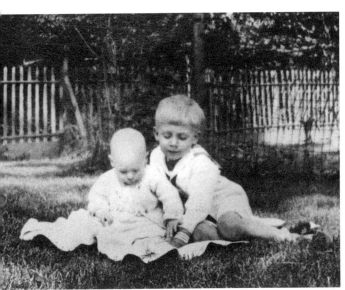

Tom and his baby brother John Paul. (Photograph courtesy of the Thomas Merton Center)

Opposite:
Ruth Jenkins Merton. (Photograph courtesy of the Thomas Merton Center)

"My mother was an American. I have seen a picture of her as a rather slight, thin, sober little person with a serious and somewhat anxious and very sensitive face. And this corresponds with my memory of her—worried, precise, quick, critical of me, her son."

(The Seven Storey Mountain)

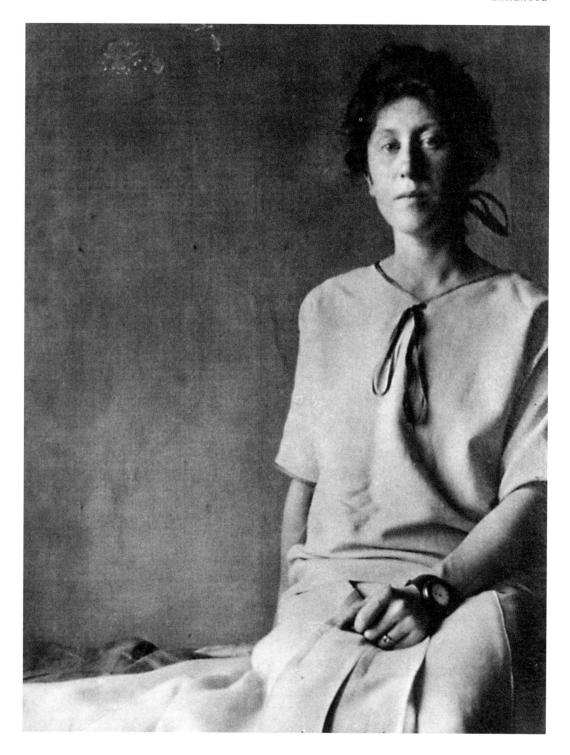

Young Tom. (Photograph courtesy of the Thomas Merton Center)

New York hospital, she wrote Tom to say good-bye. Because of hospital rules prohibiting visits by children, he wasn't allowed to see her in her last condition. "I took the note out under the maple tree in the backyard," Merton remembered, "and worked over it, until I made it all out, and had gathered what it really meant. And a tremendous weight of sadness and depression settled on me."[9] Soon after, her body cremated, there was nothing left of her but some heavy locks of red hair clipped when she was a child, now folded away in tissue paper, and her two sons: Tom, age six, and John Paul, three.

Having to cope without Ruth, Owen was willing to let her parents play a more active role in Tom and John Paul's lives. Before long Tom began to accompany his father on travels that took the two of them first to Cape Cod and then to Bermuda, places not yet trampled by tourism.

Owen not only felt at home in the Caribbean light, but fell in love with a novelist, Evelyn Scott. She was married to another artist, Owen's friend Cyril Kay Scott. A *ménage à trois* developed that lasted for nearly two years. A factor in its eventual collapse was Merton's antipathy to Evelyn Scott. "Little Tom *hated* me," she confided.[10]

Owen's bohemian freedom was shared with Tom. While John Paul was going to school on Long Island, his older brother was living a classroom-free existence, combing beaches and listening to sailors' jokes and stories.

"It is almost impossible to make much sense out of the continual rearrangement of our lives and our plans from month to month in my childhood," Merton reflected in adulthood. "Sometimes I had to go to school, sometimes I did not. Sometimes Father and I were living together, sometimes I was with strangers and only saw him from time to time. People came into our lives and went out of our lives. We had now one set of friends, now another. Things were always changing." He briefly attended school on Bermuda and then, without parental objection, dropped out, preferring sand dunes to blackboards. "I could run where I pleased, and do whatever I liked, and life was very pleasant."[11] It was only in 1923, when Owen's travels took him to France and then North Africa, that Tom was left in Douglaston.

The publishing company of Grosset & Dunlap, where "Pop" Jenkins, Tom's grandfather, worked, was a place that smelled of typewriters and paper. With its shelves of children's books, it seemed to Tom nearly as good a place to be as Bermuda.

Pop Jenkins's breakthrough in publishing had been to develop a line of books featuring numerous still photos from popular films. Jenkins indeed loved movies, a passion he passed on to his grandchildren. He had friends in Hollywood. Talk of the private lives of the stars featured at the table of the Jenkins household. In those days Long Island was a major center of movie making. At the Bayside Studios near Douglaston, Tom watched Gloria Swanson play the bride in a gypsy wedding scene. But comedy was more to his taste. Take after take, Tom witnessed W. C. Fields stagger down the steps of a tumbledown house, blunder through the bushes, and finally land on top of two cows.

While Sam and Martha Jenkins belonged to the local Episcopal church, Pop's views on religion, as far as Tom could make out, had mainly to do with what he wasn't: a Catholic or a Jew. Catholics, said Pop, were hypocrites and crooks, and Jews were nearly as bad. *Vatican* was a swear word.

An event that provided one of Merton's most haunting childhood memories occurred in Douglaston when he was eight. As the older brother, Tom was regarded with awe by John Paul, but for Tom the younger brother was a competitor and nuisance. One day Tom and two friends made a hut of scrap lumber and tar paper in the woods, a strictly private preserve off-limits to kid brothers. Stones were hurled at nonmembers who dared venture too close. A quarter century later, after subsequent events had sharpened the poignancy of the memory, Merton still recalled John Paul standing in a field a hun-

Thomas Merton with his younger brother, John Paul. (Photograph courtesy of the Thomas Merton Center)

"I suppose it is usual for elder brothers, when they are still children, to feel themselves demeaned by the company of a brother four or five years younger, whom they regard as a baby and whom they tend to patronize and look down upon." (The Seven Storey Mountain)

St. Antonin, the town where Thomas Merton and his father lived after his mother's death. (Photograph courtesy of Boston College, Burns Library)

"Here in this amazing, ancient town, the very pattern of the place, of the houses and streets and of nature itself, the circling hills, the cliffs and trees all focused my attention upon the one important central fact of the church and what it contained. Here, everywhere I went, I was forced by the disposition of everything around me, to be always conscious of the church. Every street pointed more or less inward to the center of the town, to the church."

(The Seven Storey Mountain)

dred yards away, "a little perplexed five-year-old kid in short pants and a kind of a leather jacket, standing quite still, with his arms hanging down at his sides, and gazing in our direction, afraid to come any nearer on account of the stones, as insulted as he was saddened, his eyes full of indignation and sorrow. And yet he does not go away . . . his tremendous desire to be with us and to do what we are doing will not permit him to go away. The law written in his nature says that he must be with his elder brother, and do what he is doing: and he cannot understand why this law of love is being so wildly and unjustly violated in his case."[12]

Early in 1925, after the collapse of his relationship with Evelyn and a grave illness he had contracted in Algeria (probably the first manifestation of the tumor that eventually killed him), Owen Merton had an exhibition of his paintings in London. At last, his work was being praised by such critics as Roger Fry. Owen returned to Douglaston with money, a beard, and an aura of triumph. After a few months in the Jenkins household, Owen decided the time was ripe for a return to France, taking Tom but leaving John Paul—deemed too young—in Douglaston. It must have been a hard blow for John Paul, far worse than being excluded from Tom's clubhouse. In August Owen and Tom set sail.

The new Merton home was in Saint Antonin-Noble-Val, forty miles above Toulouse in the south of France, a well-preserved medieval town whose geography and architecture still bore witness to an earlier age of faith.

"The town itself," Merton remembered, "was a labyrinth of narrow streets, lined by old thirteenth-century houses, mostly falling into ruin. . . . There was nothing left of the color and gaiety and noise of the Middle Ages. Nevertheless, to walk through those streets was to be in the Middle Ages."[13]

Like so many old European towns, its convergence point was the church. Its bell tower dominated the town. Daily life was punctuated by the ringing of the Angelus bells at 6 AM, noon, and 6 PM, "reminding people of the Mother of God who watched over them."[14] The church and even the countryside beyond the town walls seemed to announce: "This is the meaning of all created things: we have been made for no other purpose than that men may use us in raising themselves to God, and in proclaiming the glory of God."[15]

In the mountains, the two Mertons occasionally wandered in the ruins of monasteries, refreshed by "those clean, ancient stone cloisters, those low and mightily rounded arches hewn and set in place by monks."

There were encounters with people who embodied

A street sign in present-day St. Antonin marks the lane on which the two Mertons, father and son, lived and commemorates the town's most famous writer. (Photograph by Jim Forest)

13

faith, especially a Catholic family—the Privats, solid Auvergne peasants of Celtic descent—with whom Tom stayed during the summer of 1927. Merton remembered them for their kindness, their goodness, their peacefulness, their simplicity, and their devout silence about things sacred. Once, trying to prod them into defending their Catholic faith, he told them that the difference between one religion and another was no more significant than different methods of learning arithmetic. All he could get from Monsieur Privat was a quiet and sad sentence, *"Mais c'est impossible."*

Merton eventually came to regard the Privats as saints, not canonized church heroes but the invisible kind sanctified by leading ordinary lives in a God-centered way. They were "among the most remarkable people I ever knew."[16] It seemed to Merton, looking back, that their home smelled of heaven. He credited their anxious concern for his soul with making him aware that he had a soul.

It was only late in life that Tom discovered the reason for his long stay with the Privats and why, while at school, he had so often spent time in the infirmary: a doctor in Saint Antonin had discovered Tom had tuberculosis. While taking care not to alarm his son with news that he was gravely ill, Owen had arranged with the Privats to provide the rest and care needed to nurse Tom back to health.[17]

If the Privat home had the peace of heaven, the residential boarding school Tom attended in Montauban, twenty-five miles to the southwest of Saint Antonin, seemed to him, as he looked back on it from the monastery, as more closely resembling hell: a fiercely secular environment in which to hard-boil the brain. The adult Merton regarded such secular schools as typical. "Is it any wonder that there can be no peace in a world where everything possible is done to guarantee that the youth of every nation will grow up absolutely without moral and religious discipline, and without the shadow of an interior life, or of that spirituality and charity and

faith which alone can safeguard the treaties and agreements made by governments?"[18]

Nonetheless, bright boy that he was, Tom learned. He was soon speaking French like a native, including a good many words never used in print. In his autobiography, he accused the Lycée of being an academy of flippancy and cynicism, but later in life, no longer needing to see his past in such black-and-white terms, he fondly remembered Monsieur Delmas, a teacher who had introduced him to the writings of Fénelon.[19] It was while studying in Montauban that Tom Merton began to see himself as a writer. He found a circle "of more or less peaceful friends" who had "more wit than obscenity about them. . . . They had ideals and ambitions and, as a matter of fact, by the middle of the first year, I remember we were all furiously writing novels."[20]

It was during those three years in France that Tom began to glimpse his father's religious faith. "I shall never forget," he wrote in *The Seven Storey Mountain*, "a casual

Merton (top row, left) with classmates at his boarding school in Montauban. (Photograph courtesy of the Thomas Merton Center)

"Contact with that wolf-pack felt very patently like contact with the mystical body of the devil: and, especially in the first few days, the members of that body did not spare themselves in kicking me around without mercy."

(The Seven Storey Mountain)

15

Owen Merton. (Photograph courtesy of Boston College, Burns Library)

"Of us all, Father was the only one who really had any kind of faith. And I do not doubt that he had very much of

it . . . he was a man of exceptional honesty and sincerity and purity of understanding . . . a man with a wonderful mind and a great talent and a great heart: and what was more, he was the man who had brought me into the world, and had nourished me and cared for me and had shaped my soul and to whom I was bound by every possible kind of bond of affection and attachment and admiration and reverence: killed by a growth on his brain."

(The Seven Storey Mountain)

remark Father happened to make in which he told me of Saint Peter's betrayal of Christ, and how, on hearing the cock crow, Peter went out and wept bitterly. . . . We were just talking casually, standing in the hall of the flat we had taken. . . . I have never lost the vivid picture I got, at that moment, of Peter going out and weeping bitterly."[21]

He recalled on another occasion his father's indignation with a woman speaking hatefully of a neighbor. "He asked her why she thought Christ had told people to love their enemies. Did she suppose God commanded this for His benefit? Did he get anything out of it that he really needed from us? Or was it rather for our own good that he had given us this commandment? He told her that if she had any sense, she would love other people if only for the sake of the good and health and peace of her own soul."[22]

England

I believe in nothing.

The Seven Storey Mountain

Owen Merton arrived in Montauban one day in May 1928 to withdraw Tom from class and give him the news that they were moving to England. An exhibition of his paintings was being mounted in London. Owen had reluctantly decided that there were better prospects in Britain for both father and son. Leaving France was a defeat for Owen but a liberation for his thirteen-year-old son. No more Lycée! "How the light sang on the brick walls of the prison whose gates had just burst open before me."[23]

Aunt Maud and Uncle Ben had invited them to live in their red brick house, "a fortress of nineteenth-century security,"[24] in Ealing, West London. For Tom the house's great treasure was his Aunt Maud—Maud Grierson Pearce, sister of Owen's mother—a sprightly and meek lady who dressed as if Queen Victoria's Diamond Jubilee had occurred only yesterday. Her pointed nose and her thin smiling lips suggested the expression of one who had just finished pronouncing, "How nice!"[25]

Shortly after their arrival Tom confided to Aunt Maud his hope of becoming a writer. "What sort of writing," she asked. "Stories," he said. "No doubt you could do that quite well," Maud assured him, "but you ought to keep in mind that writers often find it difficult to pay their bills. Perhaps you could be a journalist as well?" Merton agreed. "A foreign correspondent?" she suggested. "Perhaps," he said.

"Then, after that, the channel steamer, Folkestone cliffs, white as cream in the sunny haze, the jetty, the grey-green downs and the line of prim hotels along the top of the rock: these things all made me happy."

(The Seven Storey Mountain)

Tom's schooling resumed at Ripley Court in Surrey. The headmistress was Aunt Maud's sister-in-law. He felt at home with chapel prayer and Anglican ritual, finding "many occasions of praying and lifting up my mind to God." It was "the first time I had ever seen people kneel publicly by their beds before getting into them, and the first time I had ever sat down to meals after a grace. . . . For about the next two years I think I was almost sincerely religious."[26] In his autobiography, however, perhaps looking back too critically, he regarded his adolescent sojourn in the Church of England less as an experience of sacramental life than an exploration of English social tradition.

Tom's major academic project at Ripley Court was to acquire enough Latin to make a decent showing in scholarship exams for public school. There were hopes in the family that, despite his bohemian origins, Tom might be accepted at an elite school such as Harrow. Sam Jenkins, his grandfather in America, was prepared to pick up the tab. But in the end Oakham was selected, "an obscure but decent little school in the Midlands," seventy miles northwest of London in Oakham.[27]

In the shelter and tranquility of Ripley Court, life had seemed as secure as Hobbiton in Tolkien's mythical Middle Earth. Then, while on Scottish summer holiday in 1929 with his father, Tom's world collapsed once more. Owen was suddenly taken ill. Doctors had discovered a malignant brain tumor. His life was at risk and his sanity affected. "ENTERING NEW YORK HARBOR. ALL WELL," said a telegram Owen sent to Tom from a London hospital.

At Oakham that fall Tom read Chaucer's *Canterbury Tales* and labored over Greek verbs in the shadow of his father's tumor. The chapel life that had blossomed for him at Ripley Court abruptly perished. Merton later credited this partly to the school chaplain, a man who liked to insert the word *gentleman* into biblical texts. The first verse of chapter 13 in Paul's first letter to the Corinthians became: "If I talk with the tongues of men and angels, and be not a gentleman, I am become as

Oakham, the English public school where Merton was enrolled.
(Photograph courtesy of Oakham School)

"Oakham, Oakham! The grey murk of the winter evenings in that garret where seven or eight of us moiled around in the gaslight, among the tuck-boxes, noisy, greedy, foul-mouthed, fighting and shouting!"

(The Seven Storey Mountain)

sounding brass." This celebration of correct manners and gentlemanliness had nothing to offer the son of a man whose father was on his deathbed.

"St. Peter and the other Apostles would have been rather surprised," Merton wrote as a monk, "at the concept that Christ had been scourged and beaten by soldiers, cursed and crowned with thorns and subjected to unutterable contempt and finally nailed to the Cross and left to bleed to death in order that we might all become gentlemen."[28]

In the chapel Tom kept a tight-lipped silence when other students recited the Creed. Angry at God for his father's illness, his counter-creed was "I believe in nothing."

Meanwhile, Sam Jenkins was making practical provisions for his grandsons. When he came to England in the summer of 1930 to explain what he had arranged, Tom was astonished to find himself the possessor of stock in Grosset & Dunlap, the owner of land on Long Island, and, with John Paul, possessor of Stone Island off the coast of Maine. On top of this, there would be an allowance for Tom from now on, to be dispensed by Tom's godfather, Dr. Thomas Bennett in London. Bennett, a family friend, was in charge of Owen's treatment; he later became Tom's guardian. Wanting to offer Tom a symbol of passage into the adult world, Pop Jenkins presented the fifteen-year-old Tom with a pipe and a pouch of Saint Julian tobacco.

Tom's residence when away from school was now the Bennett flat at 2 Mandeville Place in London's West End. A wealthy, cosmopolitan world opened its doors to Tom. The Bennetts' French maid brought him breakfast in bed. With money jingling in his pocket, he became a steady customer at many bookshops and began building a significant collection of jazz records. Whole days were spent at the movies.

"I discovered [as part of the Bennett household] that one was not only allowed to make fun of English middle-class notions and ideals but encouraged to do so.... I soon developed a habit of wholesale and glib detraction of all the people with whom I did not agree or whose taste and ideas offended me."[29]

In a climate of cultivated sarcasm and refined open-mindedness, it was hard for Merton to grasp the fine distinction between behavior that was admired in books and one's actual behavior. "I did not see ... that [the Bennetts'] interest in D. H. Lawrence as art was, in some subtle way, disconnected from any endorsement of his ideas about how a man ought to live. Or rather, the distinction was more subtle still ... it was between their interest in and amusement at those ideas, and the fact, which they took for granted, that it was rather vulgar to practice them the way Lawrence did. This was a distinction which I did not grasp until it was too late."[30]

Surrounding the Bennetts' island of affluence and good taste was the Great Depression, in which many were perishing. The beggars on London's streets gave Tom pause for thought.

It was not only the poor of England who caught his eye. In regard to India, his sympathies were with Gandhi. The Salt March and the campaign that followed it had resulted in the Round Table Conference. Gandhi was in England, providing the British public with the spectacle of a national leader who chose to live in London's slums, refused to eat meat, had a goat in his entourage, and wore next to nothing. He was, for Tom and for all of England, "a small, disquieting question mark."[31] In the fall of 1930, Tom took Gandhi's side in a formal school debate, arguing that India had every right to demand Britain's withdrawal. The opposing view—that the Indians were backward, pagan people, incapable of governing themselves—carried the day, thirty-eight to six.[32]

Owen Merton remained at the Middlesex Hospital in London. By the summer of 1930 he was on a bed of silence, a huge lump on his bandaged head and stripped of the ability to speak. Yet Tom discovered his father's eyes were full of recognition and clarity. Tom wept, and Owen wept with him.

Tom saw suffering as "a raw wound for which there was no adequate relief." In the context of war, disease, starvation, and death, all that he had heard at chapel services seemed meaningless. "You had to take it, like an animal," it seemed to Tom, avoiding what you can, and numbing yourself to the rest. "The truth that many people never understand, until it is too late," he commented later, "is that the one who does the most to avoid suffering is, in the end, the one who suffers most. . . . It is his own existence, his own being, that is at once the subject and the source of his pain, and his very existence and consciousness is his greatest torture."[33]

Within the family, it was only Owen who was able to make something of his calamity and, despite his excom-

Mahatma Gandhi.

"I remember arguing about Gandhi in my school dormitory: chiefly against the football captain, then head prefect. . . . I insisted that Gandhi was right. . . . Such sentiments were of course beyond comprehension. How could Gandhi be right when he was odd?"

(Seeds of Destruction)

"I sat there in the dark, unhappy room, unable to think, unable to move, with all the innumerable elements of my isolation crowding in upon me from every side: without a home, without a family, without a country, without a father, apparently without any friends, without any interior peace or confidence or light or understanding of my own— without God, too, without heaven, without grace, without anything."

(The Seven Storey Mountain)

munication from words, was even able to communicate a vision of eternal life to Tom. One day Tom found Owen drawing again, expressing in images the interior pilgrimage he was making. Owen's drawings, Tom recalled, "were unlike anything he had ever done before—pictures of little, irate Byzantine-looking saints with beards and great halos."[34]

In his months of desperate illness and pain Owen had found his way to pre-Reformation Christianity with its more image-centered spirituality, about which no one in the family knew anything. The one thing that was clear to Tom was that his dying father was a profoundly religious man. "Behind the walls of his isolation, his intelligence and his will ... were turned to God, and communed with God." He was finding a way "to understand and make use of his suffering for his own good, and to perfect his soul."[35]

The icons Owen had drawn were his last "words" before entering a deeper silence. On January 18, 1931, just after Tom returned from a Christmas trip to Strasbourg, France, Owen Merton died. Eleven days short of his sixteenth birthday, Tom had become an orphan.

At the time, Tom could make nothing of his father's death. For a couple of months he was sad and depressed. He coped by focusing his considerable energies on study, making rapid headway in languages—Latin, Greek, French, German, and Italian—and reading until a pair of reading glasses was needed. During the Easter holiday he managed a brief, inconsequential visit to Rome. It was a solitary trip, as were most of his walks while at school or in London.

He later regarded this period of his life, too severely, as a season of complete flattening. "It was in this year," he remembered, "that the hard crust of my dry soul finally squeezed out all the last traces of religion that had ever been in it. There was no room for any God in that empty temple full of dust and rubbish which I was now so jealously to guard against all intruders, in order to devote it to the

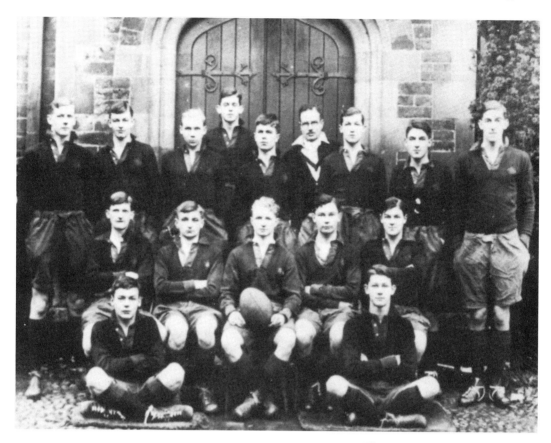

worship of my own stupid will. And so I became the complete twentieth-century man . . . a true citizen of my own disgusting century: the century of poison gas and atomic bombs. A man living on the doorsill of the Apocalypse."[36]

In fact his head wasn't quite as empty as he claimed in the high relief of his autobiography. Among other things, 1931 was the year his love for the poems of William Blake began. Seven years later, Blake became the subject of Merton's graduate studies at Columbia.

That summer Tom traveled to America for a stay with his brother and grandparents, falling intensely in love aboard ship on the way, and on the way back sharing the ship with some detectives, a gangster, a notorious playboy, and a crowd of students from Vassar and Bryn Mawr with whom he ran up a sizeable bar bill. "I cannot

Thomas Merton (top row, third from left) with his Oakham rugby team.
(Photograph courtesy of Oakham School)

"There was no rowing at Oakham, since there was no water. But the chaplain had been a rowing 'blue' at Cambridge, in his time. He was a tall, powerful, handsome man, with hair greying at the temples, and a big English chin, and a broad uncreased brow, with sentences like 'I stand for fair-play and good sportsmanship' written all over it."

(The Seven Storey Mountain)

"For it had become evident to me that I was a great rebel. I fancied that I had suddenly risen above all the errors and stupidities and mistakes of modern society . . . and that I had taken my place in the ranks of those who held up their heads and squared their shoulders and marched into the future. . . . The only future we seem to walk into, in actual fact, is full of bigger and more terrible wars, wars well calculated to knock our upraised heads off of those squared shoulders."

(The Seven Storey Mountain)

tell which is the more humiliating," he wrote in his auto-biography, "the memory of the half-baked adolescent I was in June or the glib and hard-boiled specimen I was in October when I came back to Oakham."[37]

During his weeks of travel, he decided he was an *ex officio* Communist. It was a time when Communism had become fashionable even among those coming from well-to-do homes. Tom had purchased a copy of the *Communist Manifesto*, found it more or less agreeable, and for a time kept it on view in his room, a stage prop indicating that a revolutionary was in residence. Photos of Greco-Roman Venuses took the place of movie star pin-ups.

He felt he had at last grown up. "I fancied that I had suddenly risen above all the errors and stupidities and mistakes of modern society—there are enough of these to rise above, I admit—and that I had taken my place in the ranks of those who held up their heads and squared their shoulders and marched into the future." Unfortunately, the "only future we seem to walk into," he remarked in his autobiography, "is full of bigger and more terrible wars, wars well calculated to knock our upraised heads off those squared shoulders."[38]

Liberty and independence were key words for him, qualities he exercised in ways that occasionally brought sharp reproofs from Tom Bennett. "I believed in the beautiful myth about having a good time so long as it does not hurt anybody else."[39]

Tom's literary gift having been noticed during the first year at Oakham, he became editor, and often illustrator, of *The Oakhamian* that fall. It was in that role that he had his first encounter with censorship: a colorful piece he had written about New York City reached print in grayer shades.

The Christ of the Icons

Without knowing anything about it, I became a pilgrim.

Thomas Merton
The Seven Storey Mountain

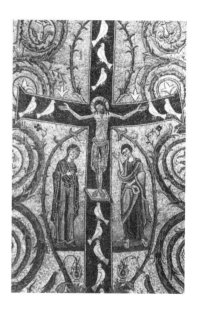

Mosaic of the crucifixion from the Basilica of San Clemente, Rome.

In the spring of 1932 Merton set off to go walking along the Rhine, an excursion that happened to coincide with Hitler's campaign for the chancellorship of Germany. Along the way he witnessed German villagers hurling bricks and fighting with pitchforks as political passions spilled over. The trip took a dangerous turn one morning when, while walking down a quiet country road lined with apple orchards, Merton was nearly run down by a car full of young Nazis "screaming and shaking their fists ... future officers of the SS."[40] Merton dived into a ditch in the nick of time, the car's amused occupants showering him with Hitler campaign leaflets as they passed.

Pain in one toe cut his holiday short. Back in London, Merton didn't bother to ask his physician-guardian, Tom Bennett, to look at the aching toe, but by the time he was back at Oakham the soreness got worse. A few days later he found himself hampered not only by his toe, but suffering a toothache. A dentist extracted a tooth, which turned out to be the cork capping an infection that had spread throughout Tom's body. The toe had become gangrenous. His body was full of poisoned blood.

For weeks Merton was in a sanatorium, during the first days barely conscious. He expected to die and viewed the prospect with absolute detachment. "As I lay in bed, in my weariness and pain and disgust, I felt for a moment the shadow of another visitor pass into the

room. It was death that came to stand by my bed. . . .
What did I think? All I remember is that I was filled
with deep and tremendous apathy. I felt so sick and disgusted that I did not very much care whether I lived or
died. . . . As far as I can recall, the thought of God did not
even enter my mind."

In fact death seemed quite a suitable revenge on life.
Merton was convinced of the ultimate meaninglessness of
life. He recovered but took no immediate pleasure in it.

In the summer he stayed with John Paul and his
grandparents in a mammoth hotel at the English resort
of Bournemouth where a summer romance brought on
emotional storms and long, solitary walks on the Dorset
downs. After that he packed his rucksack and went
camping by himself in the New Forest, savoring the
nighttime noises of frogs and streams.

In September his examination results arrived. He had
won a place at Clare College, Cambridge, to be taken up
the following fall. He left Oakham in December, and in
February 1933 he set off on an extended holiday in Italy.

What his close encounter with death hadn't done,
Rome did. For the first time since his father's fatal illness,
Merton—now eighteen—began to feel a pulse in his soul
and a longing to pray. The usual sights were not what
moved him. His adolescent opinions in high gear, he dismissed much of the city's ancient statuary as "vapid, bor-
ing, [and] semi-pornographic."[41] Nor was he impressed
with the ecclesiastical monuments of the Renaissance
and Counter-Reformation that he had first sought out as
a dutiful tourist reading his Baedeker guidebook. What
astonished him were the city's most ancient churches in
which so much of the art of Christianity's first millennium was still to be seen.

"I was fascinated by these Byzantine mosaics. I began
to haunt the churches where they were to be found,
and . . . all the other churches [among them Saints
Cosmas and Damian, Santa Maria Maggiore, Santa
Sabina, the Lateran, and Santa Costanza] that were more

*"The mosaics told me more than I had
ever known of the doctrine of a God of
infinite power, wisdom and love Who
had yet become Man, and revealed in
His Manhood the infinite of power,
wisdom and love that was His Godhead.
Of course I could not grasp and believe
these things explicitly. But since they
were implicit in every line of the picture
I contemplated with such admiration and
love, surely I grasped them implicitly. . . .
And so I could not help but catch something of the ancient craftsman's love of
Christ, the Redeemer and Judge of the
world."*

(The Seven Storey Mountain)

or less of the same period. . . . Without knowing any-thing about it, I became a pilgrim."[42]

Christ the Judge from the Basilica of San Clemente.

The icons that so arrested Merton were windows through which he felt Christ's gaze. The experience was his first glimpse of a life rooted in Christianity. As he later wrote, as a young monk:

> For the first time in my whole life I began to find out something of who this Person was that men call Christ. It was obscure, but it was a true knowledge of Him. But it was in Rome that my conception of Christ was formed. It was there I first saw Him, Whom I now serve as my God and my King, and who owns and rules my life. It is the Christ of the Apocalypse, the Christ of the Martyrs, the Christ of the Fathers. It is the Christ of Saint John, and of Saint Paul, and of Saint Augustine and Saint Jerome

and all the Fathers, and the Desert Fathers. It is Christ God, Christ King.[43]

Again and again in his later life, Merton sought to put into words what it was about icons that continued to touch him so profoundly. In letters written in 1967 and 1968, not long before his death, he explained to a Quaker correspondent that he wasn't drawn to a Christ who was merely a historical figure possessing "a little flash of the light" but to "the Christ of the Byzantine icons" who "represents a traditional experience formulated in a theology of light, the icon being a kind of sacramental medium for the illumination and awareness of the glory of Christ within us. . . . What one 'sees' in prayer before an icon is not an external representation of a historical person, but an interior presence in light, which is the glory of the transfigured Christ, the experience of which is transmitted in faith from generation to generation by those who have 'seen,' from the Apostles on down. . . . So when I say that my Christ is the Christ of the icons, I mean that he is reached not through any scientific study but through direct faith and the mediation of the liturgy, art, worship, prayer, theology of light, etc., that is all bound up with the Russian and Greek tradition."[44]

During his stay in Rome, books by D. H. Lawrence, previously much valued by Merton, suddenly seemed to him as shallow as movie posters. Eager to understand iconography, he bought a Vulgate edition of the Bible. Perhaps he remembered his father's efforts to interest him in the Bible when he was ten.

"I read more and more of the Gospels, and my love for the old churches and their mosaics grew from day to day." He realized their attraction wasn't simply his appreciation of the aesthetics of iconography, but a profound sense of peace he experienced within the walls in which the icons were housed. He felt a "deep and strong conviction that I belonged there."[45]

As the days passed, he found this sense of belonging

was true even in churches that had no Byzantine mosaics. "One of my favorite shrines was that of Saint Peter in Chains, and I did not love it for any work of art that was there, since the big attraction, the big 'number,' the big 'feature' in that place is Michelangelo's Moses. But I have always been extremely bored by that horned and pop-eyed frown. . . . Perhaps what attracted me to that Church was the Apostle himself to whom it is dedicated."[46]

Alone one night in his *pensione* room on the corner of Via Sistina and Via Tritone, trying to record in his journal his thoughts about Byzantine icons, he sensed his father's presence. The experience was over in a flash, "but in that flash, instantly, I was overwhelmed with a sudden and profound insight into the misery and corruption of my own soul. . . . And now, I think for the first time in my whole life, I really began to pray . . . praying

"There was something else that attracted me [to the churches of Rome]: a kind of interior peace. I loved to be in these holy places. I had a kind of deep and strong conviction that I belonged there: that my rational nature was filled with profound desires and needs that could only find satisfaction in churches of God."

(The Seven Storey Mountain)

St. Peter's Square, the Vatican. (Photograph courtesy of Maryknoll archives)

Interior, Basilica of Santa Sabina.
(Photograph by Jim Forest)

"I went to the Dominican's church, Santa Sabina. And it was a very definite experience, something that amounted to a capitulation, a surrender, a conversion, not without struggle, even now, to walk deliberately into the church with no other purpose than to kneel down and pray to God."

(The Seven Storey Mountain)

out of the very roots of my life and my being, and praying to the God I had never known."[47]

No doubt Merton recalled the icon drawings that his father had been making while close to death. Now, having been face-to-face with icons surviving from the church's early centuries, Tom felt stricken to tears by the state of his soul and overwhelmed by the need to pray. At the same time, he felt his father's closeness, "as real and startling as if he had touched my arm or spoken to me."

The next day, Merton climbed the Aventine Hill to visit Santa Sabina, one of Rome's oldest churches. Once inside, he knew that he had to pray there. It was impossible to play the guidebook-studying tourist any longer. Yet prayer in a public place was intensely embarrassing. Tom, age eighteen, regarded himself as urbane and sophisticated. "That day in Santa Sabina, although the church was almost empty, I walked across the stone floor mortally afraid that a poor devout old Italian woman was following me with suspicious eyes."[48] Despite his self-consciousness, he managed to cross himself with blessed water as he entered the church and then, kneeling at the communion rail, to recite the Our Father over and over again. For all his fears and embarrassment, he walked out of Santa Sabina feeling reborn. His final week in Rome was a time of discovery and joy such as he hadn't known in years.

These had been important days, but Merton's experiences in Rome were slow in bearing fruit. From Italy he went on to the United States for a family visit. He had his newly purchased Bible with him, but the embarrassment he had felt in Santa Sabina still haunted him. He read the Gospels surreptitiously, afraid someone would make fun of him. Nonetheless he quietly began to window-shop for a church. Despite the magnetic pull he had felt in the churches of Rome, anti-Catholic prejudices were widespread and had not left him untouched. Merton tried the Zion Episcopal Church, to which Sam and Martha Jenkins belonged and where his father had once been organist, but the service only irritated him, although later, when he was a student at Columbia, he returned to Zion Church and got to know the pastor, Dr. Lester Riley.[49] He next went to a Quaker Meeting in Flushing, where his mother had once prayed and meditated. He enjoyed the periods of silence while they lasted, but was annoyed by what one member had to say about the virtues of the Swiss. What had so astonished him in the ancient churches of Rome wasn't here. He didn't return.

The religious awakening in Rome seemed to fade out. In Chicago for the World's Fair, Merton got a job as barker for a striptease show called "The Streets of Paris." After the complex sexual reticence of England and the ornate eroticism of France, he found the undisguised and sweaty frankness of the American variety refreshing.

Back in New York, he joined the artist Reginald Marsh, a friend of his father's, in making the rounds of burlesque houses in Manhattan and Coney Island—places since immortalized by Marsh's art work. These were Marsh's cathedrals, where life was coarse but real. Marsh loved to draw the large-eyed, lonely men hungering for the lithesome young women beyond the footlights.

At the summer's end, Merton sailed back to England minus his Bible, his memories of prayer in Rome dormant.

Cambridge

Stab me with swords and shower my head with garbage at the horror and embarrassment I feel upon remembering Cambridge in May 1934. I would rather be instantly dead than do one thing or say one sentence or think one thought that I was likely to have been happy about at that time.

THOMAS MERTON
Run to the Mountain: The Journals of Thomas Merton, 1938-1941

Cambridge suggests England at its most attractive: beautifully proportioned classical architecture, dons in academic gowns, bright young men and women boating on the River Cam along banks crowded with daffodils, choirs singing Evensong in churches that seem to connect heaven and earth. But what Merton long remembered was the scent of decay during the "nadir of winter darkness."[50]

The bleakest year of his life began with his arrival at Clare College, Cambridge, in October 1933.

Merton found lodgings on Bridge Street. Two friends from Oakham, Ray Dickens and Andrew Winser, had rooms nearby. During their first months at Cambridge, ignoring church, the three enjoyed late Sunday morning breakfasts together. By throwing bread crumbs to ducks swimming in the River Cam just below Ray Dickens's window, they tested Pavlov's theories of conditioned behavior. If Merton prayed at all, it was a guilty secret. "When I was at Cambridge," he recalled in 1964, "I was precisely the kind of person who finds the Church unintelligible."[51] Yet, despite occasional passionate denials, religious issues remained among his interests.

Merton soon acquired companions at Cambridge who were listed by the proctor for "conduct unbecoming a gentleman." Anything but tame and shy, these "were the ones who made all the noise when there was a 'bump supper.'" Merton wrote. "We lived in the Lion Inn. We fought our way in and out of the Red Cow."[52]

In his autobiography, Merton asks, "Shall I wake up the dirty ghosts under the trees of the Backs [an area along the Cam behind the colleges], and out beyond the Clare New Building and in some rooms down on Chesterton Road?"[53]

The book as published let the ghosts slumber, leaving Merton's readers to wonder what was left unsaid. At the time, it seemed prudent to both Merton and his monastic superiors to leave out the more scandalous events in his life.[54] In an earlier draft of *The Seven Storey Mountain* manuscript, Merton wrote: "There would certainly be no point whatever in embarrassing other people with the revelation of so much cheap sentimentality mixed up with even cheaper sin. And besides, I have been told not to go into all that anyway. So that makes everything much simpler."[55]

One has to recall that in 1948, when *The Seven Storey Mountain* was published, neither *Playboy* nor anything like it was on sale at the average newsstand. Even a work of literature like James Joyce's *Ulysses* was still widely regarded as an obscene book. Merton's readers had to take his word for it that he was guilty of unspecified mortal sins "more powerful than any explosive."[56]

November 14, 1933, was a date that haunted Merton for the rest of his life, figuring in poems, journals, and especially his unpublished autobiographical novel, "Labyrinth," written in 1939. Though the section describing the main events of that night have disappeared, Merton's friend and literary agent, Naomi Burton, remembers the lost pages as describing a drunken party at

Opposite:
71 Bridge Street, where Merton lived for a time in Cambridge. (Photograph by Barry Gardiner)

Above
A page from the manuscript of "The Labyrinth," Merton's unpublished autobiographical novel. (Courtesy of the Thomas Merton Center)

"With every nerve and fibre of my being I was laboring to enslave myself in the bonds of my own intolerable disgust. There is nothing new or strange about the process. But what people do not realize is that this is the crucifixion of Christ, in which He dies again and again in the individuals who were made to share the joy and the freedom of His grace, and who deny Him."

(The Seven Storey Mountain)

Cambridge at which one of the students agreed to be nailed to a cross. "In the drunken chaos that followed," writes Michael Mott, describing Burton's recollections, "everything seemed so out of control that the mock crucifixion came close to being a real one."[57] In the text, the narrator is nearly arrested by the Cambridge police.

Circumstantial evidence suggests that what was described in the novel's lost pages actually occurred, and that it happened to Merton. On Merton's U.S. certificate of naturalization, issued in 1951, the only "visible distinctive mark" listed was a scar on the palm of his right hand. Naomi Burton recalls noticing the scar in the early sixties. With obvious embarrassment, Merton referred to it as his "stigmata."[58]

"There is certainly an odd way in which the word 'crucifixion' clings to [Merton's] references to Cambridge," Mott comments.[59] There is one such passage in Merton's novel, *My Argument with the Gestapo*, where the candles on a church altar seem to say to the book's Merton-like protagonist: "Your pride was not the world's fault, but yours, because you were the one who finally consented to be proud. Look now where the Crucifixion flowered in London like a tree, and the wounds were made in Cambridge, red as oleanders."[60]

Merton's poem "The Biography" opens in Cambridge and is about his participation in Christ's suffering and parallel crucifixion:

> *Although my life is written in Christ's Body like a map,*
> *The nails have printed in those open hands*
> *More than the abstract names of sins,*
> *More than the counties and the towns,*
> *The names of streets, the numbers of the houses,*
> *The record of the days and nights,*
> *When I have murdered Him in every square and street.*
> *Lance and thorn, and scourge and nail*
> *Have more than made His Flesh my chronicle . . .*[61]

It was a hellish interval in Merton's life, "an incoherent riot of undirected passion,"[62] said Merton; a time of "beer, bewilderment and sorrow," said his friend, Bob Lax.[63]

One factor in the events of Merton's time at Cambridge may have been the death that November of his beloved Aunt Maud Pearce. Merton had now been orphaned three times over: mother, father, and now his great aunt. "They committed the thin body of my Victorian angel to the clay of Ealing, and buried my childhood with it," he recalled. The England he had once seen through the eyes of her simplicity was buried with her. "I had fallen through the surface of old England into the hell, the vacuum and the horror that London was nursing in her avaricious heart."[64]

Drinking heavily, Merton became one of the more desperate undergraduates at Cambridge. And he lost his virginity.

Merton had been reading Freud, Jung, and Adler, struggling to understand, insofar as hangovers allowed, "the mysteries of sex-repression."[65] It seems there was very little sex repression in his life that winter. He later

Clare College, Cambridge. (Photograph by Jim Forest)

"Perhaps to you the atmosphere of Cambridge is neither dark nor sinister. . . . But for me, with my blind appetites, it was impossible that I should not rush in and take a huge bite of this rotten fruit. The bitter taste is still with me after not a few years."

(The Seven Storey Mountain)

"God in His mercy was permitting me to fly as far as I could from His love but at the same time preparing to confront me, at the end of it all, and in the bottom of the abyss, when I thought I had gone farthest away from Him."

(The Seven Storey Mountain)

recalled to a friend that his initial sexual experience was with a prostitute he encountered in Hyde Park, London. He claimed to have learned Hungarian in bed. There was a woman he saw from time to time in Cambridge who was known as "the freshman's delight."

In a journal entry written in 1965 he confessed, "I suppose I am the person who lived for a while at 71 Bridge Street, Cambridge. . . . And Clare was my College, and I was a damned fool, sitting on the steps of the boat house late at night with Sylvia."[66]

The details remain hidden, but, whether by Sylvia or someone else, he had fathered a child. Later on he told a few close friends that lawyers had been brought in and a legal settlement made with the baby's mother. (In later years there were rumors that mother and child were killed in the Blitz, but at least as late as early 1944, Merton believed they were alive. A will he wrote that February directs that half his estate should go to Tom Bennett, to be passed on "to the person mentioned to him in my letters, if that person can be contacted."[67])

Even before Merton's year at Clare College, Bennett's relationship with Merton had been under strain. Bennett had sent him an irate letter during his Italian sojourn the previous summer, pointing out that Merton had been spending money too quickly and too carelessly. Because of his rowdy late-night behavior when coming down to London from Clare, Tom was no longer welcome at the Bennett flat and had to sleep in a hotel. It was Bennett who had the irksome job of arranging the settlement for Merton's paternity.

Bennett's letters, Merton recalled, "got sharper as they went on, and finally, in March or April, I got a curt summons to come to London." After a long interval in Bennett's waiting room, Merton was received with "devastating coolness" and told to explain. "My tongue would hardly function. And the words I murmured about my 'making mistakes' and 'not wanting to hurt others' sounded extremely silly and cheap."[68] The break with his godfather was, for Tom, yet another experience of familial loss, this time not caused by death but by an act of rejection. Merton never met his guardian again.[69]

Thirty years later, writing in his journal, Merton looked back on his days at Cambridge with greater compassion than had been possible when he was a younger monk. "I suppose I regret most my lack of love, my selfishness and glibness (covering a deep shyness and a need for love) with girls who, after all, did love me, I think, for a time. My great fault was my inability, really, to believe it."[70]

For all its sorrows, Merton's year at Cambridge wasn't a total loss. Perhaps the high point was Professor Edward Bullough's class on Dante's *Divine Comedy*. Canto by canto, Merton had read his way to the frozen core of hell, at last ascending through purgatory toward the radiance of heaven. Merton's initial irritation with the poet's medieval theology gradually gave way to gladness as he followed "the slow and majestic progress of the myths and symbols in which Dante was building up a whole poetic synthesis of scholastic philosophy and theology." Reading Dante was, Merton said, "the one great benefit I got out of Cambridge."[71]

It was the *Purgatorio*'s seven storey mountain of painful ascent to heaven that later gave Merton the primary metaphor for his autobiography.

During the summer of 1934, while Merton was staying in America at the Jenkins home at Douglaston, Bennett wrote to urge his ward not to return to England. Because of poor academic results, he pointed out, Merton was sure to lose his scholarship. Even if Sam Jenkins was willing to pay the tuition to keep Tom at Clare, he had no chance of ever getting into the British diplomatic service. The sensible thing to do, Bennett advised, was to stay in America with his grandparents.

"It did not take me five minutes to come around to agreeing with him."[72] Merton felt like Br'er Rabbit being hurled into the briar patch.

Thomas Merton's passport photo at the time of his arrival in the United States. (Photograph courtesy of the Thomas Merton Center)

"Lady, when on that night I left the Island that was once your England, your love went with me, although I could not know it, and could not make myself aware of it. And it was your love, your intercession for me, before God, that was preparing the seas before my ship, laying open the way for me to another country."
(The Seven Storey Mountain)

New York City

You found yourself saying excellent things that you did not know you knew, and that you had not, in fact, known before.

THOMAS MERTON
The Seven Storey Mountain

"Did I know that my own sins were enough to have destroyed the whole of England and Germany? There has never been a bomb invented that is half so powerful as one mortal sin."

(The Seven Storey Mountain)

Though his mother had been an American citizen, Tom wasn't. After his summer on Long Island, he had to return to England to apply for permission to live in America. Back in London in late October, he filled out the forms and got the visa. No reconciliation with Tom Bennett occurred, nor, sadly, did it happen in later years. On November 29, 1934, sailing aboard the Auconia, Merton left Europe for the last time.

The Europe the nineteen-year-old Merton abandoned that winter "was a sad and unquiet continent, full of forebodings."[73] Mussolini had been leading a fascist regime in Italy since 1922. Hitler had become chancellor of Germany in 1933. The smell of another world war was in the air. Merton felt "the cold steel of the war-scare in my vitals."[74]

Taking stock of the events at Cambridge while at sea made him miserably aware that another sort of war was being waged within himself. All he had been trying to do that year was to enjoy himself without hurting anyone, yet nothing had worked out the way it was supposed to. "Everything I had reached out for turned to ashes in my hands. . . . I myself, into the bargain, had turned out to be an extremely unpleasant sort of person—vain, self-centered, dissolute, weak, irresolute, undisciplined, sensual, obscene and proud. I was a mess."

He felt the desperate need to apologize, even to confess, but weighing against that was the conviction that

Thomas Merton as he appeared in the Columbia Yearbook of 1939.
(Photograph courtesy of Boston College, Burns Library)

"Externally (I thought) I was a success. Everybody knew who I was at Columbia. Those who had not yet found out, soon did when the Yearbook came out, full of pictures of myself. It was enough to tell them more about me than I intended, I suppose. They did not have to be very acute to see through the dumb self-satisfied expression in all those portraits."

(The Seven Storey Mountain)

"confession is ill-bred, and embarrassing to everyone concerned in it." After all, as he later wrote in *My Argument with the Gestapo*, confession implies there is such a thing as sin, far from a trendy word. "Sin was a morbid concept, and if you had it in your mind, this concept would poison you entirely and you would go crazy."[75]

In the course of a stormy Atlantic crossing, his back to Rome as well as London, Merton toyed with a more rational conversion than had attracted him the day he prayed in Santa Sabina. If religion had been dismissed as irrelevant and ridiculous, Marxism was widely regarded as a kind of practical science.

Along with a variety of dissident movements, in a

Thomas Merton in the Columbia quadrangle around 1939. (Photograph from the Columbia University Yearbook, courtesy of the Thomas Merton Center)

"My active part in the world revolution was not very momentous. It lasted, in all, about three months. . . . I decided that it would be wiser if I just remained a 'fellow-traveler.' The truth is that my inspiration to do something for the good of mankind had been pretty feeble and abstract from the start. I was still interested in doing good for only one person in the world—myself."

(The Seven Storey Mountain)

vague way Merton had identified with Communism for the past two years, as did so many others at the time. The Soviet Union was widely seen as a place where an oppressive old regime had been swept aside and a new order set up in which everyone had a fair share and a job: no Great Depression, no evictions, no homeless people sleeping under bridges. Reports of concentration camps, torture, and executions were dismissed as propaganda invented by those who feared the collapse of a social order in which they happened to benefit. Despite press photos he had seen of immense propaganda posters "hanging over the walls of the world's ugliest buildings in Moscow," Merton was one of the many who embraced the idea that the Soviet Union was the refuge of "true art" while Europe and America were in the grip of "bourgeois ugliness." In the circles in which Merton was traveling, Communism was in fashion.

One of the attractive features of Communism was that it absolved him of personal responsibility for what he had done in Cambridge. "It was not so much I myself that was to blame for unhappiness, but the society in which I lived. . . . I was the product of my times, my society and my class . . . spawned by the selfishness and irresponsibility of the materialistic century in which I lived."[76]

Intellectually pardoned, and determined to turn himself in a new direction, he resolved to devote himself to helping build a new social order symbolized by the red flag. "I had my new religion all ready for immediate use"[77] and was primed to enter the fray against capitalism and to clear the ground for the classless society.

His later religious conversion did not occasion a different attitude toward capitalism. "We live in a society," he reflected in *The Seven Storey Mountain*, "whose whole policy is to excite every nerve in the human body and keep it at the highest pitch of artificial tension, to strain every human desire to the limit and to create as many new desires and synthetic passions as possible, in order to cater to them with the products of our factories and printing presses and movie studios and all the rest."[78]

New York seemed better suited to revolutionary striving than London. Radical winds would certainly blow more easily at ritual-free Columbia University, "full of light and fresh air," than at tradition-bound Cambridge. Making his way to the concrete campus past piles of dirty snow, he signed up for modern language and literature courses that would in time result in a degree and open the way for him to find work as a journalist. During the summer he had tried to find work as a reporter. The editors who interviewed him told him to finish his university studies before reapplying.

In some ways Merton's life at Columbia wasn't alto-

"When the time came for me to take spiritual stock of myself, it was natural that I should do so by projecting my whole spiritual condition with the sphere of economic history and the class struggle. In other words, the conclusion I came to was that it was not so much I myself that was to blame for my unhappiness, but the society in which I lived."
(The Seven Storey Mountain)

Statue in Columbia quadrangle.
(Photograph by Robert Ellsberg)

"Who is this man who does not have to fake and cover up a big gulf of ignorance by teaching a lot of opinions and conjectures and sudden facts that belong to some other subject? Who is this that really loves what he has to teach, and does not secretly detest all literature, and abhor poetry, while pretending to be a professor of it! His classes were literally 'education' – they brought things out of you, they made your mind produce its own explicit ideas."

(The Seven Storey Mountain)

Mark Van Doren, professor of English Literature at Columbia, who impressed and influenced Merton. (Photograph courtesy of Columbia University)

gether different than it had been at Cambridge. At parties he played the piano with wild enthusiasm, sang rowdy songs, and drank his way into many hangovers.

But there were big differences. One was that he no longer lived in his own apartment, accountable only to himself, but was part of his grandparents' household, commuting to Manhattan from Long Island. Another contrast was in the classroom. Merton rejoiced in the informality that reigned between student and teacher in America.

As the months passed, Merton was increasingly impressed that the "big sooty factory"[79] of Columbia University had on its faculty a man who was capable of teaching his students how to enter the heart of a book and how to tell a good book from a bad one: Mark Van Doren. It was partly thanks to Van Doren's first-term class in English literature that Merton discovered what was real in himself. Merton had just turned twenty. Van Doren had a special gift for posing the right question. "You found yourself saying excellent things," Merton recalled, "that you did not know you knew, and that you had not, in fact, known before. He had 'educed' them from you by his question. His classes were literally 'education'—they brought things out of you, they made your mind produce its own explicit ideas."[80] Resisting current ideological fads, Van Doren refused to trim Shakespeare to fit Marxist or Freudian patterns. He didn't want his students simply to parrot his views, but to help them find the center within themselves. He had little patience for a student who claimed he had no ideas of his own. Surely anyone old enough to be at Columbia had been in love, experienced rejection, encountered death?

It was partly thanks to Van Doren that Merton's enthusiasm for Communism dried up as quickly as it did, though not all at once. In making that move, he had to swim against the tide. Many Columbia students were Communists or at least well disposed to Communism. They controlled the student newspaper and were a lively presence on campus. Merton joined a few picket lines, carrying posters with such messages as "Books, Not Battleships." During a student peace strike, he gave a speech on Communism in England, about which he knew practically nothing, but at least he still possessed an authentic English accent. He sold some pamphlets and magazines.

One evening Merton attended a party in the Park Avenue apartment of a student whose wealthy parents were away for the weekend. "What a place for a machine-gun nest," said one of the aspiring revolutionaries.[81]

That same evening Merton signed up as a member of the Young Communist League. In those days members got "Party names" in order to hide their real identity. Merton became Frank Swift. "Swift" may have been for the writer Jonathan Swift; earlier in the evening there had been a debate as to whether or not Swift had been an atheist.[82] At the one and only meeting of his cell group that he subsequently attended, the main item for discussion was why Comrade X was missing meetings. It was the fault of Comrade X's father, it was decided. Utterly bored, Merton left early, walking into the fresh air of night. Frank Swift drowned in a glass of beer at a nearby bar—"a sweet moment of silence and relief."[83]

Merton began to develop a critique of Communism. Part of the problem for Merton was that the Communist Party was only sporadically anti-war. It was anti-war in 1935, the brief period when Merton was seriously attracted, but the Party went pro-war during the Spanish Civil War in 1936, then resumed an anti-war stance when

Merton on an outing with fraternity brothers. (Photograph from the Columbia University Yearbook, courtesy of the Thomas Merton Center)

"I suppose there were two reasons why I thought I ought to join a fraternity. One was the false one, that I thought it would help me to 'make connections' as the saying goes. The other, truer one was that I imagined that I would thus find a multitude of occasions for

parties. . . . Both these hopes turned out to be illusory."

(The Seven Storey Mountain)

Merton (seated just off-center) with his Columbia fraternity. (Photograph from the Columbia University Yearbook, courtesy of Columbia University)

"I found myself pledging one of the fraternities. It was a big, gloomy house behind the new library. . . . And there was somewhere in the building a secret room which I must not reveal to you, reader, at any price, even at the cost of life itself. And there I was eventually initiated."

(The Seven Storey Mountain)

Stalin signed the non-aggression pact with Hitler, then did another about-face when Hitler's armies attacked the Soviet Union.

Merton, whose one radical action at Cambridge had been to sign a pacifist pledge, was looking not only for something with steadier principles, but especially sought moral consistency about killing people. Merton came to realize that the Communist Party would "do whatever seems profitable to itself at the moment," which was, really, "the rule of all modern political parties."[84]

Merton's only Marxist input that summer came from the Marx Brothers. John Paul, home from school in Pennsylvania, joined him in haunting local movie theaters. Their cinematic partnership had begun the summer before. "I think John Paul and I and our various friends must have seen all the movies, without exception, that were produced from 1934 to 1937."[85] Tom's greatest heroes were Charlie Chaplin, W. C. Fields, and Harpo Marx. The only problem for the two brothers was that "we were almost always in danger of being thrown out of the theater for our uproarious laughter at scenes that were supposed to be most affecting, tender and appealing to the finer elements in the human soul—the tears of Jackie Cooper, the brave smile of Alice Faye behind the bars of a jail."[86]

Merton started classes in the fall of 1935 with a huge burst of energy, signing up for a battery of courses, among them Spanish, German, geology, constitutional law, and contemporary civilization. Intensely social person that he was, during his several years at Columbia Merton joined the Committee on Student Publications, the Pre-Journalism Society (he was president for a time), the Dean's Drag Committee, the Laughing Lion Society, the Philolexian (the university's literary association), and was part of the cross-country and track teams.

He also joined a fraternity, Alpha Delta Phi, only to be reminded how lonely one can be in the midst of a crowd. The body of a fraternity brother—a possible suicide—was found in a canal two months later.

Thomas Merton and fellow students working on the Yearbook. (Photograph from the Columbia University Yearbook, courtesy of the Thomas Merton Center)

Another encounter with death occurred when his class in contemporary civilization visited the city morgue where they he saw "rows and rows of iceboxes containing blue, swollen corpses"[87] of men and women—the murdered, the run-over, the suicides—who had been fished out of the water or found on the streets. It seemed to Merton that they were all casualties of contemporary civilization.

Despite such harrowing glimpses of despair and death, it was all-systems-go in Merton's life. "I had . . . a mysterious knack of keeping a hundred different interests going in the air at the same time"[88]—a trait that remained with him when he became a monk.

Merton's main extracurricular activity was campus journalism. Each week many hours were spent in "the noisiest and most agitated part of the campus," the fourth floor of John Jay Hall. Here were the offices of several publications: *The Columbia Review, The Spectator, The Jester*, and the yearbook. Merton was there, writing stories and humorous columns and drawing cartoons, whenever he didn't have to be somewhere else.[89] It was in these chaotic rooms that several of his life-long friendships had their genesis. Robert Giroux, who would later arrange the publication contract for *The Seven Storey Mountain* and also do the final editing, was in charge of *The Columbia Review*, and Ed Rice, later Merton's godfather, was on *The Jester* staff. Both were Catholics.

Among the others working with *The Jester* was Bob Lax, who was to become Merton's most intimate friend.[90] Lean as an exclamation mark, Lax was a gentle prophet who seemed to be meditating on some impenetrable woe. This born contemplative could "curl his long legs all around a chair, in seven different ways, while he was trying to find the right word with which to begin." He possessed "a natural, instinctive spirituality, a kind of inborn direction to the living God." Lax saw Americans as longing to do good but not knowing how, waiting for the day when they could turn on the radio "and somebody will

"I Don't Care If You Are Married"

One of Merton's cartoons for *The Jester*. (Courtesy of the Thomas Merton Center)

Thomas Merton and Robert Lax in the editorial office of *The Jester*, a Columbia student publication. (Photograph from the Columbia University Yearbook, courtesy of the Thomas Merton Center)

"The place [at Columbia] where I was busiest was the Jester *office. Nobody really worked there, they just congregated about noontime and beat violently with the palms of their hands on the big empty filing cabinets, making a thunderous sound. . . . The chief advantage of [being editors of]* Jester *was that it paid most of our bills for tuition."*

(The Seven Storey Mountain)

start telling them what they have really been wanting to hear and needing to know . . . somebody who is capable of telling them of love of God in language that will no longer sound hackneyed or crazy."[91]

Merton made an equally profound impression on Lax, whose arrival was announced audibly even more than visually: "[Merton] walked explosively: bang bang bang, as though fireworks, small, & they too, joyful, went off every time his heel hit the ground. . . . [H]e walked with joy, bounced with joy: he knew where he was going."[92]

At the beginning of the 1936 school year, Lax was elected editor of *The Jester* and Merton made art editor.[93]

Not only was work on *The Jester* staff a pleasure, but it paid most of Merton's tuition. Pocket money came from odd jobs, among them a stint working as guide and interpreter on the observation roof of the RCA building at Rockefeller Center, $27.50 a week, good money in 1936. He sold cartoons, $6 each, to a paper-cup manufacturer. As an occasional Latin tutor, he got $2.50 an hour. Paying his beer bill was no problem.

Sam Jenkins, Merton's grandfather.
(Photograph courtesy of the Thomas
Merton Center)

"Here I was, scarcely four years after I left Oakham and walked out into the world I thought I was going to ransack and rob all of its pleasures and satisfactions. I had done what I intended, and now I found that it was I who was emptied and robbed and gutted."

(The Seven Storey Mountain)

The religious sparks that had been struck in Rome in 1933 flared again in October 1936 when Merton's grandfather, Sam Jenkins, died. "He had slipped out on us, in his sleep, without premeditation, on the spur of the moment."[94] Alone with his grandfather's body in Douglaston, Merton felt he had to pray, and not just in his thoughts but on his knees. It was the sound of his grandmother's approaching steps that got him hurriedly back to his feet—still the old embarrassment about God. Martha Jenkins died the following August, Tom sitting at her side, praying silently as he listened to her struggle for breath.

With hardly a trace of his family left, Merton had his own nightmarish scrape with death soon after her burial. On his way home by train to Douglaston one night, he seemed suddenly without balance. Feeling nauseated, he walked awkwardly to the passageway between cars, then nearly tumbled onto the tracks. Hanging on until he reached Pennsylvania Station, he checked into the hotel across the street and was given a room many floors above. A house doctor gave him some medicine and urged him to get some sleep. The floor seemed to tilt steeply toward the room's one window and the window to fill the wall. It was as if some murderous gravity were pulling him toward the window and to the air beyond, enticing him to submit. His head was spinning, but he clung onto life and in the morning walked out of the hotel through the front door.

A nervous breakdown brought on by another round of family funerals? Exhaustion from the heavy load at Columbia? The start of an ulcer, as the family doctor warned? Merton only knew that he had just barely survived and that no one was left of the family that raised him except John Paul and himself.

Gilson, Huxley, Blake, and Maritain

Tell me what company you keep, and I'll tell you what you are.

CERVANTES

W alking past Scribner's Bookshop on Fifth Avenue in February 1937, *The Spirit of Medieval Christianity,* by Etienne Gilson, caught Merton's eye. The title reminded him of the ancient cloisters and churches that had attracted him as a boy in the south of France: the authority, integrity, and grace of places of worship made by believing people living in an age of faith. He bought the book.

Opening it on the train ride back to Douglaston that day and glancing through the pages preceding the text, he found something more shocking than a refrigerated body in the city morgue: the Latin phrase *nihil obstat* ("without error") and the word, above a bishop's name, *imprimatur* ("let it be printed"): official certification that the book had been read by censors and found to be consistent with Roman Catholic doctrine. For Merton these words meant the policing of the mind, the punishment of dissenters, and the enforcement of dogma.

"The feeling of disgust and deception struck me like a knife in the pit of my stomach," he recalled. "I felt as if I had been cheated! They should have warned me that it was a Catholic book! Then I would never have bought it. As it was, I was tempted to throw the thing out the window . . . to get rid of it as something dangerous and unclean."[95]

It was as if he had been given a thumbscrew used in the Inquisition. Merton could readily admire a cathedral

"I had never had an adequate notion of what Christians meant by God."
(The Seven Storey Mountain)

like the one at Chartres and even appreciate some aspects of the life of prayer and worship it suggested, but not the religious structure that motivated its builders. He marveled at the culture of Catholicism, but regarded the Catholic Church with alarm.

Happily, Merton's fascination with the book's subject matter took priority over his loathing of censorship. He read the book straight through and from it became aware that orthodox Christian theology could be as profound and clean of line as any cathedral in France or Italy.

Gilson gave words to a nonverbal aesthetic sensitivity that had already marked Merton's religious development, as it had his father's. Here was a theology with depth, spaciousness, sanity, and wholeness to match the mosaic icons that had so moved him in Rome's more ancient churches four years before.

He was especially moved by what Gilson wrote about God. Before Gilson, he admitted, "I had never had an adequate notion of what Christians meant by God. I had simply taken it for granted that the God in Whom religious people believed, and to Whom they attributed the creation and government of all things, was a noisy and dramatic and passionate character, a vague, jealous, hidden being."[96] The God in whom Catholics believed was not, as Merton previously imagined, an everlasting drill-sergeant eager to punish those who were out of step, but rather, as Merton later put it, "mercy within mercy within mercy."[97] Merton put down Gilson's book with "an immense respect for Catholic philosophy and for the Catholic faith."[98]

That spring Merton started attending Sunday services at the Zion Church in Douglaston and had long talks about books with the church's pastor, Dr. Lester Riley. While enjoying their conversations, however, Merton found Riley's sermons lacked the theological substance that excited him in Gilson. "I wanted to hear about Doctrine, and nobody told me anything about Doctrine, about what to believe."[99]

"[Huxley] showed that this negation [asceticism] was not something absolute, sought for its own sake; but that it was a freeing, a vindication of our real selves, a liberation of the spirit from limits and bonds that were intolerable, suicidal—from a servitude to flesh that must ultimately destroy our whole nature and society and the world as well."

(The Seven Storey Mountain)

In June Merton moved from Douglaston to a $7.50-a-week room on West 114th Street. It was here, at Bob Lax's urging, that he read Aldous Huxley's *Ends and Means*. The Huxley name, due to Aldous's biologist brother and scientist grandfather, was a synonym for religious skepticism. Yet here was a Huxley writing in defense of mysticism and urging his readers toward a life not only of prayer but asceticism.

Asceticism meant the art and discipline of living without society's normal comforts—simple living, or even voluntary poverty. "The very thought of such a thing was a complete revolution in my mind. The word had so far stood for a kind of weird and ugly perversion of nature, the masochism of men who had gone crazy in a warped and unjust society. What an idea! To deny the desires of one's flesh, and even to practice certain disciplines."[100]

It dawned on Merton that, in failing to link ends and means within his life, the sorrows he had experienced were as inevitable as hangovers after too much beer. Huxley helped him realize that a purposeful detachment could be a way of opening oneself to a transforming encounter with God. The only thing that baffled Merton about Huxley was his preference for the Buddha over Christ. It was thanks to Huxley, however, that Merton took his first serious look at Buddhism, a subject he returned to later in life.

Ends and Means was also a pacifist book. Huxley agreed with Gandhi: people who forget about means tend to become mean people, while murderous methods create murderous societies. Huxley saw prayer and asceticism as the necessary foundations of spiritual life. He argued that a nonviolent life is the only possible way to create a nonviolent society.

With the Spanish Civil War under way, nonviolence was far from popular among students at Columbia. Those to the right sided with Franco, those to the left with Spain's radical Republicans. The only point of agreement on both sides was the necessity of bloodshed.

Apartment on 114th St. where Merton lived after graduation from Columbia. (Photograph by Robert Ellsberg)

Head of Job. (Drawing by William Blake)

"[Blake's] rebellion, for all its strange heterodoxy, was fundamentally the rebellion of the saints. It was the rebellion of the lover of the living God, the rebellion of one whose desire of God was so intense and irresistible that it condemned, with all its might, all the hypocrisy and petty sensuality and skepticism and materialism which cold and trivial minds set up as unpassable barriers."

(The Seven Storey Mountain)

Among those who died on the Republican side in 1937 was a Columbia alumnus.

Having received his bachelor of arts diploma in February 1938, Merton entered Columbia's Graduate School of English where he chose to write his thesis on one of the great dissenters of the eighteenth century, the poet and mystic William Blake.

Blake stood in opposition to those who saw nothing more in the mystery of life than the puzzles of chemistry and who regarded mysticism as madness. With the searing conviction of a biblical prophet, Blake rejoiced that

The atoms of Democritus
And Newton's particles of light
Are sands upon the Red-Sea Shore
Where Israel's tents do shine so bright.[101]

The more he read Blake, the more impressed Merton was with the poet's unwillingness to adjust himself to an age that was simultaneously pious, grasping, self-satisfied, and indifferent to the poor. He was captivated by Blake's poetry, disarmingly simple yet with depths rarely reached by other poets. "[Blake] wrote better poetry at twelve than Shelley wrote in his whole life. And it was because, when he was twelve, he had already seen, I think, Elias standing under a tree in the fields south of London."[102]

Blake represented a quality of mind that neither gazed at the world through the rose-tinted glasses of romanticism nor, in the name of reason, looked at creation with eyes dead to God's presence and activity. Blake was also a poet of outrage. The Blake who had seen Elias under a tree also saw British fortunes being minted in "dark Satanic mills"[103] owned by pitiless men who went to church on Sunday.

"Blake saw," Merton wrote, "that, in the legislation of men, some evils had been set up as standards of right by which other evils were to be condemned: and the norms of pride or greed had been established in the judgment seat, to pronounce a crushing and inhuman indictment against all the normal healthy strivings of human nature. Love was outlawed, and became lust, pity was swallowed up in cruelty, and so Blake knew how 'The harlot's cry from street to street / Shall weave old England's winding sheet.'"[104]

"What a thing it was," Merton recalled, "to live in contact with the genius and holiness of William Blake that year. . . . By the time the summer was over, I was to become conscious of the fact that the only way to live was to live in a world that was charged with the presence and reality of God."[105]

It impressed Merton that Blake, though a religious nonconformist, held some positive opinions regarding Catholicism. The painter Samuel Palmer reported to a friend that Blake had "held forth . . . one day on the Roman Catholic Church being the only [church] which taught the forgiveness of sins."[106]

That same year a mild Hindu monk appeared in Merton's life. Bramachari had been sent from his ashram in India to take part in a Congress of Religions at the World's Fair in Chicago, but he had arrived too late. He stayed on in America, living from whatever contributions and kindnesses came his way. He was in New York thanks to Merton's friends Sy and Helen Freedgood, living quietly in their home despite the presence of a grandmother who worried that this Asian in turban, white robes, and tattered sneakers might be an enemy of the Jewish people. Merton had been part of the welcoming committee when Bramachari arrived from Chicago and in subsequent weeks spent long hours talking with him.

"He was never sarcastic, never ironical or unkind in his criticisms: in fact he did not make many judgments at all, especially adverse ones," Merton wrote a decade later. "He would simply make statements of fact, and then burst out laughing—his laughter was quiet and ingenuous, and it expressed his complete amazement at the very

The Hindu monk Bramachari. (Photograph courtesy of the Thomas Merton Center)

possibility that people should live the way he saw them living all around him."[107]

Americans often asked Bramachari about the progress of Christian missionaries in India. Bramachari's response impressed Merton. The problem was, he said, that they lived too comfortably, "in a way that simply made it impossible for Hindus to regard them as holy—let alone the fact that they ate meat." Hindus were amazed that Christians weren't ascetics.[108]

For all his friendly criticisms of meat-eating missionaries, Bramachari played a Christian missionary role in Merton's life. "He did not generally put his words in the form of advice, but the one counsel he did give me is something that I will not easily forget: 'There are many beautiful mystical books written by the Christians. You should read Saint Augustine's *Confessions*, and *The Imitation of Christ*.... Yes, you must read those books.' "[109] In his room on 114th Street Merton started reading *The Imitation of Christ* and started praying again, "more or less regularly."[110]

Summer heat drove Merton up to a bungalow Lax's family owned near Olean, in western New York, but in a week Merton was back in Manhattan "on account of being, as usual, in love."[111]

Once back in the city, one of his activities was to visit the Cloisters, a monastery-like branch of the Metropolitan Museum of Art established in Fort Tryon Park on the upper west side of Manhattan—a small paradise of medieval Christian art as well as an oasis of silence. One of its treasures had come all the way from Merton's birthplace in Prades: part of the cloister of Saint Michel de Cuxa. Here Merton had a compelling glimpse, mediated by art and architecture, of monastic life.

In September, while busy with his thesis, "Nature and Art in William Blake,"[112] Merton read another book that sharpened his attraction to Catholicism: Jacques Maritain's *Art and Scholasticism*, which also provided another lens through which to view Blake.

"By the time the summer was over, I was to become conscious of the fact that the only way to live was to live in a world that was charged with the presence and reality of God."

(The Seven Storey Mountain)

If Gilson had helped give Merton back the word *God,* Maritain resurrected the word *virtue.* He used the term without embarrassment, secure in the word's Latin meaning: strength. Merton came away from Maritain's book with a "sane conception of virtue—without which there can be no happiness, because virtues are precisely the powers by which we come to acquire happiness."[113]

The Cloisters Museum in Manhattan. (Photograph by Jim Forest)

Conversion

Even the ugly buildings of Columbia were transfigured.

Thomas Merton
The Seven Storey Mountain

Plaque outside Corpus Christi
Church on West 121st St. (Photograph
by Robert Ellsberg)

One weekend in August 1938 it struck Merton that he had "been in and out of a thousand Catholic cathedrals and churches, and yet I had never heard Mass." On those occasions when he happened to a find the liturgy under way, he fled "in wild Protestant panic." Now he began to feel "a sweet, strong, gentle, clean urge in me which said: 'Go to Mass! Go to Mass!'"[114]

Canceling a weekend date in the country with a woman he had been seeing, he had, so it seemed to him, his first sober Sunday in New York since leaving England. It was a dazzling day of blue skies and vacant avenues.

The church he walked to was Corpus Christi, a handsome building of Palladian architectural inspiration on West 121st Street. It was a parish chiefly established for Catholics attending Columbia, though it served the neighborhood as well. Wanting to watch but not be noticed, he found an obscure spot inside.

"The first thing I noticed was a young girl, very pretty too, perhaps fifteen or sixteen, kneeling straight up and praying quite seriously. I was very much impressed to see that someone who was young and beautiful could with such simplicity make prayer the real and serious and principal reason for going to church."[115] Looking around, he realized her attitude was quite typical. These were people who didn't seem to take any notice of themselves. They were matter-of-factly on their knees, all attention focused on the altar.

Afterward, walking in the sun along Broadway, Merton felt that he was in a new world. "I could not understand what it was that had happened to make me so happy, why I was so much at peace, so content with life.... Even the ugly buildings of Columbia were trans-figured."[116] Eating breakfast at Childs on 111th Street, a place that usually struck him as gloomy and small, he felt as if he were in the Elysian Fields.

If intellectually he was moving with saints and mystics, even finally overcoming his last anti-Catholic prejudices, day-to-day life in many ways was still much the same. On Labor Day he drove with a friend to Philadelphia, stopping on the way at "a big dark road-house, arguing and arguing about mysticism, and smoking more and more cigarettes and gradually getting drunk."[117] It took him days to recover from the hangover.

Yet the next Sunday he was back at Mass, and the next and the next. During those weeks it was enough just to stand by and admire the sacramental life others were leading.

In contrast to his quiet romance with Catholicism, grim events were occurring on the other side of the Atlantic: the Spanish Civil War was nearing its end, adding Spain to the list of fascist regimes in Europe, while Hitler's Germany was rapidly re-arming itself and had just annexed the Sudetenland area of Czecho-slovakia. The Nazis who had run Merton off the road in 1932 were beginning to run whole nations off the road. While Neville Chamberlain was talking about "peace in our time" on his return from Munich at the end of September, it seemed to Merton that a general holocaust was much more likely.

"I was very depressed," he wrote. "I was beyond thinking about the intricate and filthy political tangle that underlay the mess. I had given up politics as more or less hopeless, by this time. I was no longer interested in having any opinion about the movement and interplay of forces that were all more or less iniquitous and corrupt,

"How bright the little building seemed. Indeed, it was quite new. The sun shone on the clean bricks. People were going in that wide open door, into the cool darkness and, all at once, all the churches of Italy and France came back to me. The richness and fullness of the atmosphere of Catholicism that I had not been able to avoid apprehending and loving as a child, came back to me with a rush. . . ."

(The Seven Storey Mountain)

and it was far too laborious and uncertain a business to try and find out some degree of truth and justice in all the loud, artificial claims that were put forward by the various sides. . . . The future was obscured, blanked out by war as by a dead-end wall. Nobody knew if anybody at all would come out of it alive. Who would be worse off, the civilians or the soldiers? The distinction between their fates was to be abolished by aerial warfare."[118]

All the internal contradictions of the society in which Merton lived were converging within him. He could see that "my likes or dislikes, beliefs or disbeliefs meant absolutely nothing in the external, political order. I was just an individual, and the individual had ceased to count. . . . I would probably soon become a number on the list of those to be drafted. I would get a piece of metal with my number on it . . . so as to help out the circulation of red-tape that would necessarily follow the disposal of my remains."[119]

In the midst of such dark thoughts another important book landed in Merton's life, G. F. Leahy's biography of the English poet Gerard Manley Hopkins, a convert to Catholicism who became a Jesuit priest. Merton was studying Hopkins for a doctoral thesis he never completed. Sitting in his room on West 114th Street on a wet fall day, Merton started reading a chapter that described Hopkins's journey to Catholicism while a student at Oxford in 1866.

"All of a sudden," Merton recalled, "something began to stir within me, something began to push me, to prompt me. It was a movement that spoke like a voice. 'What are you waiting for?' it said. 'Why are you sitting here? Why do you still hesitate? You know what you ought to do? Why don't you do it?'

"I stirred in the chair. I lit a cigarette, looked out the window at the rain, tried to shut the voice up. 'Don't act on your impulses,' I thought. 'This is crazy. This is not rational. Read your book.' "

He tried to press on with Hopkins's life, but the inner

voice only renewed its appeal: "It's useless to hesitate any longer. Why don't you get up and go?" He read another few sentences about Hopkins's conversion, and then came his own moment of consent. "I could bear it no longer. I put down the book, and got into my raincoat, and started down the stairs. I went out into the street. I crossed over, and walked along by the grey wooden fence, towards Broadway, in the light rain. And then everything inside me began to sing."[120]

Nine blocks away was Corpus Christi and its presbytery. As it happened, its pastor, Father Ford, was just returning.

"Father," Merton asked, "may I speak to you about something?"

"Yes, sure, come into the house."

They sat in the parlor.

"Father, I want to become a Catholic."[121]

Father Ford gave him three books to read and arranged for Merton to return for instruction two evenings a week.

The news of his impending baptism (officially a "provisional" baptism because of his infant baptism in a Protestant church near Prades) was broken to Bob Lax with a frisbee-like toss of his hat. "I remember the moment," said Lax, "because he'd never before, and never since, thrown a hat in my direction."[122] On November 18, 1938, Merton was baptized.

"What do you ask from God's Church," Merton was asked. "Faith!" "What does faith bring you?" "Life everlasting."

Witnessing the rite of passage were four friends, three of them Jews: Bob Lax, Sy Freedgood, and Bob Gerdy. Only his godfather, Ed Rice, was Catholic.

Merton entered a confessional for the first time, worried that the young priest sitting on the other side of the partition might be shocked to hear some of the events and habits that were about to be recounted. "But one by one, species by species, as best I could, I

Gerard Manley Hopkins, the English poet and convert who became a Jesuit priest.

"What monsters of efficiency they must be, these Jesuits, I kept thinking to myself. . . . I tried to picture myself with my face sharpened by asceticism, its pallor intensified by contrast with a black cassock, and every line of it proclaiming a Jesuit saint, a Jesuit master-mind. And I think the master-mind element was one of the strongest features of this obscure attraction."

(The Seven Storey Mountain)

Corpus Christi Church, where Merton was baptized. (Photograph by Robert Ellsberg)

"It was a gay, clean church, with big plain windows and white columns and pilasters and a well-lighted, simple sanctuary. Its style was a trifle eclectic, but much less perverted with incongruities than the average Catholic church in America. It had a kind of a seventeenth-century, oratorian character about it, though with a sort of American colonial tinge of simplicity."

(The Seven Storey Mountain)

tore out all those sins by their roots, like teeth. Some of them were hard."

Baptized and absolved, for the first time he was not only present at Mass but was able to receive communion. "Now I had entered into the everlasting movement of that gravitation which is the very life and spirit of God . . . goodness without end. . . . He called out to me from His own immense depths."[123]

Brother John

We all had a sort of feeling that we could be hermits up on the hill.

Thomas Merton
The Seven Storey Mountain

Having been awarded his master's degree for his study of William Blake in February 1939, and now at work on his doctoral dissertation, Merton moved to a one-room apartment with a wrought-iron balcony at 35 Perry Street in Greenwich Village, Manhattan's literary heartland.

His religious life was steadily deepening. He was at Mass every Sunday, often went on weekdays as well, and occasionally stopped in church for private prayer, making the stations of the cross or reciting the rosary. His conversion had brought him that far. But preparing for confession on alternate Saturdays, it seemed to him his life still had the smell of beer and cigarettes. What conversion would mean in terms of his future life and work remained hidden.

The obvious choices were writing and teaching. His education had prepared him for the classroom. He knew from Mark Van Doren, now a friend, what a significant role a teacher could play in a student's life. Writing seemed inescapable; he would be a writer if for no other reason than that he was incapable of not writing. When not busy with academic projects, he seemed always to be at work on a novel. He was writing poetry as well. His baptism seemed to have brought with it "a sudden facility for rough, raw Skeltonic verses."[124] Rejection letters were arriving from some of the best magazines in the country. "How many envelopes I fed to the green mail-

Merton's apartment on Perry Street in Greenwich Village. (Photograph by Robert Ellsberg)

Robert Lax. (Photograph courtesy of Boston College, Burns Library)

"Bob Lax was a potential prophet, but without rage. A king, but a Jew too. A mind full of tremendous and subtle intuitions, and every day he found less and less to say about them, and resigned himself to being inarticulate. . . . Lax has always been afraid he was in a blind alley, and half aware that, after all, it might not be a blind alley, but God, infinity."

(The Seven Storey Mountain)

box at the corner of Perry Street just before you got to Seventh Avenue! And everything I put in there came back."[125]

He was dating a nurse but was in no hurry to get married. He was quietly wrestling with the idea of ordination to the priesthood and thus a life of celibacy, a word that both fascinated him and gave him the cold sweats. But he worried that, as a priest, he would no longer be able to write the way he wanted to. The word *imprimatur* was never to become a comforting sound in his ear.

For Lax, the question wasn't so much *what* to become as *who* to become. Lax, though not yet Catholic himself, had steadily encouraged Merton in his religious pilgrimage. It was Lax more than anyone who challenged Merton to aim high in the life of grace and not allow joining the church to be the high-water mark of his religious development.

Walking with Lax on Sixth Avenue one night in the spring of 1939, Lax turned toward Merton and asked, "What do you want to be, anyway?"

It was obvious to Merton that "Thomas Merton the well-known writer" and "Thomas Merton the assistant instructor of freshman English" were not good enough answers.

"I don't know," he finally said. "I guess what I want is to be a good Catholic."

"What do you mean, you want to be a good Catholic?"

Merton was silent. He hadn't figured that out yet.

"What you should say," Lax went on, "is that you want to be a saint."

That struck Merton as downright weird.

"How do you expect me to become a saint?"

"By wanting to."

"I can't be a saint," Merton responded. To be a saint would require a magnitude of renunciation that was completely beyond him. But Lax pressed on.

"All that is necessary to be a saint is to want to be one.

Don't you believe God will make you what He created you to be, if you will consent to let Him do it? All you have to do is desire it."[126]

Giving himself time to think about what sanctity might mean in his case, Merton sublet the Perry Street apartment and went off with Lax and Ed Rice to spend the summer in the Lax family cottage near Olean. Here the three of them set up their typewriters and proceeded to write novels, pausing occasionally for hamburgers, beans, milk, and bongo-playing. Rice's manuscript was called "The Blue Horse"; Lax worked on "The Spangled Palace"; and Merton struggled with a manuscript that started out as "The Straits of Dover," became "The Night Before the Battle," and was finally christened "The Labyrinth." The writing was fun and being on the side of a wooded mountain listening to birds and wind wasn't the worst thing that could happen during the weeks when Manhattan was sweating out the heat.

"We all had a sort of feeling that we could be hermits up on the hill," Merton recalled, "but the trouble was that none of us really knew how [to be hermits] and I, who was in a way the most articulate, as well as the least sensible whenever it came to matters of conduct and discussions concerning good and evil, still had the strongest urges to go down into the valleys and see what was on at the movies, or play the slot machines, or drink beer."[127]

Back in New York at the summer's end, Merton began to send his manuscript around and to pray fervently that some publisher would like it, but it found no takers. "Other people's bad books get published," he noted in his journal. "Why can't my bad book get published?"

Merton's struggle to find his voice as a writer was in part a struggle with the mystery of language and the indefinable but clear chasm that separates good writing from bad. He found himself completely at odds with those for whom good writing was built on a solid and obedient grasp of the rules of grammar. In a journal entry written in the fall of 1939, he protested the imposi-

"I made the terrible mistake of entering upon the Christian life as if it were merely the natural life invested with a kind of supernatural mode by grace. I thought that all I had to do was to continue living as I had lived before, thinking and acting as I did before, with the one exception of avoiding mortal sin."

(The Seven Storey Mountain)

Church of St. Francis of Assisi on 31st St., where Merton often prayed. (Photograph by Robert Ellsberg)

tion of rules that deny language its own life and logic "as a living, growing thing." The enslavement to the rules of grammar was, he found, an intrusion "of rules from the outside" that attempt to "standardize him, [to] stamp him with rubberstamp characteristics."[128] The tyranny of grammar reminded him of the Nazi state.

Meanwhile the situation in Europe was becoming more disastrous by the day, the Nazis confident that they were in the early stages of their thousand-year reign. As he pondered the headlines, it occurred to Merton that a Christian couldn't simply blame the politicians or accuse the abstraction called "history" for giving birth to the Nazi nightmare: "I myself am responsible for this," he realized. "My sins have done this. Hitler is not the only one who has started this war: I have my share in it too."[129]

On the first day of World War II, September 1, 1939, with bombs falling on Warsaw, Merton received communion in the Church of Saint Francis of Assisi, near Pennsylvania Station. He was aware that the same Christ he was receiving sacramentally was "being nailed again to the cross by the effect of my sins, and the sins of the whole, selfish, stupid, idiotic world of men."[130]

Days were given to his typewriter; nights to friends, movies, beer, jazz, boogie-woogie, and dancing. Merton had an impressive collection of jazz records at his apartment on Perry Street. Merton wasn't only a listener but a player when it came to jazz. Friends teased Merton not so much for playing pianos as attacking them. Jinny Burton, a woman he was dating frequently, wondered if he wouldn't be happier as a jazz pianist than a novelist. Having visited the Cuban pavilion at the World's Fair, he became adept at Spanish American dancing. There were evenings out with Jinny Burton dancing at El Chico's and Nick's.

One of the most helpful voices in Merton's life during this crucial period belonged to Dan Walsh. Walsh taught a class on Saint Thomas Aquinas which Merton was attending. A small, stocky man who looked like a benevolent prizefighter, Walsh taught with "childlike delight and cherubic simplicity," helping his students understand the spirit and theological structure of Catholicism. He had, said Merton, "the most rare and admirable virtue of being able to rise above the petty differences of schools and systems [as represented by such theologians as Augustine, Aquinas, Bonaventure, and Duns Scotus], seeing Catholic philosophy in its wholeness."[131] Walsh knew Etienne Gilson personally, whose book Merton had nearly thrown out the train window on discovering its *imprimatur*, and also knew Jacques Maritain, the French Catholic philosopher who was responsible for reviving interest in Saint Thomas Aquinas. One evening, after attending a stimulating lecture by Maritain, Merton and Walsh "went off talking about miracles and saints."[132] It was to Walsh that Merton first mentioned the possibility of becoming a priest. The two were walking together on Park Avenue. "Dan turned to me and said, 'You know, the first time I met you I thought you had a vocation to the priesthood.' "[133] Walsh surveyed the variety of religious orders within the Catholic Church, the Benedictines, Dominicans, Franciscans, Jesuits and others.

Not least in Walsh's estimation were the Trappists. Walsh had recently spent a week at a Trappist monastery in Kentucky, the Abbey of Our Lady of Gethsemani, and spoke with excitement of the Trappists' penitential way of life: hours in church each day, silence except in prayer, hard physical labor on the abbey's farmland, rigorous fasts.

Walsh asked Merton, "Do you think you would like that kind of life?"

"Oh no," Merton said with alarm, "not a chance! That's not for me! I'd never be able to stand it. It would kill me in a week." He pictured a vast gray prison with dour inmates, hoods pulled down over their faces. The Trappists' official name—the Order of Cistercians of the Strict Observance—made Merton shiver.

"Well," Walsh replied, "it's a good thing you know yourself so well."[134]

Daniel Walsh, a professor of philosophy at Columbia, was the one to whom Merton turned for advice about his religious vocation. (Photograph courtesy of Columbia University)

"[P]erhaps the impression that [Dan Walsh] made was all the more forceful because his square jaw had a kind of potential toughness about it. Yet . . . there he sat, this little, stocky man who had something of the appearance of a good-natured prize fighter, smiling and talking with the most childlike delight and cherubic simplicity about the Summa Theologica."

(The Seven Storey Mountain)

On the other hand, it was also Walsh who had said to Merton that nothing is too hard if it brings you to God.

It was after an intense night at a jazz club and a crowd of friends sleeping over in his apartment on Perry Street that Merton, once again suffering a hangover, experienced a wave of disgust at the life he was leading and turned with fresh intensity to the idea of becoming a priest. At a nearby Catholic library he found a small book about the Jesuits. Reading it until it was dark outside, he went to the Jesuit Church of Saint Francis Xavier on 16th Street. A service of adoration of the Blessed Sacrament was going on. Merton knelt, fixing his eyes on the white host in its gold monstrance on the altar, and listened once again to the questioning voice inside himself, "Do you really want to be a priest? If you do, say so." As the priest raised the monstrance and blessed the people, "I looked straight at the Host, and I knew, now, Who it was that I was looking at, and I said: 'Yes, I want to be a priest, with all my heart I want it. If it is Your will, make me a priest.' "[135]

The Jesuits appealed to Merton. Gerard Manley Hopkins had been a Jesuit. Among Jesuits, writing was a highly valued vocation, no small issue for Merton. Dan Walsh, on the other hand, suggested that the Franciscans would be the order best suited to Merton's temperament. Indeed, Merton greatly admired Francis of Assisi. Francis had lived a life of literal acceptance of the teachings of Jesus, joyfully renouncing power, refusing property, renouncing all violence, and prohibiting even his lay followers from possessing any weapons. While the Franciscan movement had been institutionalized after the founder's death, it remained welcoming, cheerful, active in the world—nothing like the prison-style monasticism Merton imagined was on offer with the Trappists.

With a letter of recommendation from Dan Walsh in hand, Merton went to talk with Father Edmund at the Franciscan monastery on 31st Street. Their discussions went well, Merton's only disappointment being that he

The Jesuit Church of St. Francis Xavier on W. 16th St. (Photograph by Robert Ellsberg)

"Do you really want to be a priest? If you do, say so."

(The Seven Storey Mountain)

would have to wait ten months, until August 1940, when the next novitiate group was formed. So eager was he to turn the page, the delay seemed like an eternity to Merton. While waiting out the year, Father Edmund urged Merton to accept a job teaching at Columbia while continuing work on his doctorate.

At the urging of a Franciscan he talked to in confession, Merton started going to Mass on a daily basis. He felt his life was being transformed. Friends remarked how happy he seemed.

While teaching an English composition course at Columbia, Merton's passion to see himself in print continued unabated. Many submissions were sent out, and nearly as many rejection slips received by return mail. His only success was with book reviews done for *The New York Herald Tribune* and *The New York Times.* He also found an agent, Naomi Burton, who liked his autobiographical novel, "The Labyrinth," and was willing to help him with his future work. She became not only his agent and friendly critic but a friend for life.

In April 1940, Merton went on an Easter trip to Cuba, his ultimate goal being the shrine of Our Lady of Charity in Cobre, a place where, in 1687, the Virgin Mary had appeared to three slave girls.

It was, Merton said, "one of those medieval pilgrimages that was nine-tenths vacation and one-tenth pilgrimage."[136] He experienced both elements with intensity. Even when walking in parts of Havana few would regard as pilgrimage places, Merton felt wrapped in a kind of innocence and simplicity he had never known in adult life.

While at Cobre, Merton made a promise to Mary that, should he ever be ordained a priest, he would offer his vocation to her.

His most profound religious encounter was not at Cobre, however, but in the far more chaotic environment of Havana. While at Mass in the Church of Saint Francis, among crowds of schoolchildren, Merton had a sudden mystical experience:

The Franciscan monastery on W. 31st St., where Merton applied for admission to the order. (Photograph by Robert Ellsberg)

Shrine of Our Lady of Cobre in Cuba, where Merton made a retreat in the spring of 1940. (Photograph by Elaine Williams, courtesy of Maryknoll archives)

The bell rang again, three times. Before any head was raised the clear cry of the brother in the brown robe cut through the silence with the words "*Yo creo . . .*" [I believe] which immediately all the children took up after him with such loud and strong and clear voices, and such unanimity and such meaning and such fervor that something went off inside me like a thunderclap and without seeing anything or apprehending anything extraordinary through any of my senses (my eyes were open on only precisely what was there, the church), I knew with the most absolute and unquestionable certainty that before me, between me and the altar, somewhere in the center of the church, up in the air (or any other place because in no place), but directly before my eyes, or directly present to some apprehension or other of mine which was above that of the senses, was at the same time God in all His essence, all His power, all His glory, and God in Himself and God surrounded by the radiant faces of the uncountable thousands upon thousands of saints contemplating His glory and praising His Holy Name. And so the unshakable certainty, the clear and immediate knowledge that Heaven was right in front of me, struck me like a thunderbolt and went through me like a flash of lightning and seemed to lift me clean up off the earth.[137]

In *The Seven Storey Mountain*, Merton again sought to describe what he had experienced:

It was a light that was so bright that it had no relation to any visible light and so profound and so intimate that it seemed like a neutralization of every lesser experience. And yet the thing that struck me most of all was that this light was in a certain sense "ordinary"—it was a light (and this most of all was what took my breath away) that was offered to all, to everybody, and there was nothing fancy or strange about it. . . . [I]t disarmed all images, all metaphors. . . . It ignored all sense experience in order to strike directly at the heart of truth. . . . [I]t . . . belonged to the order of knowledge, yes, but more still to the order of love.[138]

It was while in Cuba that it dawned on Merton that, without love and warmth, there is no truth in religious practice.

Back in New York in June, Merton received the news that certain essential papers, such as the marriage certificate of his parents, had been received and his application to enter the Franciscan novitiate had been accepted.

Summer began with a trip to Ithaca to visit John Paul, then a student at Cornell. John Paul seemed quite lost, reminding Merton of himself in Cambridge. John Paul was fascinated by the change occurring in Tom's life. The Christmas before he had given Tom a rosary as a token of support. While they were together in Ithaca, John Paul went with his brother to Mass, not just watching, but kneeling at his side.

The next stop was Olean where Merton, Lax, and Rice were once again going to work on novels, this time joined by Bob Gibney and Sy Freedgood. Merton made arrangements this time to bunk at the nearby Franciscan college, Saint Bonaventure's, using a dilapidated room in the gymnasium. This put him close to the monastery chapel where he received communion every morning. Most of the others present were young Franciscan novices. He pictured himself in brown robe and leather sandals bearing the name Brother John Spaniard.

The previous summer conversation in the writers' cottage on the hill had little to do with the events in Europe. In the summer of 1940, it was one of their chief topics. Belgium, Holland, and much of France were

The white girls open their arms like clouds,
The black girls close their eyes like wings:
Angels bow down like bells,
Angels look up like toys,

Because the heavenly stars
Stand in a ring:
And all the pieces of the mosaic, earth,
Get up and fly away like birds.
("Song for Our Lady of Cobre")

69

"So I knelt at the altar rail in the little Mexican church of Our Lady of Guadalupe . . . and asked with great intensity of desire for the publication of the book, if it should be for God's glory. The fact that I could even calmly assume that there was some possibility of the book giving glory to God shows the profound depths of my ignorance and spiritual blindness: but anyway, that was what I asked."

(The Seven Storey Mountain)

Church of Our Lady of Guadalupe on 14th St. (Photograph by Robert Ellsberg)

occupied by the German army. The heart of Rotterdam had been blitzed, the first act of city-destruction in the war. "We sat around the fireplace at night and talked about the Selective Service Law that would soon be passed in Washington, wondering how it would be and what we should do about it."[139] Lax was wondering whether this war or any war was justified. Gibney wasn't quite a pacifist but felt, even if he went into the army, he could not bear arms, a position similar to Merton's.

Merton's friends had various theories about what drew him toward some form of monastic life. Some assumed it was to obtain exemption from the draft. Ad and Joan Reinhardt teased him that he was out to get free room and board for life. Jinny Burton guessed he was looking for a quiet environment in which to devote himself to writing. Bob Gibney wondered if it wasn't just a cop-out from the real world.

Perhaps his friends' attitudes fanned Merton's own uncertainties. In any event, as the summer progressed, he began to have doubts about his Franciscan vocation. These were due in part to a vague disappointment with Franciscan life, which had begun to strike him as too tame. What troubled him most, however, was that he had given Dan Walsh and Father Edmund a streamlined version of his life story. Major pieces had been left out, most of all the fact that he had fathered a child in England. The Franciscans, he concluded, simply accepted him because he was superficially presentable, a young man with a good education and a sincere face, not the real Tom Merton, but a cardboard cut-out. As he thought it over, "it began to appear utterly impossible that anyone in his right mind could consider me fit material for the priesthood."[140]

Back in New York, he went to see Father Edmund and filled in the blank spaces. Father Edmund told Merton he needed a day to think over what he had been told. The next day he asked Merton to withdraw his application.

"It seemed to me," Merton wrote, "that I was now excluded from the priesthood forever." He walked in a

Photograph of Merton by his brother John Paul. (Courtesy of the Thomas Merton Center)

"I had to be led by a way that I could not understand, and I had to follow a path that was beyond my own choosing."
(The Seven Storey Mountain)

daze to a church on Seventh Avenue, went into a confessional, tried to tell the priest what had happened, and began to cry uncontrollably. The priest told Merton no one like him belonged in any monastery, still less in the priesthood. "He gave me to understand that I was simply wasting his time."[141] Feeling utterly abandoned, Merton wept in one of the pews until the tears were running down the fingers in which he hid his face.

Though the doors to religious community and a priestly vocation had been closed, Merton realized he could lead a more committed religious life, however privately. In addition to continuing his participation in daily Mass, he bought a four-volume breviary and cleared patches of time during the day to recite the monastic prayer offices.

"I did not have any lofty theories about the vocation of the lay-contemplative," he recalled in his autobiography. "In fact, I no longer dignified what I was trying to do by the name of a vocation. All I knew was that I wanted grace, and that I needed prayer, and that I was helpless without God, and that I wanted to do everything that people did to keep close to Him. . . . All that occupied me now was the immediate practical problem of getting up my hill with this terrific burden I had on my shoulders, step by step, begging God to drag me along."[142]

St. Bonaventure's

Destruction is all I remember.

THOMAS MERTON
My Argument with the Gestapo

"It amazed me how swiftly my life fell into a plan of fruitful and pleasant organization, here under the roof with these Friars, in this house dedicated to God."

(The Seven Storey Mountain)

In the fall of 1940 Merton took a job teaching English at Saint Bonaventure's College in Olean. The friars paid him the modest sum of $45 a month plus room and board. On the door of his room he tacked up an Annunciation by Dürer and several icons: Saint Francis receiving the stigmata, Saint Dominic the missionary preacher, and two of Mary and Jesus.

"I had three big classes of sophomores, ninety students in all, to bring through English Literature from Beowulf to the Romantic Revival in one year. And a lot of them didn't even know how to spell. But that didn't worry me very much, and it could not alter my happiness with *Piers Plowman* and *The Nun's Priest's Tale*. . . . I was back again in that atmosphere that had enthralled me as a child, the serene and simple and humorous Middle Ages . . . the twelfth and thirteenth and fourteenth centuries, full of fresh air and simplicity, as solid as wheat bread and grape wine and water-mills and ox-drawn wagons: the age of Cistercian monasteries and the first Franciscans."[143]

His students ranged from athletes to seminarians. He was surprised how much he enjoyed teaching football players. They "were the best-natured and the best-tempered and worked as hard as the seminarians. They were also the most vocal. They liked to talk about these books when I stirred them up to argue . . . [they] taught me much more about people than I taught them about books." The seminarians were quieter. "They kept pretty much to themselves, and handed in neat papers." Whatever the students' temperaments and ambitions in life, it was alarming to Merton that they all seemed to share the view "that the modern world was the highest point reached by man in his development, and that our present civilization left very little to be desired."[144]

For Merton, the age of Saint Francis ranked higher. While at Saint Bonaventure's he joined the Franciscan movement for lay associates, the Third Order. Members wore a scapular under their clothes—a cord with two small pieces of brown material similar to the fabric used in Franciscan robes. For Merton this hidden garment served as a symbol that he was a monk of some kind even if without formal membership in a religious community.

He tried to make headway in his religious life not only on his knees but at the table. He cut back on meat, but felt guilty he couldn't give it up completely. He fought with his long-running addiction to movies, doing about as well with this as with meat.

Not all his shortcomings were minor. He tried to live a celibate life but failed. The event is only hinted at in his autobiography: "If I had ever thought I had become immune from passion, and that I did not have to fight for freedom, there was no chance of that illusion any more."[145]

Merton was haunted by the expanding war in Europe. Having seen a film about the impact of the Blitz on London, he wrote in his journal: "For the first time in my life, I think, I momentarily wanted to be in the war. . . . Bombs are beginning to fall into my own life. . . . It was propaganda, but good propaganda. . . . For the first time I imagined that maybe I belonged there, not here."[146] What shocked him most was a picture of a bombed-out London shop in which, when he was sixteen, he had purchased a gray herringbone tweed suit.

The mechanized impersonality of modern war horrified Merton. "There is not even much hatred. If there were more hatred the thing would be healthier. But it

Bombing of London, the tower of St. Paul's Cathedral in the background. (Photograph courtesy of Maryknoll archives)

"Morning after morning when I glanced at the New York Times *in the library, between classes, I read the headlines about the cities that had been cut to pieces with bombs. Night after night the huge dark mass of London was bursting in wide areas of flame that turned its buildings into empty craters and cariated those miles and miles of slums. Around St. Paul's the ancient City was devastated. . . ."*

(The Seven Storey Mountain)

"I myself am responsible for this. My sins have done this. Hitler is not the only one who has started this war: I have my share in it too."

(The Seven Storey Mountain)

was just filthy, this destruction. . . . This is just a vile combat of bombs against bricks, attempts to wipe out machines and to bury men lying in tunnels under tons of stone and rubble. It is not like a fight, it is like a disease."[147]

Even in the quiet countryside surrounding Olean, Merton saw strands of connection with bomb targets: "The valley is full of oil storage tanks, and oil is for feeding bombers, and once they are fed they have to bomb something, and they generally pick on oil tanks. Wherever you have oil tanks, or factories, or railroads or any of the comforts of home and manifestations of progress, in this century, you are sure to get bombers, sooner or later. Therefore, if I don't pretend . . . to understand the war, I do know this much: that the knowledge of what is going on only makes it seem desperately important to be voluntarily poor, to get rid of all possessions this instant."[148]

He may have been influenced by Saint Francis, who once explained to his bishop why the members of his community couldn't own property: "If we held property, armed force for protection would become necessary. For property gives rise to lawsuits and to wars which in various ways destroy all love of God and of our fellowmen. Our membership, therefore, will not hold property."

Merton's thoughts about the war found their main expression in a novel he wrote while teaching at Saint Bonaventure's, "The Journal of My Escape from the Nazis" (finally published in 1969 as *My Argument with the Gestapo*). The story followed a poet's return to war-ravaged London from America. Though coming from America, the narrator, Merton in every detail but name, is a stateless person. "I have lived in too many countries," he explains, "to have a nationality."[149]

Why do you come back, he is asked. "Not to fight," he says. He admits he has come to write. What will you write? "I will say that . . . the things I remember are destroyed, but that does not mean as much as it seems,

because the destruction was already going on before, and destruction is all I remember."[150]

Later the question is posed: But isn't the war Germany's fault? "In the sense that they began fighting it, yes." Doesn't that mean Germany is guilty? "I don't know the meaning of the word guilty, except in the sense that I am also guilty for the war, partly." But it is nations that are guilty of war. "Nations don't exist. They can't be held responsible for anything. Nations are made up of people, and people are responsible for the things they do." In that case, Hitler is the guilty one. "He might be. Only I don't know enough about it. He might be more guilty than any other one person, but he isn't the only person guilty of the war. . . . All I know is, if anything happens to the world, it is partly because of me."[151]

The narrator explains to an officer who is interrogating him, "You think you can identify a man by giving his date of birth and his address, his height, his eyes' color,

Thomas Merton among fellow members of the faculty of St. Bonaventure on commencement day, 1941. (Photograph by F. Donald Kenney, courtesy of St. Bonaventure University)

"To my mind there was very little doubt about the immorality of the methods used in modern war. Self-defense is good and a necessary war is licit: but methods that descend to wholesale barbarism and ruthless, indiscriminate slaughter of non-combatants practically without defense are hard to see as anything else but mortal sins."

(The Seven Storey Mountain)

even his fingerprints. Such information will help you put the right tag on his body if you should run across his body somewhere full of bullets, but it doesn't say anything about the man himself. Men become objects and not persons. Now you complain because there is a war, but war is the proper state for a world in which men are a series of numbered bodies. War is the state that now perfectly fits your philosophy of life: you deserve the war for believing the things you believe. In so far as I tend to believe those same things and act according to such lies, I am part of the complex of responsibilities for the war too. But if you want to identify me, ask me not where I live, or what I like to eat, or how I comb my hair, but ask me what I think I am living for, in detail, and ask me what I think is keeping me from living fully for the thing I want to live for."[152]

It was an autobiographical novel written by a man using his typewriter as a confessional, confessing not only specific sins he has committed but his co-responsibility for sins that are destroying the world.

The novel was also a confession of what he would do personally in the war: he would not kill anyone or be trained in the use of deadly weapons. He found no invitation to killing in the words and life of Jesus, who had killed no one but rather lived an unarmed and healing life under the tyranny of Roman occupation. In the thirteenth century Saint Francis had renewed the nonviolent witness of the early church, writing a pacifist rule not only for his friars and nuns but for lay people too. His rule for the Third Order had forbidden members to possess weapons or use them for any reason.

When Merton registered with the Selective Service, it was as a conscientious objector, though one prepared for noncombatant service on the battlefield as an unarmed medic. In such a role, he wrote in his journal, "I would not have to kill men made in the image and likeness of God" but could obey the divine law of "serving the wounded and saving lives." Even if it turned out that he would only dig latrines, he considered this "a far greater honor to God than killing men."[153]

Writing his autobiography less than seven years later, he expanded on his decision in a text which startled many readers, appearing as it did in the early days of the Cold War:

> [God] was not asking me to judge all the nations of the world, or to elucidate all the moral and political motives behind their actions. He was not demanding that I pass some critical decision defining the innocence and guilt of all those concerned in the war. He was asking me to make a choice that amounted to an act of love for His truth, His goodness, His charity, His Gospel. . . . He was asking me to do, to the best of my knowledge, what I thought Christ would do. . . . After all, Christ did say, "Whatsoever you have done to the least of these my brethren, you did it to me."[154]

When he took his army physical, it turned out he was unsuitable for military service of any kind, with or without a gun. Soldiers had to have a certain number of teeth. Merton's encounters with dentists had left him short. He was classified 1B. Only those classified 1A were being drafted.

No room in the seminary: his student sins and their consequences too enduring. No room on the battlefield: too many morals, too few teeth.

With his images of the future abruptly altered, Merton found himself thinking about a battlefield of a different sort, the Trappist monastery in Kentucky. This would be a good place, he decided, to spend the Easter recess. He reached the abbey on April 5, 1941, the eve of Palm Sunday.

The Court of the Queen of Heaven

This is the center of America.

THOMAS MERTON
The Secular Journal of Thomas Merton

Spire of the Abbey of Gethsemani in winter. (Photograph courtesy of Boston College, Burns Library)

"Suddenly I saw a steeple that shone like silver in the moonlight, growing into sight from behind a rounded knoll. . . . Breathless, I looked at the monastery that was revealed before me as we came over the rise."

(The Seven Storey Mountain)

It was Holy Week, 1941. Huge areas of London were devastated. Coventry had been razed. The country where Merton had lived so much of his life had become a land of blood and smoke. Events that convinced others to go to war pushed Merton in the opposite direction. He believed that what Hitler represented could not be defeated by the methods the Nazis relied on: intimidation, violence, and murder. The only adequate response to evil, it seemed to Merton, was sanctity. "There is only one defense: to take the Gospel literally, and to be *saints.*"[155]

Fresh from his decision not to take part in bloodshed, Merton arrived at the Abbey of Gethsemani to share in monastic recollection of the crucifixion of Christ and to participate in the celebration of his resurrection. For all his travels, no place Merton ever visited had so astonished Merton. From the moment he arrived, he felt he had crossed a border for which he had long been searching. Under the sign of the cross, he wrote in his journal:

I should tear out all the pages of this book, and all the other pages of anything else I have ever written, and begin here. This is the center of America. I had wondered what was holding the country together, what has been keeping the universe from cracking in pieces and falling apart. It is places like this monastery—not only this one: there must be others.[156]

On Holy Saturday, five days later, he confided: "I desire only one thing: to love God. Those who love him keep his commandments. I only desire to do one thing: to follow his will. I pray that I am at least beginning to know what that may mean. Could it possibly mean that I might someday become a monk in this monastery? My Lord, and my King, and my God!"[157]

Yet there was the obvious counter-question: if his past was such that he was unacceptable to the Franciscans, would not the Trappists have similar objections?

Easter Monday, returning to the nonmonastic world after a weeklong retreat, he felt more than ever like an outsider. He noticed that even women's clothing was being drawn into the war, military insignia being added for decorative touches. Banner headlines reported that the German army had landed in Egypt.

Back at Saint Bonaventure's to teach Dante and bibliography at summer school, Merton began to look into the life and writings of Saint Thérèse of Lisieux, a Carmelite nun widely revered by Catholics simply as "the Little Flower." There was a shrine to her on campus. Her autobiography, *The Story of a Soul*, had been recommended to Merton by one of the friars he most respected, Father Irenaeus Herscher, the librarian.

At first Merton was put off. Thérèse seemed so much the pious product of nineteenth-century, middle-class provincial French culture. Gradually, however, Merton became impressed by her "little way," a path to holiness in everyday life, suffering insults and injuries without retribution, bitterness, or even self-defense. Thérèse had such a profound sense of the divine presence that even scrubbing the floor was a luminous event. Thérèse threw fresh light on what it meant to be a saint: an example of transparency and hiddenness.

While teaching summer classes, another vocational possibility was opened to Merton by a visiting speaker: Catherine de Hueck Doherty, nicknamed the Baroness because she had been born into an aristocratic Russian

St. Thérèse of Lisieux. (Photograph courtesy of the Office Central de Lisieux)

"It is a wonderful experience to discover a new saint."

(The Seven Storey Mountain)

Catherine de Hueck (center), founder
of Friendship House in Harlem.
(Photograph courtesy of Boston College,
Burns Library)

*"I don't know if you are concerned
about the past of people who come to
work for you. I got in some trouble
once. . . . If you absolutely want to
know, I will tell you, but otherwise I
can say in good conscience that I don't
believe, myself, that it would disqualify
me from working in Friendship House .
. . [though it was] enough for it to be an
impediment to my becoming a priest. . . .
It is something that definitely demands a
whole life of penance and absolute self-
sacrifice: so that if I thought the
Trappists would take me, I think I
would want to go to them. But I have to
do penance, and if Harlem won't have
me, then where may I turn?"*

*(Letter to Catherine de Hueck,
November 10, 1941)*

family.[158] She described a project she had founded,
Friendship House, a lay Catholic community in
Harlem—black territory where few whites dared to be
seen—that was trying to put into practice the church's
teaching about social justice. A plain-spoken woman,
she responded with one word—"Baloney!"—when a
Franciscan objected to her critique of friars who took a
vow of poverty but in fact lived a comfortable life far
removed from the poor. Merton was impressed that the
Baroness spoke "in a free and easy way," as he noted in
his journal, making "good, simple, unhysterical gestures.
. . . [She] talked of martyrdom without embarrassment.
. . . The way she said some things, left you ready to do
some kind of action . . . renounce the world, live in total
poverty, but also doing very definite things: ministering
to the poor in a certain definite way."[159]

Talking with Merton the following day, the Baroness
mentioned that she was looking for someone to help with
clothing distribution. Merton volunteered to help once
summer school ended and he had more free time.

She may well have wondered if this young man's offer
would not quickly evaporate. So many others had
offered to help and yet never showed up. But on August
15, there was Merton at the door of Friendship House
with a bouquet of flowers in hand.

As a student at Columbia, Merton had lived for years
just across the border from Harlem without fully seeing
what was there or understanding what a ghetto meant.
Now that he was spending time every week at
Friendship House on 135th Street at Lenox Avenue, he
was becoming aware of the mortal sin of racism. Because
of skin color, millions of people were regarded as less
than human and were even driven to regard themselves
that way. He saw Harlem as a "divine indictment against
New York City and the people who live downtown and
make their money downtown."[160] Merton's sense of outrage at what ghettoes represented didn't cool even after
years of monastic life:

Here in this huge, dark, steaming slum, hundreds of thousands of Negroes are herded together like cattle, most of them with little to eat and nothing to do. All the senses and imagination and sensibilities and emotions and sorrows and desires and hopes and ideas of a race with vivid feelings and deep emotional reactions are forced in upon themselves, bound inward by an iron ring of frustration: the prejudice that hems them in with its four insurmountable walls. In this huge cauldron inestimable natural gifts, wisdom, love, music, science, poetry, are stamped down and left to boil . . . and thousands upon thousands of souls are destroyed.[161]

Friendship House, an urban center run by a lay Catholic community on 135th St. in Harlem, where Merton worked for a short time in 1941.

Yet, despite all the evidence of social destruction and ruined lives, Merton was dazzled by Harlem's beauty, in the children most of all, but also in the elderly. He

Harlem in the 1940s. (Photograph courtesy of the Schomburg Center, New York City Public Library)

"[Catherine de Hueck] and those who joined her . . . would live and work in the slums, lose themselves, in the huge anonymous mass of the forgotten and the derelict, for the only purpose of living the complete, integral Christian life in that environment—loving those around them, sacrificing themselves for those around them, spreading the Gospel and the truth of Christ most of all by being saints, by living in union with Him, by being full of His Holy Ghost, His Charity."

(The Seven Storey Mountain)

remembered one aged woman sitting on the steps of Friendship House on a hot summer evening. "I saw in this tired, serene and holy face the patience and joy of the martyrs and the clear, unquenchable light of sanctity . . . a deep, unfathomable, shining peace."[162]

The faith of Friendship House's small volunteer community and the welcome he found in Harlem made Merton reconsider his vocation. Sipping black Russian tea with the Baroness, he talked about making Harlem his home and this work his life. Such a choice had the additional advantage that he would remain free to write, which he expected would be discouraged, if not forbidden, by the Trappists. On the other hand, not only did his attraction to Gethsemani continue to haunt him daily, but he had doubts that he would do well as the one male volunteer working daily with a community of five or six young women. "If I am with women," he wrote in his journal, "I know they are women, every minute."[163]

On retreat for five days in early September at the Trappist Monastery of Our Lady of the Valley near Providence, Rhode Island, he wrestled with the choices, struggling to understand his own motives. Writing about his quandary to the Baroness, he described himself as being tied up like a pretzel. Reading the story of the rich young man whom Jesus had called to give up everything "half kills me," he told Mark Van Doren.[164] "The sense of exile bleeds in me like a hemorrhage," he wrote in a journal entry.[165] He told another volunteer at Friendship House that he was in the midst of a "battle of angels."

Back in his room at Saint Bonaventure's, on the night of November 27 Merton wrote in his journal, "Should I be going to Harlem, or to the Trappists? Why doesn't this idea of the Trappists leave me? Perhaps what I am afraid of is to write and be rejected. . . . Perhaps I cling to my independence, to the chance to write, to go where I like in the world. . . . Going to live in Harlem . . . is a good and reasonable way to follow Christ. But going to the Trappists is exciting, it fills me with awe and desire. I return to the idea again and again: 'Give up *everything*, give up *everything*!' "[166]

After praying at the campus shrine to Saint Thérèse of Lisieux, Merton at last had the courage to talk with Father Philotheus, one of the friars, and ask his burning question: whether having fathered a child had created a canonical impediment to becoming a monk or, later on, being ordained a priest. Father Philotheus said that, in his opinion, there was no insurmountable obstacle and suggested that Merton's next step would be to go to Gethsemani during Christmas vacation to talk about the problem with the abbot.

"I rushed out of [Father Philotheus's] room," Merton

"I don't think there was ever a moment in my life when my soul felt so urgent and special an anguish. . . . 'Please help me. What am I going to do? I can't go on like this.' Suddenly, as soon as I had made the prayer, I became aware of the wood, the trees, the dark hills, the wet night wind, and then, clearer than any of these obvious realities, in my imagination, I began to hear the great bell of Gethsemani ringing in the night. . . . The bell seemed to be telling me where I belonged—as if it were calling me home. . . ."

(The Seven Storey Mountain)

wrote the Baroness on December 6, "saying all I could remember of the *Te Deum* and went and fell on my face in the chapel and began to pray and beg and implore Almighty God to let me be admitted to the Trappists."[167]

Leaving the chapel, he was at last ready to risk another rejection. That night he wrote to the abbot of Gethsemani. A few days later, the abbot's response arrived. Far from the monastery door being locked, Merton was given permission to come.

Along with the abbot's note came a letter from the draft board summoning Merton to appear for a second physical examination; the rule about teeth had changed. It was possible he could now be classified 1A—a person eligible for immediate drafting. After applying to the draft board for a delay while he was at the monastery, Merton wrote to the abbot to ask if he could come sooner than planned.

At the same time he began giving away his possessions: his manuscripts to Mark Van Doren, his journal to Catherine de Hueck Doherty,[168] his clothes to Friendship House, his books to the university library. All he retained was a Bible, his breviary, a copy of *The Imitation of Christ*, a volume of Saint John of the Cross, a collection of Gerard Manley Hopkins's poems, an anthology of William Blake, Dante's *Vita Nuova* and *Canzoniere*, the *Divine Comedy*, an edition of Italian poems, plus the clothing needed for a one-day trip, and his rosary.

It was time, he told Bob Lax, "to get out of the subway and go into the clean woods."[169]

On December 9, the day after Congress declared war on Japan, Merton closed his bank account. On December 10, he traveled by train to Kentucky with the intention not simply of visiting the Court of the Queen of Heaven, but making it his home for life.

Brother Louis

Everything I wanted to do the most, I can now try to do all the time without any interference....As soon as I got inside, I knew I was home, where I never had been or would be a stranger.

THOMAS MERTON
The Sign of Jonas

On December 13, 1941, following an interview with the abbot, Dom Frederic Dunne, Merton was accepted as a postulant choir monk—a member of the community who participates in singing the daily offices of prayer and is being prepared for ordination as a priest. He moved out of the guest house and into the monastery.

On February 21, 1942, his head shaved, he put on the white robes of a novice. Signifying the transition, he was given a new name: Frater Maria Ludovicus—Brother Mary Louis. All Trappists took Mary as a first name; she was the order's patroness. Merton's particular namesake, Louis, a ruler in the thirteenth century and the only canonized king of France, was renowned for his kindness to the poor. The name seemed apt for a French-born novice. The abbot, suffering pneumonia at the time, gave the newly vested novices an impassioned warning that they had nothing to look forward to but sickness, sorrows, humiliations, fasts, and everything human nature hates: the cross.

Changes in recent years have softened many of the sharp edges in Trappist life as Merton found it. A monk of Gethsemani today has his own small room, freedom to correspond and to follow world news, and warmth in the winter. The life Merton embraced in 1941 was more austere, even medieval.

Every detail of life made clear that this was a peniten-

Thomas Merton in his early years as a monk. (Photograph courtesy of Boston College, Burns Library)

Chapel of the Abbey of Gethsemani.
(Photograph courtesy of the Abbey of
Gethsemani)

*"This is the center of America. I had
wondered what was holding the country
together, what was keeping the universe
from cracking in pieces and falling apart.
It is places like this monastery. . . ."*
(The Seven Storey Mountain)

tial order, but doing penance was what Merton had in mind. The monks slept in their robes on straw-covered boards in dormitories that were frigid in winter and sweltering in summer. Beds were separated by shoulder-high partitions. Half the year was fasting time. A typical meal featured bread, potatoes, an apple, and barley coffee. Even on such feast days as Easter and Christmas, meat, fish, and eggs were never served. There were days when the water in the holy water fonts was frozen solid. The fire in the church's one wood-burning stove wasn't lit until ice had formed on the inside of the stained-glass windows. Hot water was on tap two days a week.

There were, and still are, long hours of communal prayer in the church: about eight hours a day. When not at prayer, there was hard physical labor: working the farm, cutting wood, maintaining the buildings. To chastise their flesh still further, there was the "discipline"—a small whip with which each monk briefly lashed his bare back on Fridays while sitting on his bed and reciting the Our Father. Even Trappist underwear was still of fifteenth-century design.

Infractions of the rule were denounced in public, at the Chapter of Faults. A novice's few personal possessions were kept in a small box in the scriptorium. Hard manual labor was done with tools that had changed little since the days of Saint Benedict. News from the outside world rarely reached the monks.

Communication was mainly by sign language using four hundred hand gestures that mainly had to do with prayer, labor, and food. Barring special permission, mail to the outside world could be sent only four times a year: Easter, Assumption, All Saints, and Christmas, and then only four half-page letters, all of which were read by a superior before being posted. Delivery of mail was normally restricted to the same four feasts. Even when a parent died, the monk stayed at the monastery.

The choir novices attended four or five classes a week: study of the Benedictine Rule, spiritual life, liturgy, and singing were the primary subjects. The novice had occasional private conferences with the novice master plus infrequent meetings with the abbot. There were a few hours of labor each day: farm work, cleaning, or cutting lumber. While the word "solitude" was often used to describe Trappist life, privacy was practically nonexistent.

It wasn't easy for Merton. He wasn't robust, treasured privacy, and he didn't like the smell of straw. But he took to Trappist life and tradition with joy, feeling he had at last found his true home. Far from feeling imprisoned, he felt free. The monastery was the one place in the world, he wrote on the anniversary of his first visit, "where everything makes sense. . . . Everything I wanted to do the most, I can now try to do all the time without any interference. . . . As soon as I got inside, I knew I was home, where I never had been or would be a stranger."[170]

Though there were periods of difficulty and uncer-

"Practically the first thing you noticed, when you looked at the choir, was this young man in secular clothes, among all the monks. Then suddenly we saw him no more. He was in white. They had given him an oblate's habit, and you could not pick him out from the rest. The waters had closed over his head, and he was submerged in the community. He was lost. The world would hear of him no more. He had drowned to our society to become a Cistercian."

(The Seven Storey Mountain)

Monks in choir. (Photograph courtesy of the Abbey of Gethsemani)

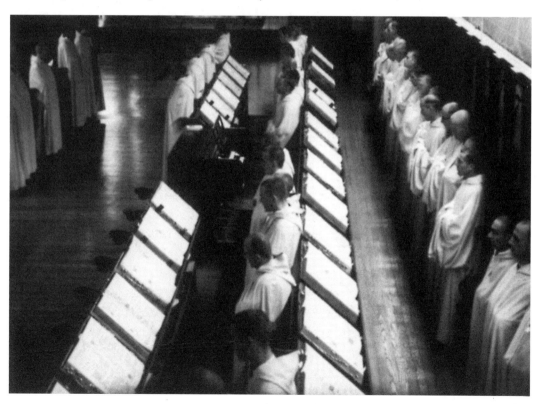

Abbey of Gethsemani. (Photograph courtesy of the Abbey of Gethsemani)

tainty, times of frustration with the demands and intrusions of community life, his writings in the first few years mainly record a life of confidence, growth, and a sense of God's presence. "What a life," he wrote Mark Van Doren five months after his arrival at Gethsemani. "It is tremendous. Not because of any acts we perform, any penance, any single feature of the liturgy or the chant, not because we sleep on boards & straw mattresses & fast & work & sweat & sing & keep silence. These things are all utterly simple acts that have no importance whatever in themselves. But the whole unity of the life *is* tremendous. . . . [T]he life is a real unity. . . . The foundation of its unity is God's unity. . . . His simplicity *is* our life. We *live*

His oneness: we *live* his singleness of concentration. . . .
No wonder it is wonderful. The life is God. . . . Christ is
the principle & end of absolutely everything that a
Trappist does, right down to breathing."[171]

"What surprises me," he wrote Lax in November, "is
not that I am happy here but that I ever tried to fool
myself I was happy anywhere else." He described Mass
as a "solemn & complicated drama of angels" with the
words of Mass proclaiming "the infinite kindness of
God." He told Lax about his fellow monks, in whom he
found the "same proportion of people with faces that
frighten you as everywhere else. The men who come
here are the same, originally, as the men in the subway.
. . . But the difference is, here they have forgotten about
being wise guys. . . . A lot of my brothers are really saints.
. . . The thing that makes the most sense," he concluded,
"is to be in the presence of God & live by His will as we
live on air & bread."[172]

One of Merton's early visitors was his brother, John
Paul. The two brothers, whose lives during childhood
had so often taken them in opposite directions, had
grown closer when Tom returned from England and
entered Columbia, though the closeness had more to do
with going to the movies than sharing a religious transformation. Several months before Merton became a
monk, John Paul had joined the Royal Canadian Air
Force. It wasn't until John Paul was in uniform that he
followed his brother into Christianity. By then he was a
Sergeant Observer, trained to be part of a bomber crew. It
was participation in this aspect of military activity, aerial
warfare, that most troubled his older brother. Finishing
his initial military training and before going to England
to join a bombing squadron, John Paul came to
Gethsemani to visit Tom in July 1942 and ended up being
baptized. For four days leading up to the event, Tom
instructed John Paul in the basics of Catholic Christianity.

Yet even with this new line of connection, there
remained separation. In one of the more poignant scenes

in *The Seven Storey Mountain*, we witness Merton trying, by sign language, to invite his brother down from the church loft to be with him: "John Paul was kneeling all alone, in uniform. He seemed to be an immense distance away." Between them was a locked door. Merton couldn't call up to tell him the way around it through the guest house. He resorted to sign language, but John Paul didn't understand the signs. "At that moment there flashed into my mind all the scores of times in our ... childhood when I had chased John Paul away with stones. . . . And now, all of a sudden, here it was all over again . . . John Paul, standing, confused and unhappy, at a distance which he was not able to bridge."[173]

In fact, with the help of the novice master, John Paul was at last escorted down from the visitors' loft and they were able to receive communion together in the chapel of Our Lady of Victories.

In Merton's poems and journal writings from his first years in the monastery, one often finds a wild joy that he is among exiles: monks who had escaped the world of war and oppression, ambition and competition. The monastery remains a kind of rough paradise, a fragment of Eden. Yet a sense of connection with those who haven't escaped the subway world remains. In a letter that first year he told his friends, "We pray all night in tears for people who are being hit and kicked and killed, and who cannot help it."

One of those killed was John Paul, now newly married to a woman he had met in England. On April 17, 1943, a telegram arrived at Gethsemani reporting that Sergeant J. P. Merton was missing in action. A death notice soon fol-

Merton's brother John Paul on his wedding day. (Photograph courtesy of the Thomas Merton Center)

lowed. Returning from a bombing raid on Mannheim, Germany, John Paul's damaged bomber came down in the North Sea. His back was broken in the crash. Begging for water, he died several hours later and was buried at sea five miles off the English coast.

The monk who hated war wrote a poem to his soldier brother, offering him his monastic life:

Sweet brother, if I do not sleep
My eyes are flowers for your tomb;
And if I cannot eat my bread,
My fasts shall live like willows where you died.
If in the heat I find no water for my thirst,
My thirst shall turn to springs for you, poor traveller....
Come, in my labor find a resting place
And in my sorrows lay your head,
Or rather take my life and blood
And buy yourself a better bed—
Or take my breath and take my death
And buy yourself a better rest.
When all the men of war are shot
And flags have fallen into dust
Your cross and mine shall tell men still
Christ died on each, for both of us.
For in the wreckage of your April Christ lies slain,
And Christ weeps in the ruins of my spring:
The money of Whose tears shall fall
Into your weak and friendless hand,
And buy you back to your own land:
The silence of Whose tears shall fall
Like bells upon your alien tomb.
Hear them and come: they call you home.[174]

Parents, grandparents, and now his brother dead, Merton had become a sole survivor.

Thomas Merton versus Brother Louis

Nobody seems to understand that one of us has got to die.

THOMAS MERTON
The Seven Storey Mountain

Opposite:
Thomas Merton in 1949, around the time that *The Seven Storey Mountain* was first published. (Photograph courtesy of the Abbey of Gethsemani)

"In one sense we are always travelling, and travelling as if we did not know where we were going. In another sense we have already arrived."

(The Seven Storey Mountain)

Entering Gethsemani, Merton assumed he was sacrificing his aspirations as a writer in order "to disappear into God."[175] He was aware that Trappists had a reputation of being suspicious of intellectual work. A Trappist monk climbed the ladder to heaven not by being noted in the outside world, but by anonymous prayer, tears, and sweat.

In fact vanishing from the literary map seemed to Merton a good idea. He was terrified of his ambition to be noticed, to be influential, to have a name, to become a famous author. In the final pages of *The Seven Storey Mountain*, he refers to his writer-self as a shadow who had followed him into the cloister. "Nobody seems to understand that one of us has to die."[176]

Yet Merton's compulsion to write wouldn't go away. It would have been easier to stop breathing. He kept a journal from his first day at Gethsemani, and soon there were poems.

As it happened, Merton's work as a writer was less an issue of ambition than of obedience. It turned out that his abbot, Dom Frederic Dunne, was the son of a bookbinder and publisher. He had grown up with a love of books and profound respect for those who write them. In fact, well before Merton's arrival, Dom Frederic had already cleared the way for another member of the community, Father Raymond Flanagan, to write and publish.

Dom Frederic Dunne, Merton's first abbot at Gethsemani. (Photograph courtesy of the Thomas Merton Center)

While aware of the novice's hesitations about writing, Dom Frederic encouraged Merton to continue with his poetry and began assigning various writing projects to him. Merton resisted periodically, on one occasion appealing to the order's Abbot General. It was in vain. While there was a brief period when his confessor ordered him to stop writing poems, the abbot decided otherwise. First Dom Frederic, and later his successor, Dom James Fox, believed that Merton had a gift from God that was valuable to the Church. They recognized an obligation to help in its nurturing. Also the community was in debt as a consequence of building projects, and it would be helpful should Merton's writings produce a little income.

In 1942, one of Merton's poems appeared in *The New Yorker* and four in *Poetry*. His first book, *Thirty Poems*, was published by James Laughlin of New Directions in 1944. Another collection of poems, *A Man in the Divided Sea*, appeared in 1946. Seven more volumes followed, including the posthumous publications of the enormous *Collected Poems*. (The best starting point for any reader eager to explore Merton's poetry is the excellent 2005 anthology, *New Selected Poems of Thomas Merton*.[177])

It was while preparing *A Man in the Divided Sea* that Merton received orders that only his secular name was to appear on the book. The ruling stood for the rest of his life. For many years no author photo was permitted on his book jackets. Not until late in his life did readers have the possibility of finding out what Merton looked like.

In March 1946, less than five years after his arrival at Gethsemani, Merton disclosed to the priest witnessing his confessions the temptation to write his life story. His confessor's response was laughter, but Dom Frederic thought it was a good idea.

In a letter to James Laughlin, Merton described the book-to-be as "a cross between Dante's Purgatory, and Kafka, and a medieval miracle play."[178] The title, already in his mind, was taken from Dante's seven-tiered image of purgatory: *The Seven Storey Mountain*. In May 1946

Merton gave Dom Frederic a memorandum (intended for the order's General Chapter, it was written in the third person) in which Merton listed various books he was prepared to write in the coming years and for which he sought the order's blessing: works on Trappist history, biographies of Cistercian saints, a book on contemplation, another on monastic community life, and a study of ancient Cistercian liturgy. The final item on the three-page list was "a biography . . . of a Gethsemani monk" who was the "son of artists, was born in Europe, and passed through the abyss of Communism and modern-day university life before being led to the cloister by the merciful love of Jesus."[179]

With Dom Frederic's backing and his own reservations about being a writer temporarily dismissed, Merton threw his considerable energies into the autobiography. Kafka, miracle plays, even Dante all fell to the side in favor of straightforward narrative. True to its title, however, the manuscript was becoming mountain-sized: "I cannot make it less than 650 typewritten pages," Merton wrote Laughlin in August.[180]

In late October 1946, Merton sent the manuscript to his agent, Naomi Burton. Several weeks passed before she had time to read it. In December she gave it to Merton's acquaintance from college days, Robert Giroux, who had gone from Columbia into the Navy and was now an editor at Harcourt Brace in New York. Having been assured by Giroux that the book was not likely to lose money, the company agreed to sign a contract with Merton. "Manuscript accepted," Giroux telegraphed Merton. "Happy new year."

The good news was followed by bad. In the spring of 1947, one of the order's censors nearly blocked publication, and not because of theological error. On top of objections to the sex and drinking recorded in the original text, he was dismayed by the prose style. He suggested Merton take a correspondence course in English grammar before attempting any more books.

Cover of *A Man in the Divided Sea,* published in 1946 by New Directions.

If on Your Cross Your life and death and
  mine are one,
Love teaches me to read, in You, the
  rest of a new history.
I trace my days back to another
  childhood . . .
Until I find a manger, star and straw,
A pair of animals, some simple men,
And thus I learn that I was born,
Now not in France, but Bethlehem.
                          ("The Biography")

Cover of the mass-market paperback edition of *The Seven Storey Mountain*.

"The Seven Storey Mountain is the work of a man I never even heard of."
(The Sign of Jonas)

Rounds of editing and rewriting were required that veiled the more controversial events in Merton's earlier life and delayed the book's publication until 1948—October 4, as it happened, the feast of Saint Francis of Assisi.

Words of praise from Evelyn Waugh were quoted on the cover. "This may well prove," he said, "of permanent interest in the history of religious experience." It was a book, said Clifton Fadiman, that deals with "not what happens *to* a man, but with what happens inside him—that is, inside his soul." "*The Seven Storey Mountain*," commented the novelist Graham Greene, "is a book one reads with a pencil so as to make it one's own."

How different *The Seven Storey Mountain* was from many other books, religious or secular, was suggested by the index, with entries that included Louis Armstrong, Saint Thomas Aquinas, William Blake, Marc Chagall, Charles Chaplin, Duke Ellington, Mahatma Gandhi, D. H. Lawrence, Harpo Marx, Pablo Picasso and Mary Pickford.

Booksellers found themselves placing order after order for more copies.

"It did not seem to me, nor to anyone in the firm," Giroux recalled, "that it would become a national phenomenon. It merely looked as if the book would 'do all right.' "[181] The first printing was 7,500 copies. However the book's prepublication orders suggested that the book was going to do better than expected. Due to orders from several Catholic book clubs, a second printing of 20,000 copies was needed prior to the official publication day. In October, the month of official publication, orders for 5,900 more copies were received; in November, 13,000; in December, 31,000. On one record day, 10,000 copies were ordered. In May 1949 Giroux hand-delivered copy number 200,000, specially bound in leather and with an engraved presentation plate, as a gift for the author.

The original cloth edition of *The Seven Storey Mountain* sold more than 600,000 copies, while in paperback sales the figure went into the millions. The book has been continually in print since 1948. A British edition followed: *Elected Silence*, borrowing a phrase from a poem of Gerard Manley Hopkins; it was edited and with a foreword by Evelyn Waugh. Translations have since appeared in at least sixteen languages. Merton found himself joking that pretty soon Hollywood would be knocking on the door and that Gary Cooper would be cast in the leading role.[182] In fact film offers were made, but Dom James and Merton were of one mind about turning them down.

What lies behind the book's remarkable popularity? Partly it is the merits of an extraordinary story told by a writer who played words as freely as Charlie Parker played the saxophone. Partly it is Merton's success in producing the most gripping account of religious conversion since Saint Augustine's *Confessions*. Partly it is because the book is a massive love letter, the ultimate object of his devotion being God and all that God has given us for our good and salvation. Merton communicated a contagious enthusiasm for the life of faith, voluntary poverty, penance, and prayer. *The Seven Storey Mountain* remains an electrifying challenge to the idea that human happiness consists mainly of a proper diet, a good job, money in the bank, a comfortable address, and an active sex life.

Timing was also a factor. Readers in 1948 were ready to listen to a monk's searing criticism of a social order which, after the ordeal of the most destructive war ever fought, now seemed aimed at producing men with identical thoughts wearing gray flannel suits while their wives cleaned house and tended the children. A war of unprecedented violence had defeated Germany, Italy, and Japan, but it had also left deep wounds in the conscience of the winners. The war crimes had not been on one side only. Obliteration bombing of cities by the Allies had produced vast numbers of civilian casualties. The Germans and Japanese were not alone in their guilt. "Everything should have been changed by the awful

"At work—writing—I am doing a little better. I mean, I am less tied up in it, more peaceful and more detached.

. . . Meanwhile, for myself, I have only one desire and that is the desire for solitude—to disappear into God, to be submerged in His peace, to be lost in the secret of His face."

(The Sign of Jonas)

Go, stubborn talker,
Find you a station on the loud world's
corners,
And try there (if your hands be clean) your
length of patience:
Use there the rhythms that upset my
sickness,
And spend your pennyworth of prayer
There in the clamor of the Christless
avenues.

And try to ransom some one prisoner.
Out of those walls, of traffic, out of the
wheels
of that unhappiness.
("The Poet, To His Book")

Cover of *Figures for an Apocalypse*,
published in 1948 by New Directions.

war," said Bob Giroux, "but it became pretty clear by 1947 that nothing at all was changing, in fact it was going to start all over again."[183]

Yet the book also had its shortcomings: occasional preachiness, sarcastic stabs at non-Catholic Christianity, condescension in describing Catholic religious communities less rigorous than the Trappists, and the suggestion that those who really wanted to reach the high wire of holiness had better head for the monastery. Later in life Merton was dismayed at how narrow and judgmental he had been and claimed that the author of *The Seven Storey Mountain* was dead and buried. Yet the book's strengths easily outweigh its weaknesses. *The Seven Storey Mountain* remains one of the most compelling autobiographies ever written.

The significance of the book for its readers was registered not only in sales. Stacks of letters were sent to Merton, far too many to answer. He was forced to respond with printed messages produced on the monastery press. His sudden fame worried him and renewed his doubts about the advisability of writing.

Yet the writing continued. A new book of poems, *Figures for an Apocalypse*, came out in 1948 and was well-received, but *Exile Ends in Glory*, a biography of Mother Berchmans, O.C.S.O., was quickly and mercifully forgotten. *The Waters of Siloe*, a history of the Trappists published in 1949, remains good reading. The same year produced another book of poetry, *Tears of the Blind Lions*, and a collection of brief meditations, *Seeds of Contemplation*, a best-seller that went through many printings and translations. *What Are These Wounds?*, a biography of Saint Lutagarde, was issued in 1950; written while Merton was in the novitiate, it is an example of sugar-coated Catholic piety at its most cloying.

His books were selling well, and some have stood the test of years, but Merton found each of them troubling. "Where did I get all that pious rhetoric," Merton wondered when he had to suffer through the public reading

Merton kneeling at right. (Photograph courtesy of the Thomas Merton Center.)

of *Exile Ends in Glory* during meals. "[This book] is one of the worst pieces of cheese that has ever been served in our rectory. . . . That was the way I thought [at the time] a monk was supposed to write."[184]

Even *Seeds of Contemplation*, a much better book, distressed him. "It lacks warmth and human affection," he noted in his journal.[185] Parts of *The Waters of Siloe* struck him as "impertinent."[186] Correcting page proofs for *Figures for an Apocalypse*, Merton found himself disgusted.[187]

"A bad book about the love of God," he scolded himself, "remains a bad book."[188]

Father Louis

*God has leavened the whole world with apostles that He scraped off
pots in the kitchens of the Greeks.*

THOMAS MERTON
The Sign of Jonas

Opposite:
Merton is ordained as Father M.
Louis, O.C.S.O., May 26, 1949, the
Feast of the Ascension. (Photograph
courtesy of the Thomas Merton Center)

Having written an autobiography that presented monastic life in general and Trappist life in particular in the best possible light, once the book was finished Merton found he was overwhelmed by distractions when singing in choir and was losing all sense of the presence of God. He was troubled by the heavy workload, one day listing in his journal twelve books and booklets that he was supposed to be writing. He suffered from insomnia and experienced growing doubts about whether he really belonged with the Trappists.

In an overcrowded monastery, meant for fifty to seventy monks but now with a population nearing two hundred, it wasn't easy to find solitude. It's unlikely anyone in the community had searched out remote corners of the abbey more thoroughly than Merton. In his ongoing quest for places where he might be alone, he sometimes found refuge in a nook in the wall of the monastery church. At times he made use of an upper room in a garden shed. Merton's main place for writing was a scriptorium that he shared with another monk. There must have been moments when he recalled with nostalgia the entire room he had all to himself on Perry Street.

The Carthusians were often in his thoughts: a way of monastic life that provided a high degree of individual privacy. The Carthusians, founded in the eleventh century

Merton in 1949. (Photograph courtesy of the Abbey of Gethsemani)

by Saint Bruno, might best be described as a community of hermits. Each choir monk has his own hermitage, usually consisting of a small dwelling set in a corner of a walled garden. Here the monk meditates, prays the Liturgy of the Hours in solitude, eats his meals, studies, writes, and works in his garden and at a manual trade. He leaves the cell only for three daily prayer services in the monastery chapel, including the community Mass, and for occasional conferences with his superior. Once a week, the monks take a four-hour walk together in the countryside during which they may speak. On Sundays and feast days a community meal is eaten in silence. Twice a year there is a daylong community recreation. Carthusians do not undertake pastoral, charitable, or missionary work and receive no retreatants other than persons who are contemplating entering the monastery. Their contribution to the outside world is their life of prayer.

The Trappists, it seemed to Merton, had practically abolished privacy and with it much of the climate of contemplative life.

In a moment of exasperation following difficulties with the order's censors, he opened fire on the Trappist sweat ethic: "Trappists believe that everything that costs them is God's will. Anything that makes you suffer is God's will. If it makes you sweat, it is God's will. But we have serious doubts about the things which demand no expense of physical energy. . . . We think we have done great things because we are worn out."[189] In his darker moments Merton wished he had been aware of the Carthusians when he was choosing between Friendship House and Gethsemani.

Part of the problem he was struggling to resolve within himself was a recurrent vagrant itch: "There is something in my nature," he wrote early in 1949, "that makes me dream of being a tramp." He thought longingly of flea-inhabited holy wanderers like Saint Benedict Joseph Labré. He found himself "woefully respectable."[190] He was feeling like "a duck in a chicken coop."[191]

Both his abbot and his confessor argued that God had brought him to Gethsemani and intended for him to remain, and most of the time Merton agreed. In January 1947, shortly before taking final vows, Merton wrote:

> It is really illogical that I should get temptations to run off to [the Carthusian] Order. . . . God has put me in a place where I can spend hour after hour, each day, in occupations that are always on the borderline of prayer. There is always a chance to step over the line and enter into simple and contemplative union with God. . . . I am such a fool that I consent to imagine that in some other situation I would quickly advance to a high degree of prayer. . . . [God] has put me in this place . . . and if He ever wants to put me anywhere else, He will do so in a way that will leave no doubt as to who is doing it.[192]

"The important thing is not to live for contemplation but to live for God," he reminded himself. "As soon as you stop traveling, you have arrived."[193]

On the feast of Saint Joseph, March 19, 1947, Merton made a lifetime commitment to poverty, chastity, obedience, continuing conversion, and stability, all in the context of the Abbey of Gethsemani. The vows were heartfelt and considered, but they didn't dismiss the doubts. Months after final vows, he was embarrassed to be found in the library by a brother monk "*in flagrante delicto*, ravished by the pictures of all the [Carthusian] Charterhouses that existed at the end of the last century."[194] News that a noted Benedictine monk had become a Carthusian filled

Where, on what cross my agony will come
I do not ask You:
For it is written and accomplished here,
On every Crucifix on every altar.
It is my narrative that drowns and is
forgotten

In Your five open Jordans,
Your voice that cries my:
"Consummatum est."

("The Biography")

"In January the novices were working in the woods near the lake. . . . The woods were quiet and the axes echoed. . . . You are not supposed to pause and pray when you are at work. American Trappist notions of contemplation do not extend to that. . . . But that January, I was still so new that I had not yet flung myself into that complex and absurd system of meditation. . . . And occasionally I looked up through the trees to where the spire of the abbey church rose up in the distance, and I thought of a line from one of the gradual psalms: 'The Lord is round about His people from henceforth, now and forever.' It was true."

(The Seven Storey Mountain)

Merton with envy, yet at the same time he sensed that his infatuation with Charterhouses was merely a temptation rather than a longing inspired by conscience.

Aware that Merton was finding it nearly impossible to sleep in the dormitory, Dom Frederic had let him use a small room over the stairs, thus giving Merton a small degree of the solitude he sought more and more urgently.

Merton's health bothered him, yet he found there was a blessing in sickness: the contemplative leisure that came with being a patient in the infirmary. "As soon as I get into a cell by myself I am a different person," he wrote in his journal during an infirmary stay. "Prayer becomes what it ought to be. . . . To have nothing to do but abandon yourself to God. . . . Plenty of time. No manuscripts, no typewriter, no rushing back and forth to church, no scriptorium, no breaking your neck to get things done before the next thing happens."[195]

In the spring of 1947, the Trappist Abbot General, Dom Dominique Nogues, came to visit Gethsemani. Because of Merton's fluency in French, he assisted the abbey's guest in all his conversations. Merton was surprised to discover that the Trappist monasteries in Europe, in order to lead a more contemplative life, were moving away from some of the more conventional devotional customs. As for Merton personally, Dom Dominique was delighted with Merton's work as a writer and assured him it was his wish that he should continue on that path.

Unfortunately the encouragement he received from superiors was often met with an equal helping of discouragement from the order's censors—fellow monks who sometimes saw themselves not simply as guardians assisting Merton against making theological errors, but as critics and editors. Time and again they found Merton's topics of writings either inappropriate or badly written or both. "I am at the mercy not only of [the censors'] theology," he explained to Naomi Burton, "but of their literary taste."[196] It seemed to Merton that even if he

wrote out the Lord's Prayer with the proposal that everyone ought to say this prayer, "one of the censors of the
order would find fault with my work."[197]

During his seventh year at Gethsemani, death with-
drew a spiritual father. Dom Frederic died on August 4,
1948. He had lived long enough to hand Merton the first
copy of *The Seven Storey Mountain*. His final advice to
Merton had been to go on writing in order "to make people love the spiritual life."[198] Merton couldn't recall anyone who had ever been kinder to him, and marveled at
the abbot's patience.

Problems Merton had been complaining to Dom
Frederic about went into recess after the abbot's death, as
if the old monk had carried them with him to heaven. In
September 1948 Merton described a deep sense of joy and
at-homeness in the monastery: "Love sails me around the
house. I walk two steps on the ground and four steps in
the air. It is love. It is consolation. . . . Love is pushing me
around the monastery, love is kicking me all around like

Several Trappist novices gather wood
near the Abbey. (Photograph courtesy of
Boston College, Burns Library)

a gong I tell you, love is the only thing that makes it possible for me to continue to tick."[199]

His elation didn't last long. By the following February Merton found that something within him seemed to have dried up and that he was hardly able to write. He felt tied up in knots.[200] "I would laboriously cover fifty pages with typescript and then tear them all up and start over again."[201]

The book he was struggling with, published in 1951 as *The Ascent to Truth*,[202] was a presentation of the spirituality of Saint John of the Cross, Merton's favorite mystic, whose dark path was Merton's as well.

One of the few books Merton had brought with him to the monastery in 1941 had been a volume of the writings of John of the Cross. It was through John that Merton had been introduced to the *via negativa*, or apophatic tradition, a spiritual path founded on the awareness that any and all attempts to define God are inadequate. One can better say what God is not, for God is not an idea, not a concept, not a theory. The light of the intellect can carry the pilgrim only so far.

"We seek no light but faith and hear no voice but that of faith," Merton wrote in one of the book's most glowing passages. "We must always walk in darkness. We must travel in silence. We must fly by night."[203]

Merton discovered in the silence and hiddenness of Mary another traveler on the dark path:

And far beneath the movement of this silent cataclysm Mary slept in the infinite tranquility of God, and God was a child curled up who slept in her and her veins were flooded with His wisdom which is night, which is starlight, which is silence. And her whole being was embraced in Him whom she embraced and they became tremendous silence.[204]

If at times his writing reached the heights of poetry, the book as a whole showed the signs of the author's con-

"The world is terrible, people are starving to death and freezing and going to hell with despair and here I sit with a silver spoon in my mouth and write books and everybody sends me fan mail telling me how wonderful I am for giving up so much. I'd like to ask them, what have I given up, anyway, except headaches and responsibilities?"

(The Sign of Jonas)

dition during much of the time he was writing it; many pages were labored, academic and dry.

Preoccupation with his impending ordination to the priesthood was contributing to the stress with which Merton was struggling. There were the occasional flare-ups of his Carthusian attraction, often in tandem with irritation with aspects of life at busy, overcrowded Gethsemani. He felt wrung out by the books already written and was embarrassed, at times revolted, by his fame. He was also trying to cope with the letters addressed to him, many of which required personal replies rather than printed cards. There were also demands on his time and energy from visitors, among them Evelyn Waugh, who told Merton that he should improve his punctuation and edit his work far more severely. On top of everything else, Merton felt so discouraged by his work as a poet that for a time he gave up writing poems. At the end of January 1949, he wondered if he was finished as a writer. "Far from disturbing me, the thought made me glad."[205] Only his journal-writing seemed to go easily, perhaps because it wasn't intended for publication. He didn't have to anticipate his reader's needs or the possible objections of superiors and censors.

Another factor contributing to the uncertainty in Merton's life at the time was Dom James Fox, the abbot who had succeeded Dom Frederic. With his election, Dom James became responsible for the care and feeding of two hundred monks, the enlargement of space to better accommodate so large a community, and the repair of buildings that were nearly derelict. The abbey's income, mainly from Mass stipends and contributions, wasn't nearly enough. Dom James was determined to make the farming profitable and to find other ways to make the abbey solvent. A graduate of the Harvard Business School and subscriber to *The Wall Street Journal*, he was well prepared for the task of getting the abbey out of the red but was not the kind of person Merton easily warmed to. The abbot's businesslike new regime irritated Merton

"The truest solitude is not something outside you, not an absence of men or of sound around you; it is an abyss opening up in the center of your own soul. And this abyss of interior solitude is created by a hunger that will never be satisfied with any created things."

(Seeds of Contemplation)

Dom James Fox succeeded Dom Frederic as Abbot of Gethsemani. (Photograph courtesy of the Thomas Merton Center)

while the increasing reliance on noisy farm machinery afflicted his ears. Merton had thought he was leaving factory clamor behind when he fled to Gethsemani.

Merton's ordination to the priesthood had been twice delayed, first at the suggestion of his confessor, then because of Dom Frederic's death. Dom James was ready to proceed, but first requested a formal declaration that he didn't intend to become a Carthusian, a promise Merton provided. To reassure Merton of his respect for Merton's needs for greater solitude, Dom James designated the monastery's rare book vault—one of the few places in the abbey that was silent and unpopulated—as Merton's new place to work. Merton was entrusted with a foot-long iron key to the vault so that he could enter it whenever time allowed.

On March 19, 1949, the feast of Saint Joseph and the second anniversary of his having taking solemn vows, Merton was ordained a deacon. Serving at Benediction the next day, he felt all in a fog but very happy. "All I could think about was picking up the Host [consecrated bread that had become the Body of Christ]. I was afraid the whole Church would come down on my head, because of what I used to be."[206] His sense of awe that he would soon preside at the liturgy deepened each day. "It seems to me impossible that I should live the next two and a half weeks without keeling over," he noted on May 8.[207]

The transition from Brother Louis to Father Louis took place on the feast of the Ascension, May 26. As Merton lay on the stone floor of the abbey church, he was overcome not with tears but laughter, as if to say: *How funny God is—choosing someone like me for something like this!*

"Even my past sins fit into the picture," he reflected in a letter to Sister Therese Lentfoehr, "throwing into high relief the tremendous mercy of God."[208] The priesthood, Merton told Mark Van Doren, would give him a completely social function that he had always been trying to

Merton's ordination in the Abbey Chapel at Gethsemani. (Photograph courtesy of the Abbey of Gethsemani)

"My priestly ordination was, I felt, the one great secret for which I had been born. Ten years before I was ordained, and seemed to be one of the men in the world most unlikely to become a priest, I had suddenly realized that for me ordination to the priesthood was, in fact, a matter of life or death. . . ."

(The Sign of Jonas)

escape. "Actually, having run into it at this end of the circle, it is making me what I was always meant to be."[209] Asked afterward if he had been nervous during the ordination, Merton replied in Trappist sign language, making a circle with thumb and forefinger, then using the forefinger of his left hand to make a center point, a silent declaration that he was finally at the place of convergence he had long been seeking.

Merton's ordination turned into a three-day homecoming festival. Friends he hadn't seen in years gathered at the monastery to share in the event and participate in his first Masses: Bob Lax, Ed Rice, Dan Walsh, Bob Giroux, Jay Laughlin, and Sy Freedgood. Not only did his guests bring news of mutual friends but they also surprised Merton with the information that India was no longer under British rule, thanks in large measure to the long struggle led by Gandhi, and Harry Truman had been elected president of the United States. "In the end I had the impression that all who came to see me were dispersing to the four corners of the universe with hymns and messages and prophecies, speaking with tongues and ready to raise the dead."[210]

Among those raised from the dead was the man himself. Ordained at last, he was able—at least for a time—to reconcile Father Louis, monk, and Thomas Merton, writer.

"My lamentations about my writing job have been foolish," he noted in his journal in July. "Writing is the one thing that gives me access to some real silence and solitude. Also I find that it helps me to pray because when I pause at my work I find that the mirror inside me is surprisingly clean and deep and serene and God shines there and is immediately found, without hunting, as if He had come close to me while I was writing and I had not observed His coming."[211] "My [writing] work is my hermitage," he noted six months later, "because it is writing that helps me most of all to be a solitary and a contemplative here at Gethsemani."[212]

Abbey Forester

God is in His transparent world, but He is too sacred to be mentioned, too holy to be observed. The big deep fish are purple in my sea.

THOMAS MERTON
The Sign of Jonas

"All for Jesus, through Mary, with a smile." This was Dom James's motto, not Merton's. Merton was forever fleeing from slogans, religious ones most of all. Dom James's smiles were sometimes galling and Merton was often irritated by the abbot's sermons. "Jesus must be our real pal," Dom James told the monks, "our most intimate buddy." The Christ to whom Merton was drawn, far from being a potential pal, was the Christ of the icons.

Yet over and over again Merton discovered his need for Dom James. For all their differences in outlook and personality, and all the familial combat between them, there was profound mutual respect. While expressing themselves in dissimilar voices, both were deeply committed both to the church and to monastic life, and neither viewed these in static terms. Merton was aware of his own rebellious nature and appreciated his need for a steadying hand. In letters to friends and in journal entries, he might passionately and loudly disagree with a decision made by Dom James, but the abbot regarded Merton as an obedient monk. Merton recognized Dom James as an authentic pastor, not seeing monks as interchangeable parts but aware of each person as original and thus requiring unique responses and attention. For example, for a member of the community obsessed with flowers, Dom James created the post of Keeper of Wayside Shrines.

Merton as a young monk. (Photograph courtesy of the Abbey of Gethsemani)

"The Christian life—and especially the contemplative life—is a continual discovery of Christ in new and unexpected places."

(The Sign of Jonas)

The abbot met a compelling need of Merton's. Hating to say no himself, Merton relied on Dom James to say no for him, complaining all the while, but then expressing relief and gratitude. Dom James provided Merton with much-needed brakes, protecting him from an impulsiveness that could have destroyed his vocation. While Merton often chafed under the abbot's overprotectiveness, what troubled him far more was his need for an overprotective abbot.

In Dom James's view, beneath Merton's restlessness and insecurity was a childhood impoverished by the absence of a sturdy, affectionate family. Yet his immense respect for Merton was indicated by the fact that he not only encouraged Merton in his vocation as a writer but entrusted him with key pastoral posts in community life. Merton also served as Dom James's confessor.

One of the problems Merton faced was work overload. This was both his own doing and Dom James's. As the end of 1949 approached, following publication of his history of the Cistercians, *The Waters of Siloe*, Merton felt exhausted. "I am a contemplative who is ready to collapse from overwork," he recorded in his journal on December 20:

> This, I think, is a sin and the punishment of sin but now I have got to turn it to good use and be a saint by it, somehow. . . . The other day while the new high altar was being consecrated I found myself being stripped of one illusion after another. There I stood and sat with my eyes closed and wondered why I read so much, why I write so much, why I talk so much, and why I get so excited about things that only affect the surface of my life—I came here eight years ago and already knew better when I arrived.[213]

One factor in his exhaustion was a new responsibility in community life. Recognizing that Merton's talents as a writer plus his education and social skills equipped him

"I find myself traveling toward my destiny in the belly of a paradox."
(The Sign of Jonas)

Merton (front center) with scholastics. (Photograph courtesy of the Thomas Merton Center)

"The one who is going to be most fully formed by the new scholastics is the Master of the Scholastics. It is as if I were beginning all over again to be a Cistercian: but this time I am doing it without asking myself the abstract questions which are the luxury and the torment of one's monastic adolescence. For now I am a grownup monk and have no time for anything but the essentials. The only essential is not an idea or an ideal: it is God Himself, Who cannot be found by weighing the present against the future or the past but only by sinking into the heart of the present as it is."

(The Sign of Jonas)

for the classroom, in December 1949 Dom James assigned him to give orientation and introductory theology classes to the novices. It was the beginning of sixteen years of teaching within the abbey community, a duty that required much of Merton's time and energy, though it had its rewards for him as well as for those he taught and often spilled over into what he was writing. Merton commented that he had learned more theology in three months of teaching than in four years of study.[214]

Merton's lectures gave particular attention to the saints at the roots of the monastic tradition—the desert seekers who were the first monks, and those who built on their example: John Cassian, Diadochus of Photike, Gregory of Nyssa, John of the Ladder, Basil the Great, and Benedict, to name only a few. The thread running through Merton's classes was to challenge those in his care with the awareness of the monastery as a school of charity. While the stress was on monastic life in community, Merton never overlooked the place of solitude in contemplative life. He also introduced his students to the hesychastic tradition (from the Greek word for silence:

"New buildings have to be put up, and the farm has to be completely reorganized and expanded, so that all this work has to be done in a hurry, many machines are needed. When you have a great crowd of postulants, much work, new buildings, and a small mechanized army of builders all working at high pressure, the silence is not always absolutely perfect."

(The Sign of Jonas)

hesychia) that is chiefly associated with monastic life in the Orthodox Church. It may have been the first time in many centuries that Western monks were being introduced to the practice of the Jesus Prayer, or Prayer of the Heart, with the frequent repetition of the words, "Lord Jesus Christ Son of God, have mercy on me, a sinner."

In his teaching no less than in his writing, Merton was drawn to early Christian sources, doing so at a time when the writings and way of life of Christians in the first several centuries was generally neglected in the Catholic Church. As he explained in an essay written for monastic circulation:

> If for some reason it were necessary for you to drink a pint of water taken out of the Mississippi River and you could choose where it was to be drawn out of the river—would you take a pint from the source of the river in Minnesota or from the estuary in New Orleans?
>
> The example is perhaps not perfect. Christian tradition and spirituality does not become polluted with development. That is not the idea at all. Nevertheless, tradition and spirituality are all the more pure and genuine in proportion as they are in contact with the original source and retain the same content.[215]

Teaching was a source of both inspiration and new discoveries for Merton, yet, in combination with the work he was doing as a writer, at times he found the load backbreaking. In a state of exhaustion that led to sickness, he spent the last days of Lent in 1950 in the infirmary. In September he was sent into the hospital in Louisville, and the following month returned to the abbey with strict orders to rest. In November he was in the hospital for nasal surgery and treatment of colitis. By December, he was back at the abbey feeling revived and eager to resume writing. Within three months, *The Ascent to Truth* was finished as well as *Bread in the*

Wilderness, a book on the Psalms. He signed a contract for four books with Harcourt Brace.

Dom James Fox was not only a businessman eager to make Gethsemani financially self-sufficient through intensive farming and food manufacture, but he was also an abbot open to change and reform in abbey life as long as the Holy Rule of Saint Benedict and Cistercian tradition weren't abandoned in the process. Soon after his election, he began allowing professed members of the community to make use of monastery property beyond the enclosure, which was the small area to which monks were limited unless required by their work. First the yard to the east of the main house was made available as a place to walk, read, and meditate. Then, in 1951, the open area was expanded to include all the property on the monastery side of the main road, land that included meadows, ponds, and woods. The novices were given access to a wooded bluff beyond the east wall of the enclosure. The abbot went a step further with Merton, permitting him to take guests walking on monastery property, a privilege later extended to other monks.

The physical world available to the monks, with

Abbey of Gethsemani as seen from above, around 1955. (Photograph courtesy of the Abbey of Gethsemani)

Now, after 20 years, the journal which Thomas Merton kept before he became a Trappist has been released for publication.

The SECULAR JOURNAL of Thomas Merton

This journal starts in Greenwich Village, moves to Cuba, returns to St. Bonaventure's and Harlem, and ends on the threshold of Gethsemani.

Cover of *The Secular Journal of Thomas Merton,* published in 1959 by Farrar, Straus & Cudahy.

Merton at the front of the line, was expanding, and just in the nick of time, because within the monastery walls "you sometimes felt like you were living in a submarine," recalls Dom John Eudes Bamberger, then a novice.[216] As the fifties got under way, there were nearly three hundred men jammed into the abbey buildings, some of them sleeping in a large tent. (But the turnover rate among novices was high. Occasionally the departures of those who decided not to stay were dramatic, like the novice who was discovered one night smoking a cigar on his straw mattress. He was leaving in the morning.)

In June 1951, in his tenth year at Gethsemani, Merton was aware of how much he had changed: "I have become very different from what I used to be. The man who began this journal is dead, just as the man who finished *The Seven Storey Mountain* when this journal began was also dead, and what is more the man who was the central figure in *The Seven Storey Mountain* was dead over and over. . . . *The Seven Storey Mountain* is the work of a man I never even heard of."[217]

Ending thirty-six years without a definite national identity, that year Merton became a United States citizen. The step was more than a formality. For all his criticisms of the United States, and despite irritation with a "baby-talk citizenship textbook" he had to read in preparation, Merton felt connected to America in a way he had never experienced with France or England. Ironically, having become a monk, he felt less estranged from the society he had walked out on. "I have come to the monastery to find my place in the world," he noted in March, "and if I fail to find this place in the world, I will be wasting my time in the monastery."[218] In the Federal Courthouse in Louisville on June 22 he discovered that a reporter had turned out to witness his participation in the ritual of national bonding. "This is a peculiar world," he commented in his journal, "in which the only man in a big crowd who has to worry about reporters is a Trappist monk who has left the world." It was precisely the surprise of an unworldly monk participating in such a worldly ceremony that made it news; also it was a story that fit in nicely with the flag-waving climate of the Cold-War fifties.

At the same time, Merton was appointed master of scholastics, that is, he was charged with the care of those monks who were being prepared for ordination. While it was a huge step away from solitude, his engagement with the scholastics introduced him to an unexpected wilderness: "What is my new desert?" he asked. "The name of it is *compassion*. There is no wilderness so terrible, so beautiful, so arid and so fruitful as the wilderness of compassion."[219]

In October 1951, Dom James found a way to give Merton greater access to the woodland and more solitude by creating the job of forester. His tasks included selecting trees to be cut down by the novices and organizing the planting of new trees. Access to the woods brought Merton a sense of relief and liberation. "It was as though I was in another country," he noted.

Now that he was the abbey's forester, Merton was in the company of trees day after day while exploring areas of the monastery's land that few of the monks had seen. One discovery was a magnificent hill that he named Mount Carmel after the mountain where Elijah heard God not as a great noise but as a whisper and on which the order of Carmelite contemplatives was founded in the twelfth century. "It is the finest of all the knobs," Merton wrote in his journal in January 1952. "It runs north and south behind the lake knob and from the top, which is fairly clear of trees, you can see

Photograph of the Abbey. (Courtesy of the Abbey of Gethsemani)

"A tree gives glory to God first of all by being a tree. For in being what God means it to be, it is obeying Him. It 'consents,' so to speak, to His creative love. It is expressing an idea which is in God, and which is not distinct from the essence of God, and therefore a tree imitates God by being a tree."

(New Seeds of Contemplation)

Opposite:
Merton. (Photograph courtesy of the Abbey of Gethsemani)

all over this part of Kentucky—miles of woods over to the northwest."

The area seemed just right for a hermitage, only at the time hermits had no place in the intensely communal life led by Trappists. "The woods cultivate me with their silences, and all day long even in choir and at Mass, I seem to be in the forest."[220]

Sitting on a cedar log under a tree in February 1952, gazing out at light blue hills in the distance, Merton saw his true self as a kind of sea creature dwelling in a water cavern which knows of the world of dry land only by faint rumor. When he got free of plans and projects—the first level of the sea with its troubled surface—then he lived in the second level, in the deep waters out of reach of storms, where there was "peace, peace, peace. . . . We pray therein, slightly waving among the fish. . . . Words, as I think, do not spring from this second level. They are only meant to drown there. The question of socialization does not concern these waters. They are nobody's property. . . . No questions whatever perturb their holy botany. Neutral territory. No man's sea. I think God meant me to write about this second level."

Still deeper down Merton was aware of a third level, swimming in the rich darkness which is no longer thick like water but pure, like air. Starlight, and you do not know where it is coming from. Moonlight is in this prayer, stillness, waiting for the Redeemer. . . . Everything is charged with intelligence, though all is night. There is no speculation here. There is vigilance. . . . Everything is spirit. Here God is adored, His coming is recognized, He is received as soon as He is expected and because He is expected He is received, but He has passed by sooner than He arrived, He was gone before He came. He returned forever. He never yet passed by and already He had disappeared for all eternity. He is and He is not. Everything and Nothing. Not light not dark, not high

not low, not this side not that side. Forever and forever. In the wind of His passing the angels cry, "The Holy One is gone." Therefore I lie dead in the air of their wings. . . . It is a strange awakening to find the sky inside you and beneath you and above you and all around you so that your spirit is one with the sky, and all is positive night.[221]

Containing the Divided Worlds

The hawk is to be studied by saints and contemplatives; because he knows his business. I wish I knew my business as well as he does his.

THOMAS MERTON
The Sign of Jonas

"The solitary is necessarily a man who does what he wants to do. In fact he has nothing else to do. That is why his vocation is both dangerous and despised."

(Thoughts in Solitude)

Some drawings by retarded children had made their way to Merton, many of them featuring Jonas, the reluctant prophet who had been hurled back into life after being in the tomb of a whale's belly. In a period when Catholic art tended to be sentimental and effeminate, these images struck Merton as the only real works of art he had seen since arriving at Gethsemani. Merton recognized Jonas as an icon of his true self while all that stood in the way of fully living his real identity was the whale from which he needed to be rescued. "Many baptized in Christ," Merton noted, "have risen from the depths without troubling to find out the difference between Jonas and whale. It is the whale we cherish. Jonas swims abandoned in the heart of the sea. . . . We must get Jonas out of the whale."[222]

In the prologue to *The Sign of Jonas*, Merton wrote:

The sign Jesus promised to the generation that did not understand Him was the "sign of Jonas the prophet"— that is, the sign of His own resurrection. . . . Every Christian is signed with the sign of Jonas, because we all live by the power of Christ's resurrection. But I feel that my own life is especially sealed with this great sign, which baptism and monastic profession and priestly ordination have burned into the roots of my being, because like Jonas himself I find myself traveling toward my destiny in the belly of a paradox.[223]

Gethsemani was part of the paradox. Abbey life was both a desert of compassion and a field of battle.

On the battlefront, Merton found himself increasingly at odds with the ways in which the monastery was making money. One of Dom James's projects to free the monastery from debt was the creation of Gethsemani Farms, a monk-staffed commercial venture that manufactured cheese, bacon, smoked hams, and bourbon-flavored fruitcakes. The products were sold by mail order as well as to guests and visitors at a shop by the gate house. Alfalfa was grown on monastery land, and, for a while, tobacco as well. A monastic factory the monks nicknamed "Little Pittsburgh" manufactured alfalfa pellets that were fed to turkeys and race horses; among those that dined on the product was a horse that won the Kentucky Derby. The campaign to make money meant a more intensive use of the workforce as well, with long hours of labor in the abbey's factories. From September through mid-December the community focused its physical energies on cheese and fruitcake production.

At times Merton felt he was just one more abbey business: royalties during the first few years following publication of *The Seven Storey Mountain* greatly helped to get the monastery out of debt. In later years, income to the community from Merton's writing averaged $20,000 to $30,000 a year.

Merton wasn't dead-set against monastic money making, but was deeply troubled by the toxic fertilizers being used on the fields, the noise of machinery, and the sense that the monastery was imitating corporate America. There were dead birds in the fields and sick monks in the infirmary with illnesses Merton didn't think had visited the monastery in the days before crop dusting. He made his views known within the community in what must have been virtuoso displays of sign language. Eventually his concerns about machinery and chemicals were taken seriously, though not before much harm had been done to land, health, and community life.

Monk inspecting cheese manufactured at the Abbey. (Photograph courtesy of Columbia University, Butler Library)

Merton's complaints about the abbey's business endeavors were another factor in his wondering whether he really belonged there. While in *The Sign of Jonas* he had praised stability—"By making a vow of stability, the monk renounces the vain hope of wandering off to find a 'perfect monastery' "—Merton was always on the lookout for monastic communities that came closer to his ideals. The ongoing struggle between Dom James and Merton centered most often on Merton's bouts of attraction to what he imagined were greener monastic pastures.

Censorship was another issue that made Merton wonder about his place with the Trappists. The signals he was given by his superiors were mixed—on the one hand, again and again he was encouraged, even ordered, to write, but then major obstacles were often thrown in the way of publishing his work.

In 1952, in the midst of a prolonged censorship battle over *The Sign of Jonas* with the Abbot General, Dom Gabriel Sortais, Merton began to hope for permission to join the Camaldoli, an order founded in the eleventh century in a valley within the Apennines. The Camaldolese model struck him as even better suited to his needs than the Carthusians. While each Carthusian had his own small house within a Charterhouse, each Camaldolese monk had his own separate hermitage. It was a community of solitaries living around a church. "The singular advantage of such a life," Merton wrote in *The Silent Life*, "is that it makes it possible for a pure contemplative life of real solitude and simplicity, without formalism and without rigid, inflexible prescriptions of minor detail, yet fully protected by spiritual control and by religious obedience."[224]

Merton's letters to the Prior General of the Camaldoli were warmly received and his interest in joining encouraged, but such a move was possible only if Merton was dispensed from the vow of stability he had taken at Gethsemani.

Not surprisingly, Dom James opposed a dispensation. He was convinced that Merton's salvation, and the salva-

Paperback cover of *The Silent Life*, first published in 1957 by Farrar, Straus & Cudahy.

tion of others, depended on his remaining at Gethsemani. Nor was the abbot alone in his opposition. One of Merton's friends and advisers, biblical scholar Father Barnabas Ahern, argued that withdrawal from Gethsemani would cause scandal, stir up restlessness in others, discredit the Trappists, and even encourage critics of the contemplative life.

While Merton's views on the issue shifted from day to day, a journal entry from the fall of 1952 describes an awareness to which he kept returning:

> If it were merely a question of satisfying my own desires and aspirations I would leave for Camaldoli in ten minutes. Yet it is not merely a question of satisfying my own desires. On the contrary; there is one thing holding me at Gethsemani. And that is the cross. Some mystery of the wisdom of God has taught me that perhaps after all Gethsemani is where I belong because I do not fit in and because here my ideals are practically all frustrated.[225]

Two weeks later he wrote that he had not yet completed the communal apprenticeship that opens the way to a hermitage: "I have in no way proved myself as a cenobite [a monk living in community]. I have been beating the air."[226] In the process of beating the air, Merton decided that, whatever happened in his future life as a monk, he must never become an abbot. On October 8, 1952, he made a private vow, witnessed by Dom James, never to accept the office.

Having managed to keep him at Gethsemani, Dom James once again helped Merton take another step into greater solitude. A vacant toolshed had been moved to the edge of the "Petrified Forest," a field east of the main monastery buildings populated by rain-worn statues of saints for which there was no room in the monastery buildings. Merton was given use of this shed for certain hours each day. He named his part-time hermitage Saint

"Receive, O monk, the holy truth concerning this thing called death. Know that there is in each man a deep will, potentially committed to freedom or captivity, ready to consent to life, born consenting to death, turned inside out, swallowed by its own self, prisoner of itself like Jonas in the whale."
(The Sign of Jonas)

Anne's, after the mother of Mary. Part of the writing of *No Man Is an Island* and *Bread in the Wilderness* occurred in Saint Anne's. This was a period of near-tranquility in his vocation, with times of deep joy.

In the fall of 1952, permission was at last given for *The Sign of Jonas* to be published. Based on the journal Merton had kept from the end of 1946 through the summer of 1952, it reached bookshops early in 1953, making Merton's vocational struggle and his attraction to religious orders stressing greater solitude publicly known. *The Sign of Jonas* quickly became one of Merton's most popular books.

The Sign of Jonas was followed by *Bread in the Wilderness*, a handsomely designed book that combined photos of a medieval Catalan crucifix with reflections on the Psalms, which he called "the most significant and influential collection of religious poems ever written." As is the case with any poem, Merton observed, the Psalms are more than declarations or statements of fact. The poet assembles words "in such a way that they exercise a mysterious and vital reactivity among themselves, and so release their secret content of associations to produce in the reader an experience that enriches the depths of his spirit. . . . A good poem induces an experience that could not be produced by any other combination of words."[227]

The year 1954 saw the publication of a short book Merton had written at the request of his superiors and wished he had been spared: *The Last of the Fathers*, on the life of Saint Bernard of Clairvaux, abbot, theologian, orator, and counselor of popes and kings. One of the towering figures of the twelfth century, Bernard's name is forever linked with one of the disasters of his age, the Second Crusade, of which he was the great preacher, though not an actual participant. Bernard, Merton pointed out, saw the Crusades as an opportunity to further Christian unity, but in practice they underlined not only how divided the Christian East was from the Christian West, but how fractured were relations between the various kingdoms of western Europe. "The French continued to be enemies of the Germans, and fought them all the way across Europe," Merton pointed out. "The whole history of the campaign [of the Crusades] was one of treachery and murder."[228]

Holy war, it turns out, is chiefly unholy war, no matter what the cause, with the Crusades a grim example of how the road to hell is paved with good intentions. As Merton was to point out in an essay on crusades written a decade later, "What was intended as a remedy for sins of violence, particularly murder, now became a consecration of violence."[229]

One of Merton's lines of research in the early fifties was to discover and make better known the occasional Trappist who, in ages past, had been permitted to become a hermit. Merton drew attention to several canonized Cistercians who had been permitted to live alone at some distance from community, including Saint Conrad of Palestine, Saint Galan, and Saint Firmian. Surely what had happened before could happen again. Could there not be a place in Trappist life for seasoned monks drawn to a greater degree of solitude?

Haunted by such saints and feeling there was no interest in renewing their tradition within the Trappist order, by the spring of 1955 Merton's wandering itch had become acute once more. This time his hopes returned to the Carthusians. Years later he would still remember the anguish he felt while planting loblolly pines "during my 1955 crisis."[230]

Dom James responded by offering Merton everything he had been campaigning for plus the possibility of doing it without changing address. Having obtained the support of the Abbot General and the order's General Chapter, Dom James was willing to release Merton from the job of master of scholastics and let him live as the community's first full-time hermit. The hermitage would be the newly built fire tower that the county had erected that summer, on top of Vineyard Knob several miles to the west of the abbey church.

(Photograph by Naomi Burton Stone)

Fire tower in the woods surrounding Gethsemani, which Merton considered as a possible site for a hermitage. (Photograph courtesy of the Abbey of Gethsemani)

Merton already enjoyed visiting this isolated place. He was initially elated, but the practical problem of getting back and forth to the monastery for Mass and one hot meal a day proved a formidable barrier. The fire tower was a long hike from the abbey. Merton's attempt to drive a jeep ended with his being sworn at, and not in sign language, by the community's mechanic. Merton had destroyed the jeep's radiator.

Merton seems to have read the accident as a sign that he was going in the wrong direction. It dawned on him that, eager though he was, in fact he was not on good enough terms with himself at this time to live in solitude. Turning his back on the fire tower, Merton proposed to the abbot that he take over the recently vacated post of master of novices. For Dom James, it was an astonishing about-face, yet one he welcomed. Merton was given the job, one of the most important in the community.

Still the issue of Merton's future was far from settled. By now his formal appeal for permission to enter another order had made its way to the Vatican. Dom James wrote to Cardinal Montini (later Pope Paul VI), among Merton's most appreciative readers in the hierarchy and a bishop likely to have sympathy for Merton's attraction to an order that stressed solitude. Merton, Dom James wrote Montini, was "inclined to give much weight to subjective matters" and was unaware that he was a public figure both in the community and in the world outside, nor could he evaluate the impact his leaving Gethsemani would have on others. "Your Excellency, before God I say to you, and I am ready to meet this decision on the Last Judgment, that I cannot see the finger of God in Father Louis's desire for change." The letter must have been convincing. Merton received neither blessing nor encouragement for a transfer.

Merton's growing interest in psychoanalysis, sparked partly by his desire to be more helpful to his novices, led to a remarkable event the next year which made Merton wonder about his own mental balance. In July 1956, an exceptional permission was given by Dom James Fox for Merton and another monk, Father John Eudes Bamberger, to travel together to Saint John's University in Minnesota to take part in a two-week seminar on psychiatry and its applications to religious life. Dom James planned to join them for the second week. Leading the conference was Dr. Gregory Zilboorg, a recent convert to Catholicism, whose books were published by one of the companies also tied to Merton.

Zilboorg came to their meeting loaded with preconceptions about Merton largely based on reading *The Sign of Jonas*. At a private meeting, Zilboorg told Merton that he was in "bad shape," a "semi-psychotic quack" as well as a gadfly to his superiors, to whom he kept coming back until he got what he wanted. His attraction to fame revealed megalomania and narcissism. He was the kind of "promoter type" who makes a killing on Wall Street one day and loses it on the horses the day after. His writing was becoming "verbological" while his "hermit trend" was pathological. As Merton listened, he couldn't help but think how much Zilboorg resembled Stalin. Yet Zilboorg was saying nothing worse than what Merton had written in his journal in his darker moments.[231]

The next day, with Dom James's arrival, Zilboorg arranged a meeting involving both the abbot and Merton at which Zilboorg declared that Merton's desire for greater solitude was of a piece with his longing for public attention. He wants a hermitage on Times Square "with a large sign over it saying 'HERMIT.'" This was too much for Merton. He was both humiliated and devastated. He sat in the room with tears running down his face muttering, "Stalin, Stalin." Dom James's worst misgivings about Merton, and Merton's about himself, had been confirmed by a famous psychiatrist.

Plans were made for Merton to come to New York for psychoanalysis with Zilboorg, but these were replaced by plans for him to see a psychologist in Louisville, Dr. James Wygal. When Zilboorg came to the abbey in

"I dreamt I was lost in a great city and was walking 'toward the center' without quite knowing where I was going. Suddenly I came to a dead end, but on a height, looking at a great bay, an arm of the harbor. I saw a whole section of the city spread out before me on hills covered with light snow, and realized that, though I had far to go, I knew where I was: because in this city there are two arms of the harbor and they help you to find your way, as you are always encountering them."

(Conjectures of a Guilty Bystander)

Merton during a conference with novices. (Photograph courtesy of Columbia University, Butler Library)

December, he said he was having second thoughts about Merton. His condition wasn't that bad after all. "It transpires that though I am indeed crazy as a loon," Merton wrote Naomi Burton at the end of the year, "I don't really need analysis."[232]

In his journal a few months later, he noted that, while there were elements of insight in Zilboorg's analysis, his soul could never fit into Zilboorg's "theater." To have attempted it would have been a "tragedy and a mess."[233]

In 1956, while blacks in Montgomery were boycotting segregated buses and the name of Martin Luther King Jr. was beginning to be set in headline type, Merton was reading Gandhi. It was an interest that dated back to student days at Oakham, though there was more to it now than taking a radical stand among classmates. It was now part of a process of exploring the social implications of the gospel as well as one of the early steps of Merton's connection with non-Christian contemplatives.

That spring also marked the beginning of Merton's immersion in Russian literature and religious writing. It was a timely interest; that fall the first Sputnik was launched. But for Merton what the Russians had to offer wasn't space travel but a profound spiritual tradition. He became convinced that restoring oneness in the church began with a recovery of oneness within oneself. A journal entry made in April 1957, in an expanded form, eventually became part of *Conjectures of a Guilty Bystander:*

> If I can unite *in myself* the thought and the devotion of Eastern and Western Christendom, the Greek and the Latin Fathers, the Russian with the Spanish mystics, I can prepare in myself the reunion of divided Christians. From that secret and unspoken unity in myself can eventually come a visible and manifest unity of all Christians. If we want to bring together what is divided, we can not do so by imposing one division upon the other. If we do this, the union is not Christian. It is political and doomed to further conflict. We must contain all the divided worlds in ourselves and transcend them in Christ.[234]

At the time, few people in the West were so well acquainted as Thomas Merton not only with the Church Fathers and mystics both East and West, but with the writings of such contemporary Orthodox theologians as Sergei Bulgakov, Vladimir Lossky, Paul Evdokimov, Oliver Clément, Alexander Schmemann, and John Meyendorff. He also carefully read the Russian philosopher Nikolai Berdyaev.

Merton found a paschal warmth in Orthodox theologians that seemed to him often missing in their Western counterparts. "One wonders," he noted in his journal, "if our theological consciousness is not after all a sign of a fatal coldness of heart, an awful sterility born of fear, or of despair."

Merton had come to appreciate the poetry of Boris Pasternak and was among the first to read his novel, *Doctor Zhivago.* He was astonished by the "striking and genuinely Christian elements" that marked the Russian author's novel, banned by Communist censors in his

"I must look for my identity, somehow, not only in God but in other men. . . . I will never be able to find myself if I isolate myself from the rest of mankind as if I were a different kind of being."
(New Seeds of Contemplation)

Russian novelist Boris Pasternak.

homeland. In August 1958, two months before it was announced that Pasternak would receive the Nobel Prize for Literature, Merton wrote to the Russian author:

> Although we are separated by great distances and even greater barriers, it gives me pleasure to speak to you as one with whom I feel to be a kindred spirit. It is as if we met on a deeper level of life in which individuals are not separate beings. In the language familiar to me as a Catholic monk, it is as if we were known to one another in God. This is a very simple and to me obvious expression for something quite normal and ordinary. . . . I am convinced that you understand me perfectly. It is true that a person always remains a person and utterly separate and apart from every other person. But it is equally true that each person is destined to reach with others an understanding and a unity which transcend individuality. Russian tradition describes this with a concept we do not fully possess in the west—*sobornost* [conciliarity; unity in the Holy Spirit].[235]

Merton told Pasternak that he was planning to study Russian "in order to try to get into Russian literature in the original. . . . I would much prefer to read you in Russian."

This was a time when private communication between citizens of the United States and the Soviet Union was practically zero. Though no doubt read and copied by Americans and Russian intelligence services, the letter reached Pasternak's *dacha* at Peredelkino, just outside of Moscow. A response was delivered to Gethsemani in early November. Six letters were exchanged before Pasternak's death in May 1960. It was a startling experience for Merton of a oneness that cut across the frontiers of politics and of ecclesiastical division.

Shortly after his expulsion from the Soviet Writers Union, Pasternak told John Harris, a mutual friend, that Merton's "high feelings and prayers have saved my life."

Waking from a Dream

The Christian life . . . is a continual discovery of Christ in new and unexpected places.

THOMAS MERTON
The Sign of Jonas

In one of Merton's letters to Boris Pasternak, written in the fall of 1958, he confided a dream he had experienced months earlier, in February:

[In my dream I was] sitting with a very young Jewish girl of fourteen or fifteen, and then she suddenly manifested a very deep and pure affection for me and embraced me so that I was moved to the depths of my soul. I learned that her name was "Proverb," which I thought very simple and beautiful. And also I thought: "She is of the race of Saint Anne." I spoke to her of her name, and she did not seem to be proud of it, because it seemed that the other young girls mocked her for it. But I told her that it was a very beautiful name, and there the dream ended. . . . Thus you are initiated into the scandalous secret of a monk who is in love with a girl, and a Jew at that! One cannot expect much from monks these days. The heroic asceticism of the past is no more.[236]

In the same letter, Merton went on to describe an experience that had occurred several weeks later, on March 18. He was in Louisville on an editorial errand, "walking alone in the crowded street and suddenly saw that everybody was Proverb and that in all of them shone her extraordinary beauty and purity and shyness, even though they did not know who they were and were per-

"The world cannot be a problem to anyone who sees that ultimately Christ, the world, his sister, his brother, and his own inmost ground are made one and the same in grace and redemptive love. If all the current talk about the world helps people to discover this, then it is fine. But if it produces nothing but a whole new divisive gamut of obligatory positions and 'contemporary answers,' we might as well forget it."
(Contemplation in a World of Action)

haps ashamed of their names because they were mocked on account of them. And they did not know their real identity as the Child so dear to God who, from before the beginning, was playing in His sight all days, playing in the world."

The event Merton shared with Pasternak was first recorded in his journal the day after it occurred. In a text developed from the journal entry, it became one of the most memorable passages in *Conjectures of a Guilty Bystander*:

In Louisville, at the corner of Fourth and Walnut, in the center of the shopping district, I was suddenly overwhelmed with the realization that I loved all those people, that they were mine and I theirs, that we could not be alien to one another even though we were total strangers. It was like waking from a dream of separateness, of spurious self-isolation in a special world, the world of renunciation and supposed holiness. The whole illusion of a separate holy existence is a dream. Not that I question the reality of my vocation, or of my monastic life: but the conception of "separation from the world" that we have in the monastery too easily presents itself as a complete illusion that by making vows we become a different species of being, pseudo-angels, "spiritual men," men of interior life. . . .

This sense of liberation from an illusory difference was such a relief and such a joy to me that I almost laughed out loud. And I suppose my happiness could have taken form in these words: "Thank God, thank God, that I *am* like other men, that I am only a man among others." . . .

It is a glorious destiny to be a member of the human race, though it is a race dedicated to many absurdities and one which makes many terrible mistakes: yet, with all that, God Himself gloried in becoming a member of the human race. A member of the human race! To think that such a commonplace realization should suddenly seem like news that one holds the winning ticket in a cosmic sweepstake.

I have the immense joy of being man, a member of the race in which God Himself became incarnate. As if the sorrows and stupidities of the human condition could overwhelm me, now I realize what we all are. And if only everybody could realize this! But it can-

Opposite:
Portrait of Merton by John Howard Griffin. (Courtesy of the John Howard Griffin Estate)

"When I wrote this book the fact uppermost in my mind was that I had seceded from the world of my time in all clarity and with total free-

dom. . . . Since that time, I have learned, I believe, to look back into that world with greater compassion, seeing those in it not as alien to myself, not as peculiar and deluded strangers, but as identified with

myself. . . . [T]he monastery is not an 'escape' from the world. On the contrary, by being in the monastery I take my true part in all the struggles and sufferings of the world."

(Preface to the Japanese edition of The Seven Storey Mountain)

A plaque at the corner of Fourth and Walnut in downtown Louisville (now Fourth and Muhammed Ali Blvd.) commemorates the site of Merton's epiphany. In 2008 this intersection was renamed Thomas Merton Square. (Photograph courtesy of the Thomas Merton Center)

not be explained. There is no way of telling people that they are all walking around shining like the sun. . . . There are no strangers!

Then it was as if I suddenly saw the secret beauty of their heart, the depths of their hearts where neither sin nor desire nor self-knowledge can reach, the core of their reality, the person that each one is in God's eyes. If only they could all see themselves as they really are. If only we could see each other that way all the time. There would be no more war, no more hatred, no more cruelty, no more greed. . . . I suppose the big problem would be that we would fall down and worship each other. . . .

At the center of our being is a point of nothingness that is untouched by sin and by illusion, a point of pure truth, a point or spark which belongs entirely to God, which is never at our disposal, from which God disposes our lives, which is inaccessible to the fantasies of our own mind or the brutalities of our will. This little point of nothingness and of absolute poverty is the pure glory of God in us. It is so to speak His name written in us, as our poverty, as our indigence, as our dependence, as our sonship. It is like a pure diamond, blazing with the invisible light of heaven. It is in everybody, and if we could see it we would see these billions of points of light coming together in the face and blaze of a sun that would make all the darkness and cruelty of life vanish completely. . . . I have no program for this seeing. It is only given. But the gate of heaven is everywhere.[237]

This was a far cry from earlier writings in which Merton had stressed the value of monastic disconnection from the world. One of the great surprises in Merton's life, astonishing at least as much to him as to those who had come to know him through his early books, were the many links he made with the nonmonastic world during the last decade of his life. On the one hand, he was being increasingly drawn toward solitude, and, at the same time, he was entering into a far deeper engagement with people and events distant from the monastery.

The same day while in Louisville, Merton stopped in a used bookshop and, for fifty cents, purchased a copy of *The Family of Man*, a collection of black-and-white photos that had been exhibited at the Museum of Modern Art in New York. Many of the images reinforced Merton's experience. "All those fabulous pictures," Merton wrote in his journal. "And again, no refinements or explanations are necessary! How scandalized some men would be if I said that the whole book is to me a picture of Christ.... God is seen and reveals Himself *as man*, that is in us and there is no hope of finding wisdom than in God-manhood."[238]

While his experience in Louisville did not suggest to him that he ought to renounce monastic life or his hope of finally becoming a hermit, his understanding of what it meant to be a monk had been transformed: the solitude he felt called to required a profound communion with others. A solitude that was indifferent to anyone's suffering was a dead-end street. He had to make of his monastic vocation a place both of non-presence and attendance, non-participation and engagement, hiddenness and hospitality, disappearance and arrival. The opposites need each other as birds need two wings.

In editing the first volume of Merton's letters, *The Hidden Ground of Love*, Monsignor William Shannon noticed that Merton's correspondence "took off after the event at Fourth and Walnut."[239] Merton began opening more and more lines of contact and dialogue with people beyond the monastery.

One of the people to whom he started writing was Dorothy Day, founder of the Catholic Worker movement. Merton had met her when she came to speak at Saint Bonaventure's while he was teaching there, but there had been no further contact between them. If

Dorothy Day, founder of the Catholic Worker movement. (Photograph courtesy of Marquette University Archives)

Merton at the time was the main symbol of Catholic withdrawal from the world, this often-jailed woman was the main representative of Catholic engagement in the world. She edited *The Catholic Worker*, an independent journal which was at the time the only pacifist publication within the Catholic Church. The many houses of hospitality that had arisen out of the Catholic Worker movement were in America's most impoverished urban neighborhoods. Dorothy Day's criticisms of an economic system that produced such a multitude of destitute, damaged, and abandoned people led many Catholics to regard her as a Communist, though for others, like Merton, she was one of the rare individuals living the gospel without compromise, much as Saint Francis of Assisi had done eight centuries earlier. Merton expressed his appreciation in a letter sent in July 1959:

> I am touched deeply by your witness for peace [her recent arrest in City Hall Park, New York, for refusing to take shelter during air raid drills]. You are very right in doing it along the lines of *Satyagraha* [literally "truth-force," Gandhi's word for nonviolence]. I see no other way, though of course the angles of the problem are not all clear. I am certainly with you on taking some kind of stand and acting accordingly. Nowadays it is no longer a question of who is right, but who is at least not criminal, if any of us can say that anymore. So don't worry about whether or not in every point you are perfectly all right according to everybody's book; you are right before God as far as you can go and you are fighting for a truth that is clear enough and important enough. What more can anybody do? . . . It was never more true than now that the world is lost and cannot see true values. Let us keep on praying for one another.[240]

Such prayers were urgently sought. At the time Merton was struggling with a desire to live his monastic

Dorothy Day being arrested following her non-compliance with a compulsory air raid drill in New York City.
(Photograph by Robert Lax, courtesy of Marquette University Archives)

life in a situation of real poverty of the sort embraced by Dorothy Day. At times it seemed to him that the Abbey of Gethsemani had become a decorative fixture of a wealthy, militaristic nation in which the cross had been turned into a flagpole for the national flag. A Benedictine abbot in Mexico had invited Merton to establish a hermitage near his monastery. The bishop of San Juan had offered him a hermitage on the island of Tortola in the British West Indies, and a similar invitation arrived from a bishop in Nevada. There was an invitation from the poet Ernesto Cardenal, a former novice at Gethsemani, to be part of an experimental monastic community on an island in Lake Nicaragua. Merton again asked his superiors, both within the order and at the Vatican, if it might not be God's will for him to make a move to one of these places. In mid-November, Dom James left hurriedly for Rome to argue the case for Merton remaining at Gethsemani.

Merton found himself looking at Gethsemani with the eyes of someone about to leave. While in Louisville, he stopped at a travel agency to find out about tickets to Latin America.

On December 17, a response from Rome reached him which he read on his knees before the Blessed Sacrament in the novitiate chapel. Cardinals Larraona and Valeri, of the Vatican's Sacred Congregation for Religious, quoted a passage from Merton's *No Man Is an Island* in which Merton affirmed his Trappist vocation, not because it was the best vocation, but because it was "the one God has willed for me."[241] (The quotation in the letter broke off before reaching that part of the original text in which Merton wrote that, if God willed something else for him, he "would turn to it on the instant.") The cardinals spoke of the scandal that would be caused were Merton to leave Gethsemani.

While the Vatican letter was not the answer he had been hoping and praying for, the cardinals' refusal to provide a *transitus* turned out to be a relief. Merton left the

"It is my intention to make my entire life a rejection of, a protest against the crimes and injustices of war and political tyranny which threaten to destroy the whole race of man and the world with him. By my monastic life and vows I am saying NO to all the concentration camps, the aerial bombardments, the staged political trials, the judicial murders, the racial injustices, [etc.]. . . . If I say NO to all these secular forces, I also say YES to all that is good in the world and in man."

(Introductions East and West)

Dom James Fox, Abbot of Gethsemani. (Photograph courtesy of the Thomas Merton Center)

chapel and went for a walk. "Coming back, I walked around a corner of the woods and the monastery swung into view. I burst out laughing. It was no longer the same place, no longer heavy. I was free from it."[242]

Two days later he presented Dom James with both a statement of submission and a declaration concerning rights of conscience. Merton stated that he would "take no further positive steps" to leave the order and "will apply no pressure to do so" apart from "manifesting my thoughts to Superiors or those who are competent." He reminded Dom James that every monk is free to receive advice from spiritual directors of his own choosing. "Do you not tend to assume that your policies represent the last word in the spiritual perfection of every one of your subjects, and that anyone who is drawn to another way is leaving the path of perfection? . . . I appeal to the right . . . to consult directors outside the monastery by letter without interference, so that this problem of mine can be settled. I am only asking for things which the Church wishes her subjects to have, not for anything unreasonable."[243]

Though resigned and even relieved to remain a monk of Gethsemani, Merton was increasingly distressed by the lack of respect for conscience and freedom within his order and within the church as a whole. Merton discovered that Dom James was blocking letters from Ernesto Cardenal despite Merton's appeal that the correspondence involved matters of conscience. Struggles with censors and superiors over his writings persisted as did his irritation with his abbey and abbot.

During the latter half of the year, apart from keeping a journal, he was spending less time writing. He set about revising and editing *Disputed Questions*, a collection of essays which included his reflections on Pasternak as well as writings about Eastern Orthodoxy and desert monasticism.

He also was at work on a book, *The New Man*, which centered on the search for the true self, made in the image and likeness of God, that is hidden beneath name, title, achievements, and illusions. He had been given a brief glimpse, while waiting for the light to change at Fourth and Walnut, of the diamond-like true self that can be experienced only in the context of seeing the divine image in the other. As he wrote in one passage in *The New Man*:

> In the mystery of social love there is found the realization of "the other" not only as one to be loved by us, so that we may perfect ourselves, but also as one who can become more perfect by loving us. The vocation to charity is a call not only to love but to be loved. The man who does not care at all whether or not he is loved is ultimately unconcerned about the true welfare of the other and of society. Hence we cannot love unless we also consent to be loved in return. The life of "the other" is not only a supplement, an adjunct to the other.[244]

As 1959 drew to a close, Merton decided, with Dom James's blessing, that it was time to begin psychoanalysis with Dr. James Wygal in Louisville. The idea had originally come up at the time Gregory Zilboorg labeled Merton the Hermit of Times Square. It wasn't that Merton was worried about pathological impulses threatening his sanity, but it would be good to have a trained, detached, and caring listener to help him see himself and those around him in fresh perspective. It proved helpful. While it seems very little actual psychoanalysis occurred in the years that followed, Jim Wygal helped Merton cope with his stress. At the same time a friendship was founded that lasted the rest of Merton's life.

Paperback cover of *The New Man*, first published in 1961 by Farrar Straus & Cudahy.

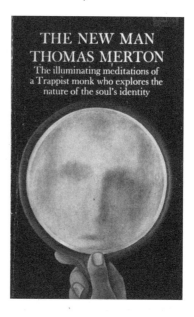

THE NEW MAN
THOMAS MERTON
The illuminating meditations of a Trappist monk who explores the nature of the soul's identity

A Hermitage on Mount Olivet

God . . . does not need to keep the birds in cages.

THOMAS MERTON
The Sign of Jonas

As the sixties began, the idea of new approaches to monastic life gained momentum among many of the monks at the Abbey of Gethsemani. Discussions took place about the value of smaller foundations following the Holy Rule of Saint Benedict. One such community, Christ in the Desert, had been set up in a remote canyon in New Mexico, which Merton, having admired it at a distance, would briefly visit in 1968. Another small foundation would soon be made in Oxford, North Carolina. But Merton personally found himself no longer obsessed with the idea of moving to a more ideal community. Instead he sought greater solitude where he was.

On March 31, 1960, Merton noted in his journal that, thanks to a decision by the abbot, he had moved into a more private cell made specially for him over the stairs by the new infirmary. Its one window gave a wonderful view of Rohan's Knob and Holy Cross. This was, Merton wrote in his journal, "a nice hermitage." Early in May, still rejoicing, he wrote about the sense he had while in his tiny cell of sitting "on the edge of the sky." He had a stool, his old scriptorium desk, a bed, three icons, and a small crucifix made by Ernesto Cardenal. "Reading in here is a totally different experience from anywhere else, as if the silence of the four walls enriched everything with great significance. One is alone, not on guard, utterly relaxed and receptive. Having four walls and silence all around enables you to listen . . . with all the pores of your skin and to absorb the truth through every part of your being. I doubt if I would be any better off [with the primitive Benedictines] in Mexico!"[245]

Another sign of new curtains rising was direct contact with the pope. It was something that Merton had hoped for in 1958, when, a few weeks after the election of John XXIII, Merton wrote him a letter describing his vision of a monastery, possibly in Latin America, where invited groups—especially writers and intellectuals—might come for retreats and discussions.[246] He also mentioned his interest in Russia.

Fourteen months later, on February 11, 1960, Merton received a packet from the Vatican that contained a portrait photograph signed by Pope John as well as John's blessing for the novitiate. Responding the same day, Merton told Pope John that he had received permission "to start, very discreetly, a small retreat project" aimed at Protestant and Catholic theologians, psychiatrists, writers, and artists—something on the lines he had described in his previous letter to John but at Gethsemani rather than in Latin America. "Our goal," Merton wrote, "is to bring together . . . various groups of people highly qualified in their own field who are interested in the spiritual life, no matter what aspect, and who will be able to profit from an informal contact, from a spiritual and cultural dialogue, with Catholic contemplatives."[247]

A nonverbal reply reached Gethsemani on April 11 with the arrival of Lorenzo Barbato, a Venetian architect who was a personal friend of the pontiff's. Barbato brought Merton a liturgical vestment, a stole, which had been used by Pope John XXIII. John wanted Merton to have it. Totally unexpected, the present was a startling indication of John's affection and respect for Merton. (The stole may be seen at the Thomas Merton Center at Bellarmine College in Louisville.)

In Barbato's care, Merton sent the pope a copy of his latest book, *The Wisdom of the Desert*,[248] a collection of say-

Pope John XXIII, who convened the Second Vatican Council. Merton sensed in Pope John a new spirit of openness to the world. (Photograph courtesy of Maryknoll archives)

"For many people he has restored hope in the Church as a living reality, as the true Body of Christ. He has made the reality of the Spirit in the world once more simply and profoundly credible even to people who are not easily disposed to believe in anything."

(Conjectures of a Guilty Bystander)

The stole worn by Pope John XXIII at his coronation, presented to Merton as a gift. (Photograph courtesy of the Abbey of Gethsemani)

"How can I express to you my gratitude and the emotion with which I received the honor bestowed on me by Your Holiness in sending me this beautiful stole, worn and blessed by Your Holiness. It is truly the greatest honor of my life . . ."

(Letter to Pope John XXIII, April 11, 1960)

ings and stories of the Desert Fathers, wilderness hermits from the early church who had become a major source of wisdom and inspiration to Merton. In an accompanying letter Merton told John of the progress being made with the ecumenical project. "A few days ago I had the pleasure of addressing more than fifty Protestant seminarians and pastors here in our monastery. They showed remarkable good will. . . . I spoke to them as a brother."[249] (Decades later, it is hard to remember the antagonistic climate that then existed between Catholics and Protestants and how astonishing, even miraculous, such dialogue was.) Aware of Pope John's special interest in the Orthodox Church, Merton went on to mention his contact with an Orthodox theologian in Paris.

Two weeks later Dom James received a letter from Cardinal Tardini, the Vatican Secretary of State, expressing the particular interest Pope John had in the "retreats with Protestants which Father Louis was organizing at Our Lady of Gethsemani."[250] Plans for the Second Vatican Council had been announced in 1959, and Pope John had decided Protestant and Orthodox Christians would also have a place in the event. The ecumenical dialogues Merton was initiating at Gethsemani couldn't be more timely.

Building on the dialogues with non-Catholics that Merton had already begun at the abbey, in April he proposed to Dom James the creation of a house, or skete, out of sight of the monastery that could function both as a center for ecumenical gatherings and also serve as a place of part-time seclusion for himself. The abbot was well disposed to the idea. Merton suggested it be built on Mount Olivet, a crest behind the sheep barn, not quite a mile from the abbey, in range of its bells. To Merton's great joy, Dom James gave his approval.

On May 18 Merton marked the trees to be cut down to make room for the "Mount Olivet Retreat Center." In October, when the contractor arrived to stake out the building site, Merton was referring to the place not as a conference center but, "let's be frank, the hermitage."[251]

By the end of the month, with construction under way, the building had a new name, after the patroness of his contemplative vocation: the hermitage of Saint Mary of Carmel. Mary was "this queen of mine to the end of the ages."[252] The completed structure was Cistercian in its plainness: a square, single-storey, two-room cinderblock dwelling with a large fireplace, a wide front window, and a long, open porch. (Later on the building would be enlarged to include a small chapel and a micro-kitchen tucked into the hallway.)

Merton lit the first blaze in the fireplace December 2. Eleven days later, on the nineteenth anniversary of his reception as a postulant, Merton took possession of the hermitage, though Dom James made clear that he was only permitted use of it for a few hours each day.

"Lit candles in the dusk," he wrote joyfully in his journal December 26. "The sense of a journey ended, of wandering at an end. *The first time in my life* I ever really felt that I had come home and that my roaming and looking were ended."[253]

Merton's hermitage on the abbey grounds. (Photograph by Michael Plekon)

"My dear Holy Father,
. . . It seems to me that, as a contemplative, I do not need to lock myself into solitude and lose all contact with the rest of the world; rather, this poor world has a right to my solitude. . . ."
(Letter to Pope John XXIII,
November 10, 1958)

Hagia Sophia

. . . as if the Blessed Virgin herself, as if Wisdom, had awakened me.

THOMAS MERTON
Journal entry, July 2, 1960

Opposite:
Merton at work in his hermitage.
(Photograph by John Howard Griffin)

"One might say I had decided to marry the silence of the forest. The sweet dark warmth of the whole world will have to be my wife."

("Day of a Stranger")

As 1961 began, Merton was home at last, if only part-time. During reading periods at the hermitage, he especially immersed himself in the writings of mystics. His love of the fourteenth-century English recluse, Julian of Norwich, dates from this period. Supplanting even Saint John of the Cross in his affections, he saw her as "without doubt one of the most wonderful of all Christian voices."[254] Julian, who sometimes wrote of "Jesus our Mother" and "Mother Jesus," helped to open the door to Merton's exploration of God's feminine dimension, at the same time creating a link to his dream of Proverb with Holy Wisdom.

One of the points of contact for Merton with Orthodox authors was their special interest in the Bible's sapiential books, the wisdom literature of the Old Testament. Several major churches in the East, including the principal church in Constantinople, were dedicated to *Hagia Sophia* (Greek for Holy Wisdom), generally understood by Orthodox Christianity as one of the titles of Christ.

It impressed Merton that several twentieth-century Russian authors, most notably Sergei Bulgakov, "have dared to accept the challenge . . . of the passages in [the Book of] Proverbs where Wisdom is 'playing in the world' before the face of the Creator. And the Church herself says this Sophia was, somehow, mysteriously to be revealed and 'fulfilled' in [Mary] the Mother of God and

"She is in all things like the air receiving the sunlight. In her they prosper. In her they glorify God. In her they rejoice to reflect Him. In her they are united with Him. She is the union between them. She is the love that unites them. She is life as communion, life as thanksgiving, life as praise, life as festival, life as glory."

("Hagia Sophia")

in the Church."[255] Merton was apparently unaware of the heated controversy within the Russian Orthodox Church regarding Bulgakov's interpretation of Holy Wisdom.

In 1958 Merton had written Boris Pasternak about his dream of Proverb, the Jewish girl whose passionate but virginal embrace had moved him so deeply. It was an encounter, he realized, with *Hagia Sophia*. The dream so impressed him that a few days later he wrote Proverb a letter expressing gratitude for her loving in him "something which I thought I had entirely lost, and someone who, I thought, had long ago ceased to be. . . . I love your name, its mystery, its simplicity, and its secret."[256]

Two weeks later, he wrote to Proverb again, assuring her that he was keeping his promise not to speak of her until he saw her again, as he felt he had the day before, March 18, among the people at Fourth and Walnut in Louisville. "I shall never forget our meeting yesterday. The touch of your hand makes me a different person. To be with you is rest and Truth. Only with you are all things found, dear child, sent by God."[257]

In April 1959, he glimpsed her again in a painting by Victor Hammer—a tall woman holding a crown over the head of Christ as a boy—when he was visiting the Hammer household in Lexington, Kentucky. As in his dream, she was a young Semitic woman.

In May, writing Hammer about the blaze the painting had lit within him, Merton suggested that the Mary-like woman in the painting could be seen as Holy Wisdom: "This feminine principle in the universe [revealed in Holy Wisdom] is the inexhaustible source of creative realization of the Father's glory in the world and is in fact the manifestation of His glory."[258]

July 2, 1960, the Feast of Our Lady's Visitation, when Merton was in the hospital in Louisville for X-rays, he had a Proverb-like dream in which he was awakened by "the soft voice of the nurse. . . . It was like awakening for the first time from all the dreams of life—as if the Blessed Virgin herself, as if Wisdom, had awakened me."[259] The gentle voice he had heard in his dream was, he knew, the voice of *Hagia Sophia*.

Visiting a Cincinnati museum in October to gather prints for the novitiate and his hermitage, he thought he had met Proverb in the flesh when he encountered "a Jewish girl sitting on top of the filing cabinets with her shoes off."[260]

Little by little Merton's prose poem *Hagia Sophia* was taking shape. The completed work began:

> There is in all visible things an invisible fecundity, a dimmed light, a meek namelessness, a hidden wholeness. This mysterious Unity and Integrity is Wisdom, the Mother of all, *Natura naturans*.[261] There is in all things an inexhaustible sweetness and purity, a silence that is a fount of action and of joy. It rises up in wordless gentleness and flows out to me from the unseen roots of all created being, welcoming me tenderly, saluting me with indescribable humility.[262]

Icon of Mother of God of the Sign.

Merton described himself waking in the hospital, at once all mankind and, at the same time, Adam, while she who is waking him was not only Eve but Mary and the feminine child, *Hagia Sophia*, playing before the Creator. She was the union between Creator and creation, the Divine nature, the mercy and tenderness of God, the Wisdom of God: *Hagia Sophia*.

The prose poem was a celebration of Merton's deepening awareness of the feminine aspects of God. It also celebrated the kenotic aspect of Christ, whose self-emptying love gloried not in wealth and power but rather in "weakness, nothingness, poverty." Christ, Merton wrote, is "a vagrant, a destitute wanderer with dusty feet . . . a homeless God, lost in the night, without papers, without identification."

Appropriately, Victor Hammer was the first to publish *Hagia Sophia*, producing an exquisite handprinted edition set in American Uncial, a typeface of his own design inspired by medieval monastic calligraphy. The text was later included in *Emblems of a Season of Fury*.

Other writings from the period reveal the political side of Merton running side-by-side with the mystical.

In "A Signed Confession of Crimes against the State," Merton celebrated the value of doing nothing and being marginal. He admits he is "sitting under a pine tree doing absolutely nothing," has done nothing for an hour, and intends to continue doing nothing. "I confess that I have been listening to a mockingbird. Yes, I admit that it is a mockingbird. . . . Clearly I am not worthy to exist another minute."[263]

Reading William Shirer's *The Rise and Fall of the Third Reich* inspired the writing of "Chant to Be Used around a Site with Furnaces," a chilling poem in monotone voice about the administration of the Holocaust, in which progress equals more efficient methods of death and those who try to save lives are the guilty ones. "All the while I obeyed perfectly," says the narrator-commander who, before his execution for war crimes, was a man of self-sacrifice whose work was conscientious and faultless. He stands not only for the administrators of Hitler's Holocaust, but for the nuclear holocaust being prepared by those who defeated the Nazis. "Do not think yourself better because you burn up friends and enemies with long-range missiles without ever seeing what you have done."[264] In 1961, the year of the U. S.-sponsored Bay of Pigs Invasion of Cuba and the Soviet-backed erection of the Berlin Wall, a future nuclear holocaust seemed increasingly likely.

In the same period Merton wrote *Original Child Bomb*, the title being an exact translation of the Japanese word for the bomb that had been dropped on Hiroshima on August 6, 1945.[265] The poem, published in March

Survivor of atomic blast at Nagasaki. (Photograph by Yosuke Yamahata/United Nations, courtesy of Maryknoll archives)

"As to the Original Child that was not born, President Truman summed up the philosophy of the situation in a few words. 'We found the bomb,' he said, 'and we used it.'"

("Original Child Bomb")

1962, was a short history written in numbered, laconic sentences about the development and first use of nuclear weapons, despite the appeal of some of the bomb's makers that it not be used without prior warning. Nonetheless, the bomb was dropped on a city considered of minor military importance:

ORIGINAL CHILD BOMB
points for meditation to be scratched on the walls of a cave
THOMAS MERTON

Title page from *Original Child Bomb*, published in 1962 by New Directions.

> The bomb exploded within 100 feet of the aiming point. The fireball was 18,000 feet across. The temperature at the center of the fireball was 100,000,000 degrees. The people who were near the center became nothing. The whole city was blown to bits and the ruins caught fire instantly everywhere, burning briskly. 70,000 people were killed right away or died within a few hours. Those who did not die at once suffered great pain. Few of them were soldiers.

Merton noted the bizarre use of Christian terms by those responsible for making, testing, and dropping the bomb. Its first test was called "Trinity." The air mission that had released the Hiroshima bomb returned to "Papacy," the code name for Tinian island.

In "A Letter to Pablo Antonia Cuadra concerning Giants," Merton saw the nuclear-armed two superpowers, the United States and the Soviet Union, as having much more in common than either side cared to admit. In fact they resembled the twin giants, Gog and Magog, of Ezekiel's prophecies. "We must become wary of ourselves when the worst that is in man becomes objectified in society, approved, acclaimed and deified, when hatred becomes patriotism, and murder a holy duty."[266]

Merton was also writing more lyric poems. "Grace's House" was inspired by a child's drawing—house, flowers, grass, sun, a chimney, smoke, trees with knotholes, clouds, a dog with collar, a mailbox with the number 5.

Between our world and hers
Runs a sweet river:

(No, it is not the road,
It is the uncrossed crystal
Water between our ignorance and her truth.)

O paradise, O child's world!
Where all the grass lives
And all the animals are aware!
The huge sun, bigger than the house
Stands and streams with life in the east
While in the west a thunder cloud
Moves away forever....

Alas, there is no road to Grace's house![267]

In "The General Dance," a canticle-like text written for *Jubilee*, the journal edited by his friend and godfather Ed Rice, Merton celebrated a God whose "delights are to be with the children of men," a world in which God has become one of us, hidden, unknown, unremarkable, vulnerable, sharing in our suffering, yet conquering death. "In Christ, God became not only *this* man, but also ... every man." To see the beauty of the world, whether a child at play or a frog leaping into a pond, is to have "a glimpse of the cosmic dance."[268]

Yet even in the midst of some of his best writing, Merton was full of doubts about his work. "I become more and more skeptical about my writing," he told Dorothy Day. "There has been some good and much bad, and I haven't been nearly honest enough and clear enough. The problem that torments me is that I can so easily become part of a general system of delusion. . . . I find myself more and more drifting toward the derided and possibly quite absurd and defeatist position of a sort of Christian anarchist."[269] (Merton was always quick to find bonding words with those to whom he was communicating; "anarchist" to Dorothy Day meant someone like herself: a person whose obedience was not to rulers, states, or any secular system, but to the gospel.)

"As for writing: I don't feel that I can in conscience, at a time like this, go on writing just about things like meditation, though that has its point. I cannot just bury my head in a lot of rather tiny and secondary monastic studies either. I think I have to face the big issues, the life-and-death issues: and this is what everyone is afraid of."

(Letter to Dorothy Day, August 23, 1961)

THE WORKER PRIESTS

By Anne Talliefer

"Man is a living paradox and the Incarnation—the Word made flesh—is the greatest paradox of all" (Henri de Lubac). Thus vocation, the call of the supernatural to the natural, the message of the Lord, when utterly pure and obediently heard is apt to surprise us shatteringly. Of all the strange vocations that of worker-priest may be among the most dispossessed

The present Anglican bishop of Tanganyka, who was then Father Trevor Huddleston, one of the great fighters against apartheid in South Africa, once said: "the trial of the worker-priests is that of Joan of Arc". Strangely enough his words are echoed in a letter written by an eminent ecclesiastic, years ago, to Father Godin, one of the founders of the movement: "It is doubtful if the Catholic Church, the Catholic hierarchy, by itself would have the courage to operate this reform. God will have to help or to constrain it to do so."

In another letter the same ecclesiastic who may or may not have been Cardinal Suhard says: "The rechristianization of France and above all of its workers demands, to begin with, a radical reform of our society. The form of slavery called proletariat must

THE ROOT OF WAR

By Thomas Merton

The present war crisis is something we have made entirely for and by ourselves. There is in reality not the slightest logical reason for war, and yet the whole world is plunging headlong into frightful destruction, and doing so **with the purpose of avoiding war and preserving peace!** This is a true war-madness, an illness of the mind and the spirit that is spreading with a furious and subtle contagion all over the world. Of all the countries that are sick, America is perhaps the most grievously afflicted. On all sides we have people building bomb shelters where, in case of nuclear war, they will simply bake slowly instead of burning up quickly or being blown out of existence in a flash. And they are prepared to sit in these shelters with machine guns with which to prevent their neighbor from entering. This is a nation that claims to be fighting for religious truth along with freedom and other values of the spirit. Truly we have entered the "post-Christian era" with a vengeance. Whether we are destroyed or whether we survive, the future is awful to contemplate.

The Christian

What is the place of the Christian in all this? Is he simply to fold his hands and resign himself —

In a letter written a few weeks later, Merton said, "I don't feel that I can in conscience, at a time like this, go on writing just about things like meditation, though that has its point. I cannot just bury my head in a lot of rather tiny and secondary monastic studies either. I think I have to face the big issues, the life-and-death issues: and this is what everyone is afraid of."[270]

In September 1961 Merton was ready to go public with his thinking on war. He did so with "The Root of War Is Fear," an essay that had once been a short chapter in *Seeds of Contemplation*, and which he had rewritten for the forthcoming *New Seeds of Contemplation*, the only book Merton ever revised. The version of the text he sent to Dorothy Day included several paragraphs written especially for *The Catholic Worker*:

Partial front page of the October 1961 issue of *The Catholic Worker*, which featured "The Root of War," Merton's first contribution to the pacifist newspaper.

151

The present war crisis is something we have made entirely for and by ourselves. There is in reality not the slightest logical reason for war, and yet the whole world is plunging headlong into frightful destruction, and doing so with the purpose of avoiding war. . . . This is true war-madness, an illness of the mind and spirit that is spreading with a furious and subtle contagion all over the world. Of all the countries that are sick, America is perhaps the most grievously afflicted. On all sides we have people building bomb shelters where, in case of nuclear war, they will simply bake slowly instead of burning quickly or being blown out of existence in a flash. And they are prepared to sit in these shelters with machine guns with which to prevent their neighbor from entering. This in a nation that claims to be fighting for religious truth along with freedom and other values of the spirit. Truly we have entered the "post-Christian era" with a vengeance. Whether we are destroyed or whether we survive, the future is awful to contemplate.

What is the place of the Christian in all this? Is he simply to fold his hands and resign himself for the worst, accepting it as the inescapable will of God and preparing himself to enter heaven with a sigh of relief? Should he open up the Apocalypse and run into the street to give everyone his idea of what is happening? Or, worse still should he take a hard-headed and "practical" attitude about it and join in the madness of the war makers, calculating how, by a "first strike" the glorious Christian West can eliminate atheistic Communism for all time and usher in the millennium? I am no prophet and seer but it seems to me that this last position may very well be the most diabolical of illusions, the great and not even subtle temptation of a Christianity that has grown rich and comfortable, and is satisfied with its riches.

What are we to do? The duty of the Christian in this crisis is to strive with all his power and intelligence, with his faith, his hope in Christ, and love for God and man, to do the one task which God has imposed upon us in the world today. That task is to work for the total abolition of war. There can be no question that unless war is abolished the world will remain constantly in a state of madness and desperation in which, because of the immense destructive power of modern weapons, the danger of catastrophe will be imminent and probable at every moment everywhere. Unless we set ourselves immediately to this task, both as individuals and in our political and religious groups, we tend by our very passivity and fatalism to cooperate with the destructive forces that are leading inexorably to war. It is a problem of terrifying complexity and magnitude, for which the Church itself is not fully able to see clear and decisive solutions. Yet she must lead the way on the road to

Merton with his Aunt Kit, during a visit to Gethsemani in 1961. (Photograph courtesy of the Thomas Merton Center)

the nonviolent settlement of difficulties and toward the gradual abolition of war as the way of settling international or civil disputes. Christians must become active in every possible way, mobilizing all their resources for the fight against war.

First of all there is much to be learned. Peace is to be preached, nonviolence is to be explained as a practical method, and not left to be mocked as an outlet for crackpots who want to make a show of themselves. Prayer and sacrifice must be used as the most effective spiritual weapons in the war against war, and like all weapons, they must be used with deliberate aim: not just with a vague aspiration for peace and security, but against violence and war. This implies that we are also willing to sacrifice and restrain our own instinct for violence and aggressiveness in our relations with other people. We may

(Photograph courtesy of the Thomas Merton Center)

"We find ourselves confronting the possibility of nuclear war with more than the common and universal urgency, because we Christians are at least dimly aware that this is a matter of choice for us and that the future of Christianity on earth may depend on the moral quality of the decision we are making."

(Thomas Merton on Peace)

never succeed in this campaign but whether we succeed or not, the duty is evident. [271]

Merton was aware that many who treasured *The Seven Storey Mountain* would be troubled, even irate, when confronted with a view so critical of what America was doing. With John F. Kennedy's inauguration in January 1961, the United States government was led by a Catholic who enjoyed overwhelming Catholic support. Quite apart from this, U.S. policy traditionally had the determined support of the American Catholic population and hierarchy, eager to demonstrate their loyalty in the face of widespread anti-Catholic sentiment.

On October 23, a few weeks after *The Catholic Worker* essay was published, he wrote in his journal:

I am perhaps at the turning point in my spiritual life, perhaps slowly coming to a point of maturation and the resolution of doubts—and the forgetting of fears. Walking into a known and definite battle. May God protect me in it. *The Catholic Worker* sent out a press release about my article, which may have many reactions. . . . I am one of the few Catholic priests in the country who has come out unequivocally for a completely intransigent fight for the abolition of war and the use of nonviolent means to settle international conflicts. Hence by implication not only against the bomb, against nuclear testing, against Polaris submarines, but against all violence. This I will inevitably have to explain in due course. Nonviolent action, not mere passivity. How am I going to explain myself and defend a definite position in a timely manner when it takes at least two months to get even a short article through the censors of the Order, is a question I cannot attempt to answer. [272]

Silencing

Everything the enemy does is diabolical and everything we do is angelic. [The enemy's] H-bombs are from hell and ours are instruments of divine justice.

THOMAS MERTON

"The Root of War Is Fear" was followed quickly by more essays on the same theme in *The Catholic Worker* and such other publications as *Commonweal, Blackfriars, Fellowship,* and *Jubilee.*

Merton was also writing letters. At a time when "better dead than red" was a popular slogan in America, he wrote to Pope John XXIII to voice alarm at the way in which many Americans linked their opposition to Communism with a readiness to use the U.S. nuclear arsenal to destroy the Soviet Union. Regarding their hawkish position as a sign of loyalty both to the church and nation, Catholics were prominent among the most intransigent. The U.S. economy itself depends increasingly on preparation for war, Merton went on, so that steps toward disarmament were seen not only as unpatriotic but also as economically threatening. "A very small peace movement, bringing Protestants and Catholics together, has come into being in the United States," he told the pope. "I try to be a part of this movement as much as I can, here in the cloister, through my prayers and writings and also through the conversations I have with those who come here."[273] Monsignor Capovilla, private secretary to Pope John, recalls that the letter impressed the pope, and Monsignor William Shannon said, "It may have had some influence on the writing of *Pacem in Terris*."[274]

The topics Merton was writing about, as 1961 came to

The cross that stood before Merton's hermitage. (Photograph by Jim Forest, courtesy of Boston College, Burns Library)

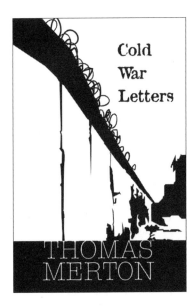

Cover of *Cold War Letters*, finally published in 2006 by Orbis Books.

"We are living in a condition where we are afraid to see the total immorality and absurdity of total war. . . . The burden of protest in these letters is simply that such a state of affairs is pure madness, that to accept it without question as right and reasonable is criminally insane and that in the presence of such fantastically absurd and suicidal iniquity the Christian conscience cannot keep silent."
(Cold War Letters)

an end, were not welcomed by the Trappists' Abbot General, Dom Gabriel Sortais,[275] nor did most of the order's censors see such controversial writing as appropriate for a monk. As the year came to an end, Merton noted in a letter that the censorship he was encountering was "completely and deliberately obstructive, not aimed at combing out errors at all, but purely and simply at preventing the publication of material that 'doesn't look good.' And this means anything that ruffles in any way the censors' tastes or susceptibilities."[276] It was not only the censors who were irritated. An editorial in *The Washington Catholic Standard* in March 1962 described Merton as "an absolute pacifist" and accused him of disregarding "authoritative Catholic utterances and [making] unwarranted charges about the intention of our government towards disarmament."

As such criticism mounted, Merton was forced to withdraw his name as editor of *Breakthrough to Peace*, a book of essays on the arms race which he had conceived and assembled for New Directions, but at least the project itself was not derailed and his introduction remained part of the book, which was published in September 1962. Merton's name was featured on the cover not as editor but as author of the introduction.[277]

Looking for a way to share his thinking about the religious dimension of social and political problems without having to pass through the labyrinths of censorship, Merton produced *Cold War Letters*, a book-sized mimeographed collection of letters. (It was published by Orbis Books in 2006.[278]) Some of his correspondents were enlisted to help circulate the text. It was Merton's first experience of being read in *samizdat* (Russian for self-published), thus forging another link with Russian writers like Boris Pasternak. In doing this, Merton had the support of his abbot. Dom James assented to the circulation of Merton's more controversial writings in mimeographed form, deciding that censorship was required only for material that had the potential of reaching the general public.

```
    jhs


              COLD WAR LETTERS:     PREFACE


        These copies of letters written over a period of little more than one year pre-

    ceding the Cuban Crisis of 1962, have been made for friends who might be expected

    to understand something of the writer's viewpoint, even when they might not agree

    with all he has said, still less with all that he may have unconsciously implied.

        As a matter of fact, the letters themselves have been copied practically without

    change, except that the more irrelevant parts have been cut out. There have been

    none of the careful corrections, qualifications, and omissions which would be re-

    quired before such a book could possibly be considered for general circulation, or

    even for any but the most limited and private reading. As it stands, it lies open

    to all kinds of misinterpretation, and malevolence will not find it difficult to

    read into these pages the most sinister of attitudes. A few words in a preface may

    then serve to deny in advance the possible allegations of witch hunters.

        There is no witch here, no treason and no subversion. The letters form part of

    no plot. They incite to no riot, they suggest no disloyalty to government, they

    are not pandering to the destructive machinations of revolutionaries or foreign

    foes. They are nothing more than the expression of loyal but unpopular opinion, of
```

Many hours were devoted to work on a book, *Peace in the Post-Christian Era*, that Merton hoped would be moderate enough to pass inspection by the Abbot General and the order's censors. The manuscript had just been completed when a letter arrived ordering Merton to give up all such writing projects.

"Now here is the axe," he wrote me April 29, 1962. "For a long time I have been anticipating trouble with the higher superiors and now I have it. The orders are, no more writing about peace. . . . In substance I am being silenced on the subject of war and peace."

The decision, he said, reflected "an astounding incomprehension of the seriousness of the present crisis

An excerpt from Merton's *Cold War Letters*, a manuscript that was privately distributed in mimeographed form at a time when his writings on war and peace were subject to censorship.

in its religious aspect. It reflects an insensitivity to Christian and Ecclesiastical values, and to the real sense of the monastic vocation. The reason given is that this is not the right kind of work for a monk and that it 'falsifies the monastic message.' Imagine that: the thought that a monk might be deeply enough concerned with the issue of nuclear war to voice a protest against the arms race, is supposed to bring the monastic life into *disrepute*. Man, I would think that it might just possibly salvage a last shred of repute for an institution that many consider to be dead on its feet. . . . That is really the most absurd aspect of the whole situation, that these people insist on digging their own grave and erecting over it the most monumental kind of tombstone."

"My peace writings have reached an abrupt halt. Told not to do any more on this subject. Dangerous, subversive, perilous, offensive to pious ears, and confusing to good Catholics who are all at peace in the nice idea that we ought to wipe Russia off the face of the earth. Why get people all stirred up?"
(Letter to Daniel Berrigan, December 7, 1961)

Beneath the surface of the disagreement between Merton and the Abbot General was a different conception of the identity and mission of the church. In his letter, Merton stated, "The vitality of the Church depends precisely on spiritual renewal, uninterrupted, continuous, and deep. Obviously this renewal is to be expressed in the historical context, and will call for a real spiritual understanding of historical crises, an evaluation of them in terms of their inner significance and in terms of man's growth and the advancement of truth in man's world: in other words, the establishment of the 'kingdom of God.' The monk is the one supposedly attuned to the inner spiritual dimension of things. If he hears nothing, and says nothing, then the renewal as a whole will be in danger and may be completely sterilized."[279]

Those silencing him, he went on, regarded the monk as someone appointed not to see or hear anything new but "to support the already existing viewpoints . . . defined for him by somebody else. Instead of being in the advance guard, he is in the rear with the baggage, confirming all that has been done by the officials. . . . He has no other function, then, except perhaps to pray for what he is told to pray for: namely the purposes and the objectives of an ecclesiastical bureaucracy. . . . He must in no event and under no circumstances assume a role that implies any form of spontaneity and originality. He must be an eye that sees nothing except what is carefully selected for him to see. An ear that hears nothing except what it is advantageous for the managers for him to hear. We know what Christ said about such ears and eyes."

Merton asked if he shouldn't "just blast the whole thing wide open, or walk out, or tell them to jump in the lake?" Wouldn't it be justified to disobey such manifestly unjust orders? After all, as he pointed out, obedience is synonymous with love. But would disobedience or a public denunciation be seen as a witness for peace and for the truth of the church, in its reality, rather than some figment of the imagination? Wouldn't such action rather be seen by his fellow monks as an excuse for dismissing a minority viewpoint and be regarded by those outside as fresh proof that the church had no love for private conscience? Whose mind would be changed?

"In my own particular case," he concluded, public protest and disobedience "would backfire and be fruitless. It would be taken as a witness against the peace movement and would confirm these people in all the depth of their prejudices and their self complacency. It would reassure them in every possible way that they are incontrovertibly right and make it even more impossible for them ever to see any kind of new light on the subject. And in any case I am not merely looking for opportunities to blast off. I can get along without it.

"I am where I am. I have freely chosen this state, and have freely chosen to stay in it when the question of a possible change arose. If I am a disturbing element, that is all right. I am not making a point of being that, but simply of saying what my conscience dictates and doing so without seeking my own interest. This means accepting such limitations as may be placed on me by authority, and not because I may or may not agree with the ostensible reasons why the limitations are imposed, but out of love for God who is using these things to attain ends which I

Photograph by Jim Forest. (Courtesy of Boston College, Burns Library)

"In the name of lifeless and graven letters on parchment we are told that our life consists in the peaceful and pious meditation on Scripture and a quiet withdrawal from the world. But if one reads the prophets with his ears and eyes open he cannot help recognizing his obligation to shout very loud about God's will, God's truth, and justice of man to man."

(Letter to Daniel Berrigan, November 27, 1962)

159

myself cannot at the moment see or comprehend. I know He can and will in His own time take good care of the ones who impose limitations unjustly or unwisely. That is His affair and not mine. In this dimension I find no contradiction between love and obedience, and as a matter of fact it is the only sure way of transcending the limits and arbitrariness of ill-advised commands."[280]

Behind the silencing, he wrote a few weeks later, was the charge that he had been writing for "a Communist-controlled publication," as *The Catholic Worker* was said to be by some of its opponents.[281]

In mid-May Merton received a letter from the Abbot General in which Dom Gabriel stressed the difference between religious orders which teach and those which pray. "I am not asking you to remain indifferent to the fate of the world," he insisted. "But I believe you have the power to influence the world by your prayers and by your life withdrawn into God more than by your writings. That is why I am not thinking about hurting the cause you are defending when I ask that you give up your intention of publishing the book you have finished, and abstain from now on from writing on the subject of atomic warfare, preparation for war, etc."[282]

Merton obeyed, if in a limited way. Never submitted to a publisher, the book remained generally unknown, but not entirely, for Merton again resorted to *samizdat* methods of communicating his views. With the abbot's permission, several hundred copies of *Peace in the Post-Christian Era* were produced by mimeograph and mailed to friends who in turn shared their copies with others. (It was eventually published in 2004, by Orbis Books.[283]) Though reaching far fewer readers than any of his other books, the text was studied all the more attentively by those who obtained it. For example, Bob Grip tells me he came upon a copy of the mimeographed edition of *Peace in the Post-Christian Era* on a windowsill in the library of the Vatican's North American College in Rome.[284]

Merton was not altogether sorry about what had hap-

"It is unfortunate that so much of monastic obedience has become merely formal and trivial. There is no use in lamenting this, but nevertheless, renewal in this area must mean, above all, a recovery of the sense of obedience to God in all things and not just obedience to rules and superiors when obedience is demanded: and after that, go wool-gathering where you may!"

(A Vow of Conversation)

pened. He rejoiced in discovering access to uncensored channels of communication; he had become "a firm believer in the power of the offbeat essay printed or mimeographed in a strange place."[285] (At least one other book of Merton's, *Art and Worship*, has yet to reach the public, not because of censorship by his order, but because the book's intended publisher thought Merton's views were too old-fashioned. The book was set in type and due to be published in 1959. One reader of the manuscript, the art critic and historian Eloise Spaeth, could not bear Merton's " 'sacred artist' who keeps creeping in with his frightful icons." Unfortunately this book was never put out in a mimeographed edition, though a few chapters were published as magazine articles.[286])

One of the problems with *Peace in the Post-Christian Era,* he realized, was that it had been written with a constant eye to what might be allowed through official channels. "What a mess one gets into," he wrote me that July, "trying to write a book that will get through the censors, and at the same time say something. I was bending in all directions to qualify every statement and balance everything off, so I stayed right in the middle and perfectly objective . . . [at the same time trying] to speak the truth as my conscience wanted it to be said."[287]

Another of the other burning issues that Merton felt obliged to write about in the early sixties was racism, a topic he hadn't addressed since describing his experiences of Harlem in *The Seven Storey Mountain*. In the fifties, a vigorous civil rights movement had come into being, starting with the bus boycott in Montgomery, Alabama, followed by waves of freedom rides, sit-ins, and finally mass marches. The impetus came largely from within southern black churches. Again and again, nonviolent protest by blacks and their allies were met by brutality from local whites and the police. In "Letters to a White Liberal," Merton warned that the defeat of nonviolent protest would give rise to violent protest that might even unleash a new civil war. As he pointed out, "Where

Cover of Merton's *Peace in the Post-Christian Era*. It was finally published by Orbis Books in 2004.

"The monk is the one supposedly attuned to the inner spiritual dimension of things. If he hears nothing and says nothing, then the renewal [of the Church] as a whole will be in danger and may be completely sterilized. But these authoritarian minds believe that the function of the monk is not to see or hear any new dimensions, simply to support the already existing viewpoints. . . . The function of the monk . . . then becomes simply to affirm his total support of officialdom."
(Letter to Jim Forest, April 29, 1962)

The Second Vatican Council.
(Photograph courtesy of Maryknoll archives)

minds are full of hatred and where imaginations dwell on cruelty, torment, punishment, revenge and death, then inevitably there will be violence and death."[288]

Increasingly Merton turned to smaller journals for publication of his essays, aware that the terms of the order's Statute of Censorship permitted publication without censorship of "brief articles destined for periodicals of limited circulation and influence" so long as the local superior gave permission. Another option was to rename himself something other than Thomas Merton. Thus the uncensored Merton occasionally addressed wider audiences by writing under the thin cover of a revealing pseudonym. One piece in *The Catholic Worker* was signed Benedict Monk. And to those acquainted with Merton's Marx Brothers sense of humor, who but Merton would sign himself Marco J. Frisbee?

Despite his problems with censorship, Merton was made hopeful by the process of church renewal inspired by Pope John XXIII. A Vatican Council, the first one in nearly a hundred years, had been announced by the pope in January 1959 and began in October 1962. Though the first session was mainly devoted to revamping the liturgy, subsequent sessions were to consider such matters as the church's role in the modern world.

In December 1962 Merton sent a selection of his peace writing to Hildegard and Jean Goss-Mayr, secretaries of the International Fellowship of Reconciliation. The couple had received permission from Dom Gabriel Sortais to circulate Merton's peace essays among the theologians and bishops drafting a text on the church's social mission.

In April 1963, two months before his death, Pope John published what became the most widely discussed papal encyclical of modern times: *Pacem in Terris (Peace on Earth)*. Stressing that the most basic human right is the right to life, John spoke out passionately against such threats to life as the arms race, said that war was no longer an apt means for vindicating violated rights, and called for legal protection of conscientious objectors to military service. Far from sanctioning blind obedience to those in authority, the pope stressed the individual responsibility to protect life and uphold morality: "If civil authorities legislate or allow anything that is contrary to the will of God, neither the law made nor the authorization granted can be binding on the conscience of the citizens since God has more right to be obeyed than man."[289]

Days after the encyclical was released, Merton wrote the Abbot General to say "it was a good thing that Pope John didn't have to get his encyclical through our censors: and could I now start up again."[290] Specifically he asked Dom Gabriel for permission to return to work on *Peace in the Post-Christian Era* so that it might finally be published. Unmoved, Dom Gabriel renewed the prohibition. Merton commented in his journal, "At the back of [Dom Gabriel's] mind obviously is an adamant convic-

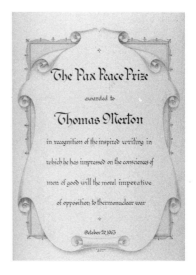

The Pax Peace Prize
awarded to
Thomas Merton
in recognition of the inspired writing in which he has impressed on the consciences of men of good will the moral imperative of opposition to thermonuclear war
October 22, 1963

Award presented to Merton in 1963 by Pax, a Catholic peace group.

tion that France [of which Dom Gabriel was a citizen] should have the bomb and use it if necessary. He says that the encyclical [*Pacem in Terris*] has changed nothing in the right of a nation to arm itself with nuclear weapons for self-defense."[291]

In the summer of 1963 the silenced Merton was honored for what he had managed to publish before *Pacem in Terris* changed the direction of Catholic social thought. Awarded a medal by Pax, a Catholic peace group that had grown out of the Catholic Worker and which eventually became the U.S. section of Pax Christi International, Merton wrote a letter of acceptance in which he commented that "a monastery is not a snail's shell nor is religious faith a kind of spiritual fallout shelter into which one can plunge to escape the criminal realities of an apocalyptic age." The monk, like anyone else, had to make decisions for or against life; these were, in fact, decisions for or against God. "I have attempted to say this in the past as opportunity has permitted, and opportunity has not permitted as much as I would have liked. But one thing I must admit: to say these things seems to me to be only the plain duty of any reasonable being. Such an attitude implies no heroism, no extraordinary insight, no special moral qualities, and no unusual intelligence. . . . These propositions are . . . clear as day light. . . . If I said it before *Pacem in Terris*, that still does not make me terribly original." The same was said, after all "by popes before Pope John, and by theologians, and by the Fathers of the Church, and by the Gospels themselves." Medals, he said, shouldn't be needed for those repeating ancient truths.[292]

In November 1963 Dom Gabriel Sortais died. The new Abbot General, Dom Ignatius Gillet, was, in time, to prove more open to Merton's peace writing.

One of the achievements of 1963 had been a reflection on his life and vocation written in the form of an introduction to the Japanese edition of *The Seven Storey Mountain*. Merton felt that too often his autobiography had revealed a deficit of compassion. He also saw it as a young man's book. It would be quite a different work had it been written twenty years later. The great decisions of his life—becoming a Christian, a monk, and a priest—were not at issue, but, he wrote,

> I have learned to look back into the world with greater compassion, seeing those in it not as alien to myself, not as peculiar and deluded strangers, but as identified with myself. In freeing myself from their delusions and preoccupations, I have identified myself, nonetheless, with their struggles and their blind, desperate hope of happiness.
>
> But precisely because I am identified with them, I must refuse all the more definitely to make their delusions my own. I must refuse their ideology of matter, power, quantity, movement, activism and force. I reject this because I see it to be the source and expression of the spiritual hell which man has made of his world: the hell which has burst into flame in two total wars of incredible horror: the hell of spiritual emptiness and sub-human fury which has resulted in crimes like Auschwitz or Hiroshima. This I can and must reject with all the power of my being. This all sane men seek to reject. But the question is: how can one sincerely reject the effect if he continues to embrace the cause? . . .
>
> The monastery is not an "escape from the world." On the contrary by being in the monastery I take my true part in all the struggles and sufferings of the world. To adopt a life that is essentially non-assertive, a nonviolent life of humility and peace, is in itself a statement of one's position. But each one in such a life can, by the personal modality of his decision, give his whole life a special orientation. It is my intention to make my entire life a rejection of, a protest against the crimes and injustices of war and political tyranny which threaten to destroy the whole race of man and the world with him. . . .

Photograph by Jim Forest.

By my monastic life and vows I am saying **no** to all the concentration camps, the aerial bombardments, the staged political trials, the judicial murders, the racial injustices, the economic tyrannies, and the whole socio-economic apparatus which seems geared for nothing but global destruction in spite of all its fair words in favor of peace. I make monastic silence a protest against the lies of politicians, propagandists and agitators, and when I speak it is to deny that my faith and my Church can ever seriously be aligned with these forces of injustice and destruction.

My life, then, must be a protest against [those who invoke their faith in support of war, racial injustice and tyranny] also, and perhaps against these most of all. . . .

The time has come for judgment to be passed on this history. I can rejoice in this fact, believing that the judgment will be a liberation of Christian faith from servitude to and involvement in the structures of the secular world. And that is why I think certain forms of Christian "optimism" are to be taken with reservation, in so far as they lack the genuine eschatological consciousness of the Christian vision, and concentrate upon the naive hope of merely temporal achievements—churches on the moon!

If I say **no** to all these secular forces, I also say **yes** to all that is good in the world and in man. I say **yes** to all that is beautiful in nature, and in order that this may be the yes of a freedom and not of subjection, I must refuse to possess anything in the world purely as my own. I say yes to all the men and women who are my brothers and sisters in the world, but for the yes to be an assent of freedom and not of subjection, I must live so that no one of them may seem to belong to me, and that I may not belong to any of them. It is because I want to be more to them than a friend that I become, to all of them, a stranger.[293]

Pastor to Peacemakers

Our job is to love others without stopping to inquire whether or not they are worthy. That is not our business. What we are asked to do is to love and this love will render both ourselves and our neighbors worthy, if anything can.

THOMAS MERTON

Despite his close identification with pacifist groups, Merton preferred not to label himself a pacifist and never rebuked those who had reluctantly resorted to violence in self-defense. He also accepted the possibility that just wars may have occurred in earlier times, when the technology of warfare didn't inevitably cause numerous noncombatant casualties, and might still occur in the modern context in the case of oppressed people fighting for liberation. But, as he wrote Dorothy Day in 1962, the issue of the just war "is pure theory. . . . In practice all the wars that are [happening] . . . are shot through and through with evil, falsity, injustice, and sin so much so that one can only with difficulty extricate the truths that may be found here and there in the 'causes' for which the fighting is going on."[294]

Neither did he insist that a Christian was obliged to be a conscientious objector, yet the highest form of Christian discipleship, he was convinced, required the renunciation of violence: "The Christian does not need to fight and indeed it is better that he should not fight, for insofar as he imitates his Lord and Master, he proclaims that the Messianic Kingdom has come and bears witness to the presence of the *Kyrios Pantocrator* [Lord of Creation] in mystery, even in the midst of the conflicts and turmoil of the world."[295] What he found valuable in the just-war tradition was not its acceptance of violent methods, but its insistence that evil must be actively opposed. It was this

that drew him to Gandhi, Dorothy Day, and groups involved in active nonviolent combat for social justice.

While his vocation made an active role in the peace movement impossible, through correspondence and occasional face-to-face visits Merton played a pastoral role among peace activists that was perhaps even more important than his public role as an author, and one in which he could communicate without having to worry about getting his words past the censors.

For all his respect for peace activists, however, he was aware that engagement in any movement, however justified its concerns, was not without danger. He retained a vivid memory of equivalent activities from his student days at Cambridge and Columbia. "I have the feeling of being a survivor of the shipwrecked thirties," he noted, "one of the few that has kept my original face before this present world was born."[296]

There was always the danger in any movement, including those with a religious dimension, of its participants becoming zealots, thus losing contact with conscience and their own perceptions and instead being carried along by group-defined attitudes and ideology in which critical thought is supplanted by slogans, rhetoric, and peer group pressure. As Merton wrote in *Seasons of Celebration*, one had to be "on guard against a kind of blind and immature zeal—the zeal of the enthusiast or of the zealot . . . who 'loses himself' in the cause in such a way that he can no longer 'find himself' at all." Such a person is "alienated by the violence of his own enthusiasm: and by that very violence he tends to produce the same kind of alienation in others."[297]

If the deadening influence of ideology was one problem, he found that the absence of compassion crippled many protest actions. Those involved in protest tend to become enraged with those they see as being responsible for injustice and violence and even toward those who uphold the status quo. Without compassion, Merton pointed out, the protester tends to become more and

Opposite:
Merton during a retreat for peacemakers in 1965. (Photograph by Jim Forest, courtesy of Boston College, Burns Library)

"Do not depend on the hope of

results. . . . These are not in your hands or mine, but they can suddenly happen, and we can share in them. . . ."
(Letter to Jim Forest,
February 21, 1966)

"We live in the time of no room, which is the time of the end. . . . Into this world, this demented inn, in which there is absolutely no room for Him at all, Christ has come uninvited. But because He cannot be at home in it, because He is out of place in it, and yet He must be in it, His place is with those others for whom there is no room."

(New Seeds of Contemplation)

more centered in anger and, far from contributing to anyone's conversion, can easily become an obstacle to changing the attitudes of others.

As he put it in one letter, "We have to have a deep patient compassion for the fears of men, for the fears and irrational mania of those who hate or condemn us. . . . [These are, after all] the ordinary people, the ones who don't want war, the ones who get it in the neck, the ones who really want to build a decent new world in which there will not be war and starvation."[298]

Most people, Merton pointed out, are irritated or frightened by agitation even when it protests something—militarism, nuclear weapons, social injustice— which objectively endangers them. "[People] do not feel at all threatened by the bomb . . . but they feel terribly threatened by some . . . student carrying a placard."[299]

Without love, especially love of opponents and enemies, he insisted that neither profound personal nor social transformation can occur. As Merton wrote to Dorothy Day in 1961:

Persons are not known by intellect alone, not by principles alone, but only by love. It is when we love the other, the enemy, that we obtain from God the key to an understanding of who he is, and who we are. It is only this realization that can open to us the real nature of our duty, and of right action. To *shut out* the person and to refuse to consider him as a person, as an other self, we resort to the "impersonal law" and to abstract "nature." That is to say we block off the reality of the other, we cut the intercommunication of our nature and his nature, and we consider only our own nature with its rights, its claims, its demands. And we justify the evil we do to our brother because he is no longer a brother, he is merely an adversary, an accused. To restore communication, to see our oneness of nature with him, and to respect his personal rights and his integrity, his worthiness of love, we have to see ourselves as similarly accused along with him . . . and needing, with him, the ineffable gift of grace and mercy to be saved. Then, instead of pushing him down, trying to climb out by using his head as a stepping-stone for ourselves, we help ourselves to rise by helping him to rise. For when we extend our hand to the enemy who is sinking in the abyss, God reaches out to both of us, for it is He first of all who extends our hand to the enemy. It is He who "saves himself" in the enemy, who makes use of us to recover the lost groat which is His image in our enemy.[300]

Where compassion and love are absent, actions that are superficially nonviolent tend to mask deep hostility, contempt, and the desire to defeat and humiliate an opponent. As he wrote in one of his most insightful letters:

One of the problematic questions about nonviolence is the inevitable involvement of hidden aggressions and provocations. I think this is especially true when there are . . . elements that are not spiritually developed. It is an enormously subtle question, but we have to consider the fact that, in its provocative aspect, nonviolence may tend to harden opposition and confirm people in their righteous blindness. It may even in some cases separate men out and drive them in the other direction, away from us and away from peace. This of course may be (as it was with the prophets) part of God's plan. A clear separation of antagonists. . . . [But we must] always direct our action toward opening people's eyes to the truth, and if they are blinded, we must try to be sure we did nothing specifically to blind them.

Yet there is that danger: the danger one observes subtly in tight groups like families and monastic communities, where the martyr for the right sometimes thrives on making his persecutors terribly and visibly wrong. He can drive them in desperation to be wrong, to seek refuge in the wrong, to seek refuge in

Thomas Merton's sandals. (Photograph by Jim Forest, courtesy of Boston College, Burns Library)

"The contemplative life has nothing to tell you except to reassure you and say that if you dare to penetrate your own silence and dare to advance without fear into the solitude of your own heart . . . you will truly recover the light and capacity to understand what is beyond words and beyond explanations because it is too close to be explained. . . ."
(The Monastic Journey)

Thomas Merton with Father Daniel
Berrigan, S.J., a founder of the
Catholic Peace Fellowship.
(Photograph by Jim Forest, courtesy of
Boston College, Burns Library)

violence. . . . In our acceptance of vulnerability . . . we
play [on the guilt of the opponent]. There is no finer
torment. This is one of the enormous problems of our
time . . . all this guilt and nothing to do about it except
finally to explode and blow it all out in hatreds, race
hatreds, political hatreds, war hatreds. We, the righteous, are dangerous people in such a situation. . . . We
have got to be aware of the awful sharpness of truth
when it is used as a weapon, and since it can be the
deadliest weapon, we must take care that we don't kill
more than falsehood with it. In fact, we must be careful how we "use" truth, for we are ideally the instruments of truth and not the other way around.[301]

Merton saw that the peace movement often tended to identify too much with particular political groups and ideologies. Ideally its actions should communicate liberating possibilities to others no matter how locked in they were to violent structures. He wrote late in 1962:

It seems to me that the basic problem is not political, it is apolitical and human. One of the most important things is to keep cutting deliberately through political lines and barriers and emphasizing the fact that these are largely fabrications and that there is another dimension, a genuine reality, totally opposed to the fictions of politics: the human dimension which politics pretends to arrogate entirely [to itself]. . . . This is the necessary first step along the long way . . . of purifying, humanizing and somehow illuminating politics.[302]

Peacemaking, he said, was rooted in spiritual life.

We have to pray for a total and profound change in the mentality of the whole world. What we have known in the past as Christian penance is not a deep enough concept if it does not comprehend the special problems and dangers of the present age. Hair shirts will not do the trick, though there is no harm in mortifying the flesh. But vastly more important is the complete change of heart and the totally new outlook on the world of man. . . . The great problem is this inner change. . . . [Any peace action has] to be regarded . . . as an application of spiritual force and not the use of merely political pressure. We all have the great duty to realize the deep need for purity of soul, that is to say the deep need to possess in us the Holy Spirit, to be possessed by Him. This takes precedence over everything else.[303]

He was convinced that engagement was made stronger by detachment. Not to be confused with a lack

"Daniel Berrigan's visit was most stimulating. He is a man full of fire, the right kind, and a real Jesuit, of which there are not too many, perhaps. . . . He is alive and full of spirit and truth. I think he will do much for the church in America and so will his brother Phil, the only priest so far to have gone on a Freedom Ride. They will have a hard time, though, and will have to pay for every step forward with their blood."

(The Road to Joy)

of interest in achieving results, detachment meant knowing that no good action is wasted even if the immediate consequences are altogether different from what one hoped to achieve.

In his longest letter to me on this theme, he advised:

Do not depend on the hope of results. When you are doing the sort of work you have taken on, essentially an apostolic work, you may have to face the fact that your work will be apparently worthless and even achieve no result at all, if not perhaps results opposite to what you expect. As you get used to this idea, you start more and more to concentrate not on the results but on the value, the rightness, the truth of the work itself. And there too a great deal has to be gone through, as gradually you struggle less and less for an idea and more and more for specific people. The range tends to narrow down, but it gets much more real. In the end, it is the reality of personal relationships that saves everything.

You are fed up with words, and I don't blame you. I am nauseated by them sometimes. I am also, to tell the truth, nauseated by ideals and with causes. This sounds like heresy, but I think you will understand what I mean. It is so easy to get engrossed with ideas and slogans and myths that in the end one is left holding the bag, empty, with no trace of meaning left in it. And then the temptation is to yell louder than ever in order to make the meaning be there again by magic. Going through this kind of reaction helps you to guard against this. Your system is complaining of too much verbalizing, and it is right.

The big results are not in your hands or mine, but they suddenly happen, and we can share in them; but there is no point in building our lives on this personal satisfaction, which may be denied us and which after all is not that important.

The next step in the process is for you to see that

your own thinking about what you are doing is crucially important. You are probably striving to build yourself an identity in your work, out of your work and your witness. You are using it, so to speak, to protect yourself against nothingness, annihilation. That is not the right use of your work. All the good that you will do will come not from you but from the fact that you have allowed yourself, in the obedience of faith, to be used by God's love. Think of this more, and gradually you will be free from the need to prove yourself, and you can be more open to the power that will work through you without your knowing it.

Fireplace in Merton's hermitage. (Photograph by Jim Forest)

The great thing after all is to live, not to pour out your life in the service of a myth: and we turn the best things into myths. If you can get free from the domination of causes and just serve Christ's truth, you will be able to do more and will be less crushed by the inevitable disappointments. Because I see nothing whatever in sight but much disappointment, frustration and confusion. . . .

The real hope, then, is not in something we think we can do but in God who is making something good out of it in some way we cannot see. If we can do His will, we will be helping in this process. But we will not necessarily know all about it beforehand.[304]

Monk in the Rain

Just get warm in any way you can and love God and pray.

Thomas Merton
A Vow of Conversation

"What a thing it is to sit absolutely alone, in the forest, at night, cherished by this wonderful, unintelligible, perfectly innocent speech, the most comforting speech in the world, the talk that rain makes by itself all over the ridges, and the talk of the watercourses everywhere in the hollows! Nobody started it, nobody is going to stop it. It will talk as long as it wants, this rain. As long as it talks I am going to listen."

(Raids on the Unspeakable)

As Merton struggled to define his responsibility for a world that seemed hurrying toward annihilation, the battle to come closer to his true self continued unabated.

His health was often a burden. Late in 1963 pain in his left arm and the base of his neck required traction at Saint Joseph's Infirmary in Louisville. His stomach was often problematic. Treating various ailments, doctors prescribed an impressive array of pills. At the abbey, Merton was put on a special diet.

The world's health was even worse. America, burdened with racism and trapped in the Cold War, seemed crowded with people primed to kill. The bombing of a black church in Birmingham in which four children perished deepened Merton's sense of identification with those who were the victims of violence; he put a photo of one of the children, eleven-year-old Carol Denise McNair, in his journal. During hunting season the woods echoed with the cracks of rifle fire. There were flights of B-52 bombers flying high overhead each day with their cargo of nuclear bombs and there was the steady rumble of artillery fire from Fort Knox many miles away. The fighting in Vietnam was beginning to boil into full-scale war. In November 1963, President John F. Kennedy was shot dead in Dallas, while the following summer Harlem exploded in riots and three civil rights volunteers were murdered in Mississippi.

Firehoses turned on civil rights demonstrators in Birmingham, Alabama. (Photograph courtesy of Maryknoll archives)

"The race question cannot be settled without a profound change of heart, a real shakeup and deep reaching metanoia on the part of White America. It is not just a question of a little more good will and generosity; it is a question of waking up to crying injustices and deep-seated problems which are ingrained in the present set-up and which instead of getting better are going to get worse."

(Seeds of Destruction)

The turmoil of the sixties in both the church and the world was pulling some experienced monks away from Gethsemani, among them Merton's friend and confessor, Father John of the Cross. Like a child in the dark, Merton felt vulnerable, especially during periods on his own at the isolated hermitage where Dom James was allowing him more and more time. As the fall began he was sleeping there every night.

The publishing restrictions that the former Abbot General had imposed on Merton in 1962 were lifted by his successor, Dom Ignace Gillet, in 1964. A major part of the material Merton had circulated only in mimeographed form at last became the substance of a book issued that fall as *Seeds of Destruction*.

Returning to his long-running interest in Gandhi, in 1965 Merton edited a slim book on the nonviolent liberator of India, *Gandhi on Non-Violence*. In an introductory essay Merton marveled at Gandhi's ability to see the oneness that erases the border between the sacred and the secular and to seamlessly join in his own life contemplative and active ele-

Cover of *Gandhi on Non-Violence*, a volume edited by Merton and published by New Directions in 1965.

"In Gandhi's mind, non-violence was not simply a political tactic which was supremely useful and efficacious in liberating his people from foreign rule.

. . . On the contrary, the spirit of non-violence sprang from an inner realization of spiritual unity in himself. *The whole Gandhian concept of non-violent action and* satyagraha *is incomprehensible if it is thought to be a means of achieving unity rather than as* the fruit of inner unity already achieved."

(Gandhi on Non-Violence)

ments. Merton connected Gandhi with Pope John. Both men realized, Merton observed, that "there can be no peace on earth without the kind of inner change that brings man back to his 'right mind.'"[305] *Gandhi on Non-Violence* remains perhaps the best brief introduction not only to Gandhi but to a method of effective social struggle that refuses to use evil means to achieve social healing.

A book by Hannah Arendt led Merton to consider Gandhi's polar opposite, Adolf Eichmann, the chief bureaucrat of the Holocaust in which millions, Jews most of all, had died in concentration camps. The result was an essay with an ironic title: "A Devout Meditation in Memory of Adolf Eichmann." Eichmann, who had been declared sane by examining psychiatrists, seemed to Merton an archetype of all those who were perfecters of efficient new technologies of killing. Personally, they may have nothing against those who die from their actions; it was enough that those in authority required such methods. Merton wrote:

The sanity of Eichmann is disturbing. We equate sanity with a sense of justice, with humaneness, with prudence, with the capacity to love and understand other people. We rely on the sane people of the world to preserve it from barbarism, madness, destruction. And now it begins to dawn on us that it is precisely the sane ones who are the most dangerous. It is the sane ones, the well-adapted ones, who can without qualms and without nausea aim the missiles and press the buttons that will initiate the great festival of destruction that they, the sane ones, have prepared. . . . No one suspects the sane, and the sane ones will have perfectly good reasons, logical, well-adjusted reasons, for firing the shot. They will be obeying sane orders that have come sanely down the chain of command.[306]

Merton the writer was being joined by Merton the artist. A "love affair" with photography began in the fall

of 1964. Starting with a borrowed Kodak Instamatic camera, Merton used black-and-white film to photograph trees and tree stumps, paint buckets, the weathered side-board of old wooden buildings such as he found not only at the monastery but at Shakertown in Pleasant Hill, Kentucky.[307]

The Shaker aesthetic touched him profoundly: "The peculiar grace of a Shaker chair is due to the fact that it was made by someone capable of believing that an angel might come and sit on it."[308]

Applying black ink to white paper, Merton used Japanese brushes to produce images that he christened "calligraphs"—images, often abstract, that had in common with his photographs a remarkable and refreshing quietness. The images in both cases were "words out of silence." A first public exhibition of his calligraphs occurred in November, with another show soon after. Merton's purpose in allowing the exhibitions was to sell prints in order to found a scholarship for a black student.

Photograph by Thomas Merton.
(Courtesy of the Merton Legacy Trust)

"There are drops of dew that show like sapphires in the grass as soon as the great sun appears, and leaves stir behind the hushed flight on an escaping dove."
(The Sign of Jonas)

Photograph by John Lyons. (Courtesy of the Thomas Merton Center)

"Everything the Fathers of the Church say about the solitary life is exactly true. The temptations and the joys, above all, the tears and the ineffable peace and happiness."

(A Vow of Conversation)

With additional financial support provided by Dom James from monastery funds, the scholarship was created.

Merton's exploration of the nonverbal may have been connected with his exploration of the feminine dimension of creation. Certainly his sense of having been too critical of his mother and having never properly known women continued to haunt him, most of all in vivid dreams that he took pains to record in his journals.

In March 1964 he described a dream in which a distinguished woman Latinist from Harvard came to the monastery and "sang in Latin with meters, flexes and puncta." The novices giggled. Her presence, Merton realized when the abbot entered the room, constituted a violation of the cloister as an enclosed space barred to women. She had to be hustled out. Merton escorted her down the stairs noticing that, in her expulsion from the monastery, her clothes had become soiled and torn. "She was confused and sad"[309]—and so was Merton. The dream suggests Merton's troubled awareness that there is something lop-sided about a males-only enclave in which Eve is still seen as the great temptress from whom men seeking salvation had to flee for their lives.

Perhaps his Latin-speaking lady was a Western cousin of Proverb—or perhaps she represented the Latin liturgy, now being swept away. While sympathetic with the problem faced by those for whom Latin was incomprehensible, Merton missed the Latin, and was also unimpressed with the translation of the liturgy into contemporary English.

One night in late November, Merton dreamt again of his beloved Proverb. This time she was a Chinese princess who had come to spend the day with him. Merton felt "overwhelmingly the freshness, the youth, the wonder, the truth of her, her complete reality, more real than any other, yet unobtainable."[310] The dream was also a recognition of the wisdom of the Far East, which increasingly was opening itself to Merton.

Perhaps it was Proverb who made him so receptive to the Noah-like downpour that came the next night and which inspired one of Merton's finest essays, "Rain and the Rhinoceros." It was a celebration not only of rain but all that society ignores and neglects—at least until a price tag can be put on it. Merton recognized in rain a language of God. "Think of it: all that speech pouring down, selling nothing, judging nobody, drenching the thick mulch of dead leaves, soaking the trees, filling the gullies and crannies of the wood with water, washing out the places where men have stripped the hillside! . . . this wonderful, unintelligible, perfectly innocent speech, the most comforting speech in the world, the talk that rain makes."[311]

In the midst of rain and dreams Merton received a group of peacemakers for a retreat on "the spiritual roots of protest." Merton had arranged the event with the Catholic Peace Fellowship, of which he was an adviser and sponsor, and the Fellowship of Reconciliation.

The basic question Merton had asked those involved to consider was: "By what right do we protest?" It was an

"No matter what mistakes and delusions have marked my life, most of it I think has been happiness and, as far as I can tell, truth."

(A Vow of Conversation)

Photograph by John Lyons. (Courtesy of the Thomas Merton Center)

Franz Jägerstätter, an Austrian Catholic beheaded by the Nazis for his refusal to serve in Hitler's army.

unsettling challenge to people who could be regarded as professional protesters. One of those involved in the retreat, A. J. Muste, had been involved for at least half a century in a wide range of campaigns for unions and worker rights and against war and racism. Dan and Phil Berrigan, both Catholic priests, would only a few years later be on the cover of *Time* magazine, their names synonymous with acts of civil disobedience protesting the Vietnam War.

In his contribution to the four-day conversation, Merton focused on the "solitary witness" of Franz Jägerstätter, a modest but determined Austrian farmer who had been beheaded by the Nazis for his refusal to serve in the army of the Third Reich. A devout Catholic, Jägerstätter had received no support from his pastor or bishop; rather he had been admonished that it was his duty to take the military oath. Who was he, a mere peasant, to take his conscience so seriously? What Austrian bishops and theologians had failed to see with moral clarity was seen by a barely educated man who willingly gave up his life rather than collaborate in evil. For Merton, this married man and father was a saint uniquely matched to a century of total war.[312]

On December 15-16, Merton was permitted his first full day and night at the hermitage, coming down to the abbey only to say Mass and to eat a hot meal. "Everything the [Desert] Fathers say about solitary life is exactly true," he wrote in his journal. "The temptations and the joys, above all the tears and the ineffable peace and happiness. The happiness that is so pure because it is simply not one's own making, but sheer mercy and gift! And the sense of having arrived at last in the place destined for me by God, and for which I was brought here twenty-three years ago!"[313]

In the hermitage the night of January 30, 1965, the eve of his fiftieth birthday, Merton took fresh stock of himself. He was disturbed to recall the selfishness, glibness, and lack of love that had been typical of his relations with women throughout adolescence and adulthood. He had been "a damned fool" while at Clare College, Cambridge, "very selfish and unkind to Joan." He recalled late nights with Sylvia on the steps of the Clare boathouse. Was one of these women the mother of his child? He doesn't say, only remarking that profound shyness repeatedly had hidden "an urgent need for love."[314]

In the same journal entry, he reaffirmed his vocation to solitude. His happiest moments in life had been while alone. Alone, he needed no masks. The joy given to him in those hidden places had allowed him to glimpse his true identity.

Yet Merton was not alone in his dreams. Early in February 1965, he dreamed about a black woman who had been his foster mother in a forgotten childhood. He owed her his life and love. "It was really she and not my natural mother who had given me life. . . . Her face was ugly and severe, yet a great warmth came from her to me and we embraced with love. I felt deep gratitude, and what I recognized was not her face but the warmth of her embrace and of her heart. . . . Then we danced a little together, I and my black mother."[315]

In June, wide awake, he remembered the Proverb-like Anne Winser, a thirteen-year-old girl he had seen briefly in his mid-teens while a guest of her older brother on the Isle of Wight. "I remember the quiet rectory in the shady valley of Brooke. She was the quietest thing in it. A dark and secret child. . . . I hardly remember even thinking of her or noticing her, yet the other day I realized that I had never forgotten her and that she had made a deep impression."

Anne Winser represented "the part of the garden I never went to," the feeling that "if I had taken another turn in the road, I might have ended up married to Anne." She was the "true (quiet) woman with whom I never really came to terms in the world, and because of this, there remains an incompleteness in me that cannot be remedied."[316]

One of Merton's ink-brush "calligraphs." (Courtesy of the Thomas Merton Center)

Father Louis, Hermit

Those who travel the most see the least.

THOMAS MERTON
Honorable Reader

H anging on the inside of the closet door in the bedroom of his hermitage was a sheet of parchment in which Pope Paul VI offered his blessing to "Father Louis, Hermit."

"The hermit project has been voted and approved officially by the Council of the community and is accepted and understood by most everyone," Merton wrote me on August 20, 1965. "It begins officially tomorrow. I can use any prayers."[317] His only responsibilities within the community would be to say daily Mass in the library chapel, eat a hot meal at the infirmary, and to give a lecture on Sundays that interested members of the community could attend.

"Life is this simple," he said in his final talk as master of novices. "We are living in a world that is absolutely transparent and God is shining through it all the time. This is not just a fable or a nice story. It is true. If we abandon ourselves to God and forget ourselves, we see it sometimes, and we see it maybe frequently. God manifests Himself everywhere, in everything—in people and in things and in nature and in events. It becomes very obvious that He is everywhere and in everything and we cannot be without Him. You cannot be without God. It's impossible. It's simply impossible. The only thing is that we don't see it. What is it that makes the world opaque? It is care."[318]

It wasn't "care" in the sense of concern for others that

Merton in the fall of 1965. (Photograph by Jim Forest, courtesy of Boston College, Burns Library)

"I exist under trees, I walk in the woods out of necessity. I am both a prisoner and an escaped prisoner. I cannot tell you why, born in France, my journey ended here in Kentucky. It makes no difference. Do I have a 'day'? Do I spend my 'day' in a 'place'? I know there are trees here. I know there are birds here. I know the birds in fact very well, for there are precise pairs of birds (two each of fifteen or twenty species) living in the immediate area of my cabin. I share this particular place with them: we form an ecological balance."
("Day of a Stranger")

he was referring to, but "care" in the sense of anxiety or fear.

Leaving the novitiate and feeling—at least for the moment—blessedly free from care, Merton picked up some old work clothes and walked up to his cinderblock hermitage, an austere building which at the time lacked any plumbing. Water had to be carried. Merton shared the nearby wooden outhouse with a black snake.

"I am living as a stylite on top of a hermit hat," Merton wrote Bob Lax in October. "I am utterly alone from human company. . . . I make no more cookies in the cookie factory."[319]

"In the refectory is read a message of the Pope, denouncing war, denouncing the bombing of civilians, reprisals on civilians, killing of hostages, torturing of prisoners (all in Vietnam). Do the people of this country realize who the Pope is talking about? They have by now become so solidly convinced that the Pope never denounces anybody but Communists that they have long since ceased to listen. The monks seem to know. The voice of the reader trembles."

("*Day of a Stranger*")

Yet far from feeling settled down, Merton was never more willing to think about moving somewhere else than during those early months as a hermit at Gethsemani. As much as he had longed for radical solitude, its achievement was not without disorientation and suffering. He often felt isolated and lonely. An invitation from Ernesto Cardenal asking for his participation in a monastic experiment at Solentiname in Nicaragua filled Merton with a longing to say yes. He wrote to Cardinal Paul Philippe, secretary of the Congregation of Religious in Rome, and to Pope Paul VI asking if he might be "loaned" to Solentiname while remaining a monk of Gethsemani. The response, while sympathetic, advised Merton to stay where he was. It was, of course, the answer he expected. He had been able to say yes to Cardenal and could blame his not actually going on Rome.

Merton's health took a turn for the worse. The most aggravating problem was dysentery, caused, it was discovered, by pollution in a stream near the hermitage which had been Merton's initial source of water. He also suffered from dermatitis and for a time had to wear dermal gloves.

While Merton was struggling with his new life as a hermit, on the other side of the world the awful slaughter in Vietnam steadily gained momentum. One of those most sensitive to the war was Roger LaPorte, a former Cistercian novice who had become one of the young volunteers at the Catholic Worker in New York. Roger identified so deeply with those who were being burned alive by American bombs that on the night of November 9, 1965, he sat down in front of the United States Mission to the United Nations, poured gasoline on himself, struck a match, and became a voluntary victim of the war. He died of his burns two days later. It was an action none of his friends guessed Roger was planning and left the Catholic Worker community in a state of profound shock.

When the news reached Gethsemani November 11, Merton was stunned. He immediately telegrammed the

Catholic Peace Fellowship, the peace group with which Merton was most closely engaged:

JUST HEARD ABOUT SUICIDE OF ROGER LAPORTE. WHILE I DO NOT HOLD CATHOLIC PEACE FELLOWSHIP RESPONSIBLE FOR THIS TRAGEDY, CURRENT DEVELOPMENTS IN PEACE MOVEMENT MAKE IT IMPOSSIBLE FOR ME TO CONTINUE AS SPONSOR OF FELLOWHIP. PLEASE REMOVE MY NAME FROM LIST OF SPONSORS. THOMAS MERTON.

"The spirit of this country at the present moment is to me terribly disturbing," he told me in a letter sent the same day. "It is not quite like Nazi Germany, certainly not like Soviet Russia, it is like nothing on earth I ever heard of before. This whole atmosphere is crazy, not just the peace movement, everybody. There is in it such an air of absurdity and moral void, even where conscience and morality are invoked (as they are by everyone). The joint is going into a slow frenzy. The country is nuts."[320]

A week later Merton reversed his decision, apologizing for his resignation. "I am, so to speak, making my novitiate as a 'hermit' of sorts and I have my hands full with this. It is a full time job just coping with one's own damn mind in solitude."[321]

Early in December, in another letter, Merton wrote:

Roger's immolation started off a deep process of examination and it will lead far. Wrong as I think his act was objectively, I believe it did not prejudice the purity of his own heart and I never condemned him. What I condemned and . . . still question is a pervasive . . . spirit of irrationality, of power seeking, of temptation to the wrong kind of refusal and impatience and to pseudo charismatic witness which can be terribly, fatally destructive of all good. . . . [There is] a spirit of madness and fanaticism [in the air] . . . and it summons me to a deep distrust of all my own acts and involvements in this public realm. . . . The real road

Pope Paul VI. (Photograph courtesy of Maryknoll archives)

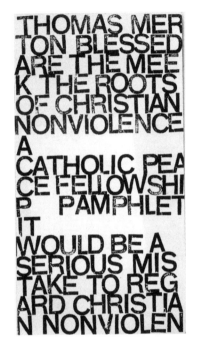

Cover of a pamphlet by Merton, "Blessed Are the Meek," issued by the Catholic Peace Fellowship.

"Nonviolence must simply avoid the ambiguity of an unclear and confusing protest that hardens the warmakers in their self-righteous blindness. This means that in this case above all nonviolence must avoid a facile and fanatical self-righteousness, and refrain from being satisfied with dramatic, self-justifying gestures. . . . Christian nonviolence . . . is convinced that the manner in which the conflict for truth is waged will itself manifest or obscure the truth."

("Blessed Are the Meek")

[for me] lies . . . with a new development in thought and work that will be, if it is what it should be, much more true and more valid for peace than any series of ephemeral gestures I might attempt to make. But anyway, now is a time for me of searching, digging and if I mention angst it is not to dramatize myself in any way but to assure you that I conceive my real and valid union with you all to take this form of silently getting ground up inside by the weights among which you are moving outside. It is to be understood that if I get any word, I hope reasonable word, to utter, I will not hesitate to utter it as I have always done before.[322]

Through the Catholic Peace Fellowship, Merton released a press statement in December in which he made public both the fact that he had become a hermit and that he was remaining a sponsor of the Catholic Peace Fellowship. He took the occasion to express his conviction "that what we need most of all today [in working for peace in Vietnam] is patient, constructive and pastoral work rather than acts of defiance which antagonize the average person without enlightening him."

The crisis precipitated by Roger LaPorte's self-immolation led Merton to write a major essay on nonviolence, "Blessed Are the Meek," published as a booklet by the Catholic Peace Fellowship in 1966, and later included in both *Faith and Violence* and *The Nonviolent Alternative*. Merton saw active nonviolence as a way of living the Sermon on the Mount. The meek whom Jesus identified as blessed are not the naturally quiet and obedient people who would never dare to protest. Rather they are the ones who are meek before the word of God and who live without arrogance in God's truth no matter what the cost. Nonviolence is a discipline, Merton stressed, of refusing to hate or to be held captive by enmity. It is a commitment to see the human face of an adversary, and to make every effort to enter into dialogue. "The chief difference between nonviolence and violence," he commented, "is that the lat-

ter depends entirely on its own calculations. The former depends entirely on God and on his Word."[323]

In the midst of that stressful period a gift arrived which Merton regarded as a providential sign: an eighteenth-century hand-painted icon of the Virgin and Child. The donor, Marco Pallis, was a friend in England with whom Merton had been corresponding since 1963. For Merton, the present was like a kiss from God. He wrote Pallis in response:

How shall I begin? I have never received such a precious and magnificent gift from anyone in my life. I have no words to express how deeply moved I was to come face to face with this sacred and beautiful presence granted to me. . . . At first I could hardly believe it. . . . It is a perfect act of timeless worship. I never tire of gazing at it. There is a spiritual presence and reality about it, a true spiritual "Thaboric" light, which seems unaccountably to proceed from the Heart of the Virgin and Child as if they had One heart, and which goes out to the whole universe. It is unutterably splendid. And

Front porch of Thomas Merton's hermitage. (Photograph by Merton, courtesy of the Thomas Merton Center)

"I confess that I am sitting under a pine tree doing absolutely nothing. I have done nothing for an hour and firmly intend to continue to do nothing for an indefinite period."

("A Signed Confession of Crimes Against the State")

Icon of the Virgin and Child given to
Merton by Marco Pallis, *detail*.
(Photograph by Jim Forest)

silent. It imposes a silence on the whole hermitage. . . . [This] icon of the Holy Mother
came as a messenger at a precise moment
when a message was needed, and her presence before me has been an incalculable aid in
resolving a difficult problem.[324]

As 1966 began, Merton felt able to regard
Dom James, who had played so important a
role in clearing the way for Trappists to
become hermits, in a more balanced light.
"For all his limitations and idiosyncrasies,
[Dom James] has done immense good to this
community by stubbornly holding everything together," Merton wrote in his journal.
"He . . . is an extraordinary man, many
sided, baffling, often irritating, a man of
enormous will, but who honestly and in his
own way really seeks to be an instrument of
God. And in the end that is what he has
turned out to be. I am grateful to him."[325]

Though Merton sometimes felt muddled and distracted,
his hermitage life had achieved a certain rhythm and
wholeness. He described an ordinary day in a letter to
Abdul Aziz, a Muslim Sufi scholar with whom he had been
corresponding since 1961. He got up about 2:30 in the
morning to recite the normal psalm-centered offices of
monastic prayer. Next came an hour or so of meditation followed by Bible reading. Then he made himself a light
breakfast—tea or coffee, perhaps a piece of fruit or some
honey. He read while eating, studying until about sunrise.
With sunrise there was further prayer and then some manual work—sweeping, cleaning, cutting wood—until about
9 o'clock when he paused for another office of psalms. After
that he wrote letters before going to the monastery to say
Mass. Mass was followed by a cooked meal alone at the
monastery. Returning to the hermitage, he returned to
reading, then said another office at 1 o'clock before another

hour or more of meditation. Only then did he allow himself a period for writing, usually not more than an hour and a half. At about 4 o'clock he said another office of psalms and then made a light supper, typically tea or soup and a sandwich. After supper he had another hour of meditation before going to bed at around 7:30.

In the same letter Merton described his method of meditation:

Strictly speaking I have a very simple way of prayer. It is centered entirely on attention to the presence of God and to His will and His love. That is to say that it is centered on faith by which alone we can know the presence of God. One might say this gives my meditation the character described by the Prophet as "being before God as if you saw Him." Yet it does not mean imagining anything or conceiving a precise image of God, for to my mind this would be a kind of idolatry. On the contrary, it is a matter of adoring Him as invisible and infinitely beyond our comprehension, and realizing Him as all. . . . There is in my heart this great thirst to recognize totally the nothingness of all that is not God. My prayer is then a kind of praise rising up out of the center of Nothing and Silence. If I am still present "myself" this I recognize as an obstacle. . . . If He wills He can then make the Nothingness into a total clarity. If He does not will, then the Nothingness actually seems to itself to be an object and remains an obstacle. Such is my ordinary way of prayer or meditation. It is not "thinking about" anything, but a direct seeking of the Face of the Invisible. Which cannot be found unless we become lost in Him who is Invisible.[326]

Writing, as he was, to a Muslim friend, as usual Merton sought as much as possible to find common ground. In a letter written a few years earlier to a Christian correspondent in England who had sought advice about prayer, Merton had emphasized the value of the Jesus Prayer:

"My own peculiar task in the church and in my world has been that of the solitary explorer who, instead of jumping on all the latest bandwagons at once, is bound to search the existential depths of truth in its silences, its ambiguities, and in those certainties which lie deeper than the bottom of anxiety. . . . It is a kind of submarine life in which faith sometimes mysteriously takes on the aspect of doubt when, in fact, one has to doubt and reject conventional and superstitious surrogates that have taken the place of faith."

(Faith and Violence)

Cover of *Raids on the Unspeakable*,
published in 1964 by New Directions.

*"Your idea of me is fabricated with
materials you have borrowed from other
people and from yourself. What you
think of me depends on what you think
of yourself. Perhaps you create your idea
of me out of material that you would
like to eliminate from your own idea of
yourself. Perhaps your idea of me is a
reflection of what other people think of
you. Or perhaps what you think of me is
simply what you think I think of you."*
(No Man Is an Island)

I heartily recommend . . . the Russian and Greek business where you get off somewhere quiet, . . . breathe
quietly and rhythmically with the diaphragm, holding
your breath for a bit each time and letting it out easily:
and while holding it, saying "in your heart" (aware of
the place of your heart, as if the words were spoken in
the very center of your being with all the sincerity you
can muster): "Lord Jesus Christ, Son of God, have
mercy on me a sinner." Just keep saying this for a
while, of course with faith, and the awareness of the
indwelling [of the Holy Spirit], etc. It is a simple form
of prayer, and fundamental, and the breathing part
makes it easier to keep your mind on what you are
doing. That's about as far as I go with methods. After
that, pray as the Spirit moves you, but of course I
would say follow the Mass in a missal unless there is a
good reason for doing something else, like floating
suspended ten feet above the congregation.[327]

After many years of aspiring to a life of solitude, now
he was struggling with the actual reality of what he
sought. It was at times a hard apprenticeship, and on
other days effortless. "There is no question," he noted in
his journal early in 1966, "that the solitary life is fraught
with problems and 'dangers,' but on the other hand I see
that it is necessary for me to meet these precisely as they
come to me in solitude. . . . I see that it is to face what I
cannot face that I am in solitude, and everything in my
life is affected by the change—my ordinary attitudes, my
attitude toward the world, my attitude toward myself,
my work toward my spiritual goal—my life in Christ.
. . . To go out to walk slowly in the wood—this is a more
important and significant means to understanding, at the
moment, than a lot of analysis and a lot of reporting on
the things 'of the spirit.'"[328]

A Proverb Named Margie

What is sweet about this bitter
Division? It is death
It is the devil's kingdom
We are two half people wandering
In two lost worlds.

THOMAS MERTON
"Evening: Long Distance Call," in *Eighteen Poems*

Merton was suffering persistent back pain as 1966 began. On March 23 he entered Saint Joseph's Hospital in Louisville for spinal surgery. Recovering from the operation a week later, he met a student nurse with gray eyes and long black hair who bore a striking resemblance to the Proverb of his dreams. Her name was Margie.[329] They talked about *The Sign of Jonas*, the Peanuts comic strip, and *Mad* magazine. Merton started looking forward to her visits and their animated conversations. A few days later, when Margie left Louisville for a weekend in Chicago, Merton felt overwhelmed by loneliness.

He lay awake half the night in his hospital bed tormented "by the gradual realization that we were in love and I did not know how I could live without her."[330] Before returning to the monastery he left a letter for her confiding his need for friendship and telling her how to write to him, marking the envelope "conscience matter" so that it wouldn't be read by anyone else at the abbey.

Thus began one of the most joyful, bewildering, and anguished periods of Merton's life. He fell in love while in a particularly vulnerable state and, with his usual enthusiasm, was swept far out to sea by the experience. In earlier years, Merton had been able to say, "When I am alone, I am no longer lonely."[331] Now he felt a deep wound in contemplating a future lived only in the company of men. In a journal entry written on Easter

"When a wound is beginning to heal, they strip off the bandages, and the adhesive tape seems to take most of the skin with it. . . . When a man becomes a Cistercian, he is stripped not only of his clothes, or part of his skin, but of his whole body and most of his spirit as well. And it is not all finished the first day: far from it! The whole Cistercian life is an evisceration, a gutting and scouring of the human soul."

(Unpublished manuscript for
The Seven Storey Mountain,
from A Thomas Merton Reader)

Sunday, just after his return to the monastery from the hospital, he confessed "a deep emotional need for feminine companionship and love, and seeing that I must irrevocably live without it ended by tearing me up more than the operation itself."[332] Still recovering and living temporarily in the abbey infirmary, he felt dazed.

A week later there was a four-page letter from Margie. Merton responded with a letter in which he said he had fallen in love with her. "I will do the only thing possible," he wrote in his journal, "and risk loving with Christ's love when there is so obvious a need for it."[333]

Thomas Merton seated at the edge of Monk's Pond on the monastery grounds. (Photograph courtesy of the Thomas Merton Center)

Back in the hermitage, the male-female pairings of birds attracted his attention. "Today I saw this male . . . on a fencepost singing joyfully—but at first no female. Then I saw her flying in and out of a big rose bush in the hedge, where the new nest is, and was happy."[334]

"I have got to dare to love," he wrote two days later, "and to bear the anxiety of self-questioning that love arouses in me."

Ignoring monastery rules, he managed to reach Margie by telephone, making an appointment to see her on April 26, when he would be in Louisville for a post-operative examination. They had lunch in a local restaurant where Merton showed her a poem he had written for her, "With the World in My Blood Stream." (Seventeen more poems for Margie were to follow.) Margie told Merton he didn't know what he was getting into, while Merton assured her that they could love each other without a sexual relationship. They could aim for spiritual love. The rest could be controlled, Merton assured her. "I have vows and I must be faithful to them," he noted in his journal.[335] Yet the relationship was now far from cerebral: "I have kissed her and in the chastity and tenderness of it . . . felt this deep, total, vibrant resonance and response of a whole warm little being, totally surrendered."[336]

On May 5 James Laughlin and Chilean poet Nicanor Parra came to visit Merton. They had a picnic not far from the abbey. Using Laughlin's loose change, Merton called Margie from a pay phone along the road, arranging for Margie to join them for a meal later in the day. The four of them ate in the Luau Room at the Louisville airport. Merton, unshaven and wearing T-shirt and overalls, must have been the oddest sight in the restaurant in many a day—looking like a convict, he noted in his journal, and probably feeling like one too. With Merton concentrating his attention mainly on her, it must have been awkward for Margie. Finally Merton and Margie went

"All monks, as is well known, are unmarried and hermits more unmarried than the rest of them. Not that I have anything against women. I see no reason why a man can't love God and a woman at the same time. If God was going to regard women with a jealous eye, why did he go and make them in the first place?"

("Day of a Stranger")

"Love is our true destiny. We do not find the meaning of life by ourselves alone – we find it with another. We do not discover the secret of our lives merely by study and calculation in our own isolated meditations. The meaning of our life is a secret that has to be revealed to us in love, by the one we love."

(Love and Living)

off for a walk, then sat for a while on a knoll of grass at the edge of the airport, in view of others but to some extent alone. "Suppose the clear light of that evening were love itself," Merton wrote of their time together that day, "and suppose we just became that light, that love: as if the clear beauty of the evening incarnated itself and its beauty and its meaning in us . . . and the meaning of everything that ever happened was suddenly centered in us because we were now love. It was our turn to express and show forth in worship the essence of all truth and life and meaning by our love."

It seemed to Merton that he had discovered the one person with whom he could be fully himself without a facade. For the first time in his remembered life, Merton felt he was wholly known not only by God but by another person. "This is God's own love He makes in us," he wrote in a poem that night.[337] In his journal he wondered about the possibility of "chaste marriage."

Together again on May 7 for a picnic with several friends on the edge of Dom Frederic's Lake on the monastery grounds, Merton and Margie managed to have a walk together. Merton tried to explain that he was a person who needed to live alone, yet who now found himself feeling he couldn't live apart from her. As they sat on the embankment of a creek, they imagined Merton getting a job in Louisville, buying a car, and being together whenever they wanted. His definition of the meaning of the vow of chastity was shrinking steadily, yet he was aware that, while he was drifting further and further from what was expected of him as a monk living under vows, he was intensely alive, not least when praying.

On May 9, Merton wrote in his journal of his awareness "that the deepest capacities for human love in me have never been tapped, that I too can love with an awful completeness." If the way should ever open in the Catholic Church for married clergy, "I should take it."

In Louisville May 14 for medical reasons, he had lunch with Margie. Besides sharing their mutual enthusiasm for

Joan Baez's ballad, "Silver Dagger," they talked about what living together might mean. ("Silver Dagger" became a binding song for them. Merton had a record player in the hermitage. For a time, they each played the song at 1:30 AM, when Margie's shift at the hospital was finished. Merton's time of rising was brought forward an hour.)

Five days later they met for a walk and picnic in the woods near Vineyard Knob, on the grounds of Gethsemani but well off the community's beaten track, sharing a bottle of wine that Margie had brought for the occasion. "We ate herring and ham (not very much eating!) And drank our wine and read poems and talked of ourselves and mostly made love and love and love for five hours. And though we had over and over reassured ourselves and agreed that our love would have to continue always chaste and this sacrifice was essential, yet in the end we were getting rather sexy—yet really instead of being all wrong it seemed eminently right. We now love with our whole bodies anyway."[338]

In a poem written after the picnic, "Certain Proverbs Arise Out of Dreams," Merton asked, "Why has God created you to be in the center of my being?"[339]

Joy and guilt followed each other in quick succession just as fantasies of marriage alternated with decisions to bring their relationship to an end so that he could get on with his vocation as it was supposed to be lived.

Frightened by where the momentum of love was taking them, Merton called off plans for another meeting a few days later. He was face to face with the terrible choice that had to be made: continuing monastic life, or marriage.

Merton on a visit to the Shaker village at Pleasant Hill. (Photograph by James Laughlin, courtesy of the Thomas Merton Center)

A portrait of Merton by John Lyons.
(Photograph courtesy of the Thomas
Merton Center)

Their next meeting, in connection with another medical appointment, was in the safe confines of
Cunningham's Restaurant in Louisville. Both sensed the
climate of their relationship had changed. "I can never be
anything else but a solitary," Merton wrote in his journal
that night. "My loneliness is my ordinary climate. That I
was allowed to have so many moments of complete
accord and harmony and love with another person, with
her, was simply extraordinary. I like people, but usually I
am tired of being with others after about an hour. That I
could be with her for hours and hours and not be tired
for an instant with her—it was a miracle, but it did not
mean that I was not essentially a solitary."

A week later they met again in Louisville, this time at
the office of Merton's friend, the psychiatrist Jim Wygal,
despite his disapproval of what Merton was doing. For
Merton's part, he was freshly aware of how deeply he

loved Margie and how empty the future seemed when he imagined it without her.

Aware that his vow of chastity was going up in smoke, he went to his confessor, for the first time revealing to a brother monk the great event going on in his life. Despite this, as became clear when Merton managed to call Margie later that day, the idea of marriage kept charging back across all his arguments and resolutions.

Part of another call to Margie the next day, June 12, happened to be overheard by the monk running the switchboard. He felt it his duty to inform Dom James, as Merton learned from the cellarer the next day. As no one knew better than Merton, something like this was bound to happen in a tiny monastic village. There was as much relief as anxiety in his response to the news.

Not waiting for the abbot to summon him, Merton went to see Dom James and told him in general terms what was going on, refusing however to reveal Margie's name. Merton was astonished and relieved with Dom James's reaction. He didn't hit the ceiling but responded with warmth and concern, only urging Merton to make a complete break. It wasn't an entirely candid conversation on Merton's side—he denied that he was thinking about marriage, though this had been exactly what Margie and Merton had lately been talking about on the phone. Dom James wondered if it would help Merton to return for a time to the community, perhaps living in the infirmary, but gave his blessing to Merton remaining in the heritage.

When Merton called Margie to tell her what had happened, she was appalled by how inhuman it all was. Merton wrote a bitter poem about being careful with love for "it fills the world with destruction / Millions of small pocket cyclones / Have fouled up communication with / Inexhaustible demanding rage."[340]

The next day Dom James told Merton that it wasn't just advice not to have any more contact with "that woman." It was an order.

"When people are truly in love, they experience far more than just a mutual need for each other's company and consolation. In their relation with each other they become different people: they are more than their everyday selves, more alive, more understanding, more enduring, and seemingly more endowed. They are made more into new beings. They are transformed by the power of their love."

(Love and Living)

On June 22 Merton resolved that the "whole thing has to be given up."

Dreaming two nights later, he saw his mother's face appearing in a tangle of dark briars behind luminous roses with silky petals, an image contrasting with his briars-only portrait of her in *The Seven Storey Mountain*. Margie had shifted his way of seeing women, even his own mother. Then he dreamed that, while in the hospital, he was "short and rude" with a student nurse—an "ideal" celibate defending his vow of chastity, but hardly the sort of human being Merton longed to be.

Despite the abbot's order, it seemed to Merton a requirement of charity to see Margie face-to-face one more time. In Louisville for X-rays on June 25, Merton met her and found her distraught. She had decided to seek a job in the hospital of her hometown where she planned to volunteer her services in "special cases"—work involving sacrifice. Merton gave her *A Midsummer Diary*, written during the past ten days. It had the caustic subtitle, "Or the account of how I once again became untouchable."

While he wondered if he would ever see her again when they parted that day, they were together again July 16 when Merton was in Louisville for treatment of a sprained ankle. She picked him up at the doctor's office and they went off with a bag of cherries for a picnic in Cherokee Park. It was one of their happiest visits despite the awful awareness that a future together was hopeless. "We rock and swim / In love's wordless pain," Merton wrote in a poem about the day. "Halfway between / Heaven and hell / Zion and the green river / We rock together / In that lovely desperate grip."[341]

Dom James talked with Merton again July 28, not about Margie but about other indications of disarray in Merton's life: an unauthorized visit to the nearby convent of the Sisters of Loretto, and a swim Merton had taken with a visitor in one of the monastery ponds. Wondering if the strain of the hermitage wasn't too much, Dom James again suggested returning to life in community.

*Don't sing love songs,
you'll wake my mother.
She's sleeping here
right by my side.
And in her right had
a silver dagger,
she says that I can't
be your bride.*

*Go court another tender maiden
and hope that she will be your wife.
For I've been warned and I've decided
to sleep alone all of my life.*

*("Silver Dagger,"
traditional Appalachian ballad)*

Perhaps Merton could teach scripture as master of juniors? The main effect of the meeting was to make real to Merton the fact that his vocation as hermit was at risk.

Meeting again a week later, Dom James teased Merton about his relationship with Margie, which Dom James imagined was entirely over. The abbot said he should write a book called *How to Get Hermits into Heaven*. Merton was furious. On leaving Dom James's office, Merton said, "When the baby is born you can be the godfather!" Dom James took it as a joke, but Merton saw the worry on his face.

Rather than risk seeing Margie again, Merton sent her a letter "saying in effect Goodbye." She was due to graduate and would soon be leaving Louisville. Imagining her opening the letter and reading it, he was stricken, tried in vain to reach her by phone, then wrote her a poem. He felt howls of pain "rending their way up out of the very ground of my being. . . . I thought I was being torn in half." A week later, when he managed to reach her by phone, he learned that letters she had sent him were not getting through even though marked "conscience matter." Her voice, he wrote in his journal, was choked with emotion.

On September 8, following a private retreat, Merton made a permanent commitment to a hermit's vocation: "I, Brother M. Louis Merton, solemnly professed monk of the Abbey of Our Lady of Gethsemani, having completed a year of trial in the solitary life, hereby make my commitment to spend the rest of my life in solitude in so far as my health may permit." Dom James signed as a witness.

Even then Merton and Margie managed two brief, final visits in late October. Margie was in Louisville for exams and Merton was staying at Saint Anthony's Hospital for treatment of intestinal troubles. After that there was only very occasional contact by telephone; Merton's last call to Margie was a few months before his death.

In the end, Merton renewed his commitment to

We are beyond the ways of the far ships
Here in this coral port,
Farther than the ways of fliers,
Because our destinies have suddenly transported us
Beyond the brim of the enamel world.
(Figures for an Apocalypse)

remain a monk and persevered as a hermit. It was among the hardest choices of his life. His love for Margie hadn't ended. A man with no sense of the impossible, Merton had crashed at full-speed, in a love as desperate as Romeo's. Even so a kind of healing had happened to him. "There is something deep, deep down inside us, darling, that tells us to let go completely," he had written in a letter to Margie that summer, though it is unclear whether the letter was ever sent. "Not just the letting go when the dress drops to the floor and bodies press together with nothing between, but the far more thrilling surrender when our very being surrenders itself to the nakedness of love and to a union where there is no veil of illusion between us."

What had occurred that summer was known only to a few close friends, all of them quite worried by what was going on. Yet it wasn't Merton's intention that it remain a secret. Copies of the poems were given to James Laughlin for safekeeping and eventual publication. The journals became part of the archive of the Merton Literary Trust that Merton had set up with Monsignor Alfred Horrigan and Father John Loftus at Bellarmine College in Louisville. Though publication of the journals was to be delayed for twenty-five years after his death, he wanted nothing suppressed, including his love for Margie: "It needs to be known too, for it is part of me. My need for love, my loneliness, my inner division, the struggle in which solitude is at once a problem and a 'solution.' And perhaps not a perfect solution either."

It was in this period of his life that Merton wrote a short, deeply felt essay on purity in which he expressed his exasperation with those moralists who define purity in negative terms mainly having to do with sex, who insist that the achievement of purity was synonymous with freeing oneself from one's body, or—for the married—at least reducing sex to a purely biological event that might sometimes have to be endured, but should not be enjoyed.

"This whole attitude of abstraction, of hatred and denigration of the body," Merton wrote, "has finally led to a pathological and totally unrealistic obsession with bodily detail . . . [in consequence of which] love becomes no longer an expression of the communion between persons. . . . Instead of saying that an act is pure when you remove all that is material, sensuous, fleshly, emotional, passionate, etc., from it, we will on the contrary say that a sexual act is pure when it gives a rightful place to the body, the senses, the emotions . . . , the special needs of the person, all that is called for by the unique relationship between the two lovers, and that is demanded by the situation in which they find themselves. . . . It is precisely in this spirit of celebration, gratitude, and joy that true purity is found."[342]

We hear a similar voice in a brief essay, "Love and Need," also written in 1966:

(Photograph courtesy of the Thomas Merton Center)

When people are truly in love, they experience far more than just a mutual need of each other's company and consolation. In their relations with each other they become different people: they are more than their everyday selves, more alive, more understanding, more enduring. . . . They are made over into new beings. They are transformed by the power of their love.[343]

203

A Member of the Family

In an age where there is much talk about "being yourself" I reserve to myself the right to forget about being myself, since in any case there is very little chance of my being anybody else.

THOMAS MERTON
"Day of a Stranger," in *A Thomas Merton Reader*

"Another of your most important duties [as a designated trustee of Merton's literary estate] will be to see that the author, during his declining years, is occasionally revived by picnics. And that he has access to suitable sources of creative inspiration from time to time."

(Letter to Tommie O'Callaghan, October 17, 1967)

As 1967 began, Merton sent out a mimeographed letter to friends in which he commented that he was becoming more conscious of "the futility of a life wasted in argument when it should be given entirely to love." He hoped he would "be able to give up controversy some day."[344]

A new kind of love began making its way into his life. A spark of friendship with Frank and Tommie O'Callaghan blazed so warmly that Merton became, in effect, not only a frequent guest in their large, child-crowded home, but a member of the family. Often in Louisville for medical appointments, Merton's main place of refuge was the O'Callaghan house, eating there, playing with the children, sometimes staying the night. In warm weather he occasionally joined in family picnics. A similar bond was formed in Bardstown with Thompson and Virginia Willett, another couple with lots of children. If Merton was not to marry, at least he was able to experience a steady familial warmth.

An aspect of Merton's attraction to both families was the vital Catholicism he found in these households, neither rigidly conservative nor rabidly modern. In a journal entry made in 1966, he noted: "Lately with all the emphasis on being 'contemporary' I have perhaps felt a little guilty about my love of the Middle Ages."[345]

Merton felt increasingly out of gear with the new breed of "progressive" Catholics, one of whose tenets was that the ideal place for a monk in the modern world was a prison cell, or at least placing himself at risk of confinement through engagement in the battle against injustice and war. Such correspondents as Philip Berrigan and Rosemary Radford Ruether had come to the conclusion that the monastic life could no longer be regarded as a genuine Christian vocation but rather as escapism. As Ruether put it in one letter,

Above:
Merton on a "family picnic" with Sister Therese Lentfoehr and Tommie O'Callaghan. (Photograph courtesy of Tommie O'Callaghan)

"I love the monastic life dearly . . . but today it is no longer an eschatological sign and witness in the Church. For those who wish to be at the 'kingdom' frontier of history, it is the steaming ghetto of the big city."[346]

In his response, while acknowledging that he was a maverick in the Trappist order, Merton said he believed he was where God intended him to be. "I honestly believe that this is the right place for me . . . insofar as it is the right battleground. . . . I myself would be leading a less honest and more faked life if I were back in the cities. . . . In staying here I am not just being here for myself but for my friends, my Church, and all those I am one with. . . . Lots of people would like me to get out and join them in this or that, but I just don't see that I could do it without getting into some kind of absurd role and having to act a part and justify some nonsense or other that I don't really believe in."[347]

He noted in his journal that he found himself "shy" about tackling Christological problems in his correspondence with Ruether.[348] It was a bracing exchange of letters that lasted six months, yet seems to have left Merton feeling increasingly cut off from those who saw themselves as Christianity's avant-garde.

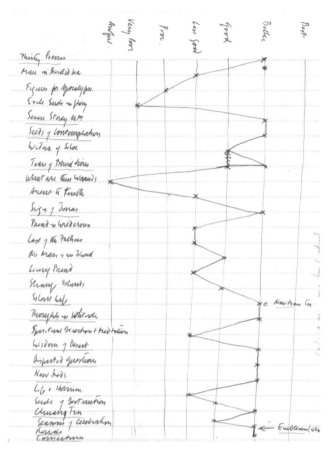

In a graph Merton rated his own books ranging from "awful" to "best." (Courtesy of the Thomas Merton Center)

"I am pursued by the vilifications of progressed Catholics," Merton wrote Bob Lax. "Mark my words, there is no uglier species on the face of the earth... mean, frivolous, ungainly, inarticulate, venomous, and bursting at the seams with progress into the secular cities and the Teilhardian subways. The Ottavianis [referring to the cardinal who headed the Vatican's Holy Office; his name was synonymous with conservatism] are bad, but these are infinitely worse. You wait and see."[349]

Merton found many changes in the liturgy at best funny, at worst tasteless and ugly. He could hardly believe his ears when the monks started to sing "The Church's One Foundation" at a service of profession for a new member of the community: "Renewal? For me it's a return to the deadly past. Victorian England." He lamented the ruthless discarding of the old simply because it was old and was depressed by the abrasiveness of many who regarded themselves as renewers and modernizers.

In an act of detached self-evaluation as a writer, in 1967 Merton made a graph in which he evaluated the books he had so far published, ranking them awful, bad, poor, fair, good, better, best. He judged only one—*What Are These Wounds?*—as awful, with *Exile Ends in Glory* a runner-up. *Spiritual Direction and Meditation* and *Seasons of Celebration* were listed as poor. *Ascent to Truth, Bread in the Wilderness, Last of the Fathers*, and *Life and Holiness* landed in the fair column. *No Man Is an Island, Strange Islands, The New Man, Disputed Questions, New Seeds of*

Contemplation, and *Mystics and Zen Masters* he regarded as good. In the better category were *Thirty Poems, The Seven Storey Mountain, Seeds of Contemplation, Waters of Siloe, Tears of the Blind Lions, The Sign of Jonas, The Silent Life, Thoughts in Solitude, Wisdom of the Desert, Seeds of Destruction, The Way of Chuang Tzu, Raids on the Unspeakable*, and *Conjectures of a Guilty Bystander*. (In a similar but not identical graph, Merton remembered to include *Emblems of a Season of Fury*, a collection of poems, including it to the "better" category.)[350] No title made it to the top rung. Merton felt he hadn't yet achieved what he was reaching for. The following year, after reading the manuscript of James Baker's dissertation about Merton, he recorded in his journal an even more rigorous critique of his writings to date. The Baker text, though highly sympathetic, "showed me clearly so many limitations in my work. So much has been provisional, inconclusive, half-baked. I have always said too much too soon. And then had to revise my opinions. My own work is to me extremely dissatisfying. It seems trivial."[351]

On a picnic. (Photograph courtesy of Tommie O'Callaghan)

In the same period that Merton was looking back on his earlier books, he discovered his long struggle with censors had come to an end. That summer Father Paul Bourne, the monk who had carried the main responsibility for vetting Merton's books, wrote to say censorship had been suspended. It took Merton some time to be convinced that the red light had truly turned green.

Bursitis forced another operation on Merton in late February. Because he was troubled with allergies, Merton's doctor banned beer, beef, and dairy products. To make hermitage life physically less demanding for Merton, Dom James arranged for plumbing to be installed. By the summer Merton had a sink, running water, water heater, hot plate, and refrigerator.

As the months passed there was a steady trickle of visitors, among them Islamic scholar Sidi Abdeslam, philosopher Jacques Maritain, singer and peace activist Joan Baez, various writers and theologians—Jonathan

Merton in his hermitage with a gathering of old friends, including John Howard Griffin (at left, who snapped the photo with a self-timer), and philosopher Jacques Maritain (at right). (Photograph by John Howard Griffin. Used with permission)

Williams, Guy Davenport, Will Campbell, James Holloway, Rosemary Haughton, and Walker Percy—and such friends as Bob Lax, Sy Freedgood, Naomi Burton Stone, Dan Berrigan, John Howard Griffin, Ralph Eugene Meatyard, and Ron Seitz.

One gets a glimpse of Merton shortly after his fifty-second birthday in an essay in which Guy Davenport describes the best display of manners on the part of restaurant staff he had ever witnessed. The venue was the Imperial Ramada Inn in Lexington, Kentucky. Gathered around the table were "the photographer Ralph Eugene Meatyard (disguised as a businessman), the Trappist Thomas Merton (in mufti, dressed as a tobacco farmer with a tonsure), and an editor of *Fortune* [none other than

Merton's old friend, Sy Freedgood] who had wrecked his Hertz car coming from the airport and was covered with spattered blood from head to toe. Hollywood is used to such things (Linda Darnell having a milk shake with Frankenstein's monster between takes), and Rome and New York, but not Lexington, Kentucky. Our meal was served with no comment whatever by the waitresses, despite Merton downing six martinis and the *Fortune* editor stanching his wounds with all the napkins."[352]

While company was always stimulating, Merton's travel itch remained intense. Dom James, however, was more reluctant than ever to permit anything more than brief local outings. When Merton told Dom James in January 1967 about an invitation to visit the Trappist abbey of Melleray in France, the abbot responded, "God has given you this hermitage not to quit it for greater expansion of exterior activities, but to remain in it for a greater deepening of your interior activities."[353]

Despite his aches, pains, and occasional disappointments, Merton was in good spirits. His sense of humor was evident not only in letters but even in photos. With a borrowed camera, he took a photo in April showing a heavy construction skyhook hanging over the Kentucky countryside. "The only known photograph of God," Merton noted on the back.

While only allowing himself a couple of hours a day for writing and editing, in those small spaces he achieved a great deal, including a series of literary studies focusing on Albert Camus, William Faulkner, William Styron, and Simone Weil.[354] There was also his essay on Ishi, the last surviving member of a tribe of Native Americans in California.[355] He produced new essays on monastic life and the contemplative vocation[356] as well as a preface for the Japanese edition of *The New Man*.[357] He edited *A Vow of Conversation*, drawn from his journals of 1964-65, but decided to hold off publication, partly because he was sure the book would provoke a rash of critical reviews—not so much of the book as of himself from progressive Catholics

Merton called this "the only known photograph of God." (Photograph courtesy of the Thomas Merton Center)

Zen and the Birds of Appetite
Thomas Merton

Cover of *Zen and the Birds of Appetite*, published by New Directions in 1968.

Ride your horse along the edge of the sword.
Hide yourself in the middle of the flames.
Blossoms of the fruit tree will bloom in the fire.
The sun rises in the evening.

(*Zen saying*)

who would consider a hermit's vocation irrelevant if not counter-revolutionary. Soon after that he finished *Zen and the Birds of Appetite*. A frequent contributor to small magazines, that year he launched one of his own, *Monks Pond*, the first of four issues appearing in December 1967.[358]

There were also his Sunday lectures at the monastery, mainly drawn from notes on his current reading. The Sufi movement within Islam, and the Cargo Cults of the South Pacific were among the major topics.[359]

During restricted daily periods for correspondence, letters issued from his typewriter like snowflakes in a blizzard. Suzanne Butorovich, only sixteen when she sent her first letter in June 1967, became one of his favorite correspondents. She asked Merton if he liked pop music and what he thought of the Beatles and LSD. (Merton liked the Beatle song "Taxman," recommended Bob Dylan's latest album, and said he didn't need LSD because "the birds turn me on." One letter to her revealed his method of cooking kasha.)[360] In letters to June Yungblut, a Quaker living in Atlanta, he prepared for a retreat at Gethsemani for civil rights activists that was to involve Martin Luther King Jr., but the event perished with Dr. King's assassination in 1968.

One of the great joys of 1967 was the ordination of Dan Walsh, the person who first told Merton about the Abbey of Gethsemani and made him consider a vocation with the Trappists. Walsh had been a longtime resident in the monastery guest house. It had been the idea of the Archbishop of Louisville that this dedicated theologian ought to become a priest. The event occurred at Saint Thomas Seminary May 16, followed by a big party at the O'Callaghan house. Merton was among the most festive. "There was a lot of celebrating," Merton wrote me the following day. "In fact I celebrated on too much champagne, which is a thing a Trappist rarely gets to do, but I did a very thorough job. At one point in the afternoon I remember looking up and focusing rather uncertainly upon four faces of nuns sitting in a row looking at me in

Merton, assisted by Brother Maurice Flood, gives communion to Jacques Maritain. Kneeling at the left is Merton's old professor, Daniel Walsh. (Photograph by John Howard Griffin, courtesy of the Thomas Merton Center)

a state of complete scandal and shock. Another pillar of the Church had fallen."[361]

Still more important was the permission Merton received from Dom James to celebrate Mass in the hermitage. Using a specially made cedarwood altar, Merton said his first Mass there on July 16, the Feast of Our Lady of Carmel, to whom the hermitage was dedicated. The hermitage now sheltered every aspect of Merton's life. Early in 1968 a six-by-eight foot chapel was added to the hermitage.

In September 1967, Dom James made the startling announcement that he was retiring. He had decided to follow Merton's example and become a hermit, the monastery's third. (The second was Father Flavian Burns.) Alarmed at rumors that some of the monks were thinking of electing Merton as Dom James's successor, Merton posted a statement on the community bulletin board—"My campaign Platform for non-Abbot and permanent keeper of my present doghouse"—in which he

"People ask me if now that we have a new Abbot, I will be able to 'get out' more. Will I be able to visit campuses and engage in conferences and dialogue, etc.? . . . For my part, I do not think that even if it were possible for me, I would be justified in going around appearing in public, or semi-public, and giving talks. I feel it would not be consistent with my real vocation. . . . I am committed to a life of solitude and meditation which I hope that I can share with others by a certain amount of writing. And that is about it."

(Circular Letter to Friends, Pre-Lent 1968)

assured everyone that "the responsibility of presiding over anything larger than a small chicken coop is beyond my mental, moral and physical capabilities." In any event he wasn't equipped, he declared, to cope with 125 confused and anxiety-ridden monks. Further, his ideas on monastic development had become foggy due to the encroachments of age and mental deterioration. If elected, however, he promised plenty of beer.[362]

If not an abbot, Merton proved to be something of an abbot-maker, helping convince his fellow hermit, Father Flavian Burns, to stand. Merton worried that Dom James's successor might be ill-disposed to hermits and therefore wanted a candidate who was sure to let the hermits continue. One of the factors that had made Dom Flavian overcome his hesitations and stand for election as abbot was to safeguard Merton's vocation as a writer. As he told Michael Mott, Merton "had the unique ability not only to search, but to record the search for others."

When the monks cast their votes on January 13, 1968, Father Flavian was chosen by a large majority.[363] But a week before the event Merton had made a firm decision that he would remain a monk of Gethsemani no matter who was chosen, holding on just as Pasternak had clung to Russia, refusing to leave no matter how chilly the local monastic weather might become. He had not come to Gethsemani, he recalled, to have his own way.

Dom Flavian had a different view of his office than Dom James and a readiness to let Merton accept some of the invitations he received. "The paradox is that it is to a great extent because I am here that I am invited to go," he had told one correspondent, "while it is because I am here I can't go."[364] Under Dom Flavian a new era dawned in Merton's life. He had the chance to become a traveling hermit. Merton was in the long-awaited, exhilarating but also quite alarming position of having no one to say no on his behalf.

Asia on My Mind

I have my own way to walk and for some reason or other Zen is right in the middle of it wherever I go.

Thomas Merton

THE WAY OF CHUANG TZU

THOMAS MERTON

Cover of *The Way of Chuang Tzu,* published in 1965 by New Directions.

Most invitations that came to Merton were easily turned down, but one that came at the beginning of 1968 seemed heaven-sent: Would Merton come to Bangkok in December to take part in a conference of Benedictine and Trappist abbots? Late in March Merton told Dom Flavian that he would like to accept and, while traveling, visit "some Zen places" elsewhere in Asia. Though with hesitation, Dom Flavian eventually agreed.[365]

Merton had been attentive to Asia since he was fifteen, when he had taken Gandhi's side in a student debate. Living in New York seven years later, the Hindu monk from India, Bramachari, had deeply impressed Merton, as had A. K. Coomaraswamy's writings on art and asceticism.

In the late fifties Merton's thinking led him back toward Asia. In 1956 he had begun reading everything he could find by D. T. Suzuki, the Japanese Zen Buddhist scholar. Three years later Merton initiated a correspondence with Suzuki, confessing he did not pretend to understand Zen but nonetheless owed a great debt to Suzuki. "Time after time, as I read your pages, something in me says, 'That's it!' Don't ask me what. I have no desire to explain it to anybody. . . . So there it is, in all its beautiful purposelessness."[366] He wondered whether, should Suzuki come to the United States, he might not visit the Abbey of Gethsemani? Merton had permission

Merton with Zen scholar D. T. Suzuki, during their meeting in 1964. (Photograph courtesy of the Thomas Merton Center)

When Chuang Tzu was about to die, his disciples began planning a splendid funeral.

But he said: "I shall have heaven and earth for my coffin; the sun and moon will be the jade symbols hanging by my side; . . . What more is needed?"

But they said: "We fear that crows and kites will eat our Master."

"Well," said Chuang Tzu, "above ground I shall be eaten by crows and kites, below it by ants and worms. In either case, I shall be eaten. Why are you so partial to birds?"

(The Way of Chuang Tzu)

to meet Suzuki in that event. He took the occasion to send Suzuki a collection of sayings of the Desert Fathers, the Zen masters of the early church.

While Suzuki never came to Gethsemani, Merton made a short trip to New York in June 1964 to meet him. It was Merton's first (and last) visit to New York since entering the monastery. Before Dom James gave permission, Merton had to promise that he would keep his visit secret and not make contact with old friends in Manhattan.

The two men drank green tea and talked. Though ninety-four years old and deaf, Suzuki was still the lively, responsive man Merton had anticipated. The main thing for Merton was "to see and experience the fact that there really is a deep understanding between myself and this extraordinary and simple man whose books I have been reading now for about ten years with great attention." Suzuki told Merton a story about a great master's dream in which his mother appeared to him with two mirrors, one in each sleeve. One was black, the other contained all things; the master found "himself among them, looking out." Being with Suzuki and his assistant, Miss Okamura, Merton "felt as if I had spent a few moments with my own family." They reminded him of his friends in Kentucky, Victor and Carolyn Hammer, people especially linked in Merton's life with *Hagia Sophia*. [367]

Suzuki's essays had renewed Merton's interest in Chuang Tzu, a Chinese philosopher who lived around the fourth century BC: Merton had first become aware of Chuang Tzu many years earlier when writing his thesis on William Blake. In 1961 he had enlisted the help of John Wu in preparing *The Way of Chuang Tzu*. "I have enjoyed writing this [book] more than any other I can remember. . . . I simply like Chuang Tzu because of what he is," Merton commented in the book's preface.

It is sometimes assumed that Merton's interest in Buddhism and other Asian religions suggests he was engaged in a search for a spiritual home that met his needs better than Christianity, or perhaps was seeking to put the two religions into a blender and pour out of it his own "baptized Buddhism." In fact for Merton the faith into which he had been baptized was never at issue. As he put it in a journal entry dated June 26, 1965, written on the Feast of the Sacred Heart of Jesus: "There is one more thing—I may be interested in Oriental religions, etc., but there can be no obscuring the essential difference—this personal communion with Christ at the center and heart of reality as a source of grace and life."

But it seemed to Merton that, thanks to the activity of the Holy Spirit, there was great wisdom to be found in other religious traditions and thus it was of mutual benefit for friendships to take root across the borders of religious difference. Suzuki was one such friend. Another was Thich Nhat Hanh, a Buddhist monk, Zen master, and poet from Vietnam. Nhat Hanh spent two days at the abbey in May 1967.

Merton immediately recognized Nhat Hanh as someone very like himself. It was like meeting Chuang Tzu in the flesh. As the two monks talked, the different religious systems in which they were formed provided bridges toward each other. "Thich Nhat Hanh is my brother," Merton said in a letter printed in a program for a poetry reading in New York, attended by Dan Berrigan, Abraham Heschel, Robert Lowell, and Arthur Miller, at which Nhat Hanh was introduced to the American public. "He is more my brother than many who are nearer to me in race and nationality, because he and I see things exactly the same way."

When Merton asked Nhat Hanh what the war was doing to Vietnam, the Buddhist said simply, "Everything is destroyed." This, Merton said to the monks at his

Thomas Merton with Thich Nhat Hanh, a Vietnamese Buddhist monk. (Photograph by John Heidbrink)

"He is more my brother than many who are nearer to me in race and nationality, because he and I see things in exactly the same way. . . . Do what you can for him. If I mean something to you, then let me put it this way; do for Nhat Hanh whatever you would do for me if I were in his position. In many ways I wish I were."

(Faith and Violence)

A Vietnamese mother and her family flee combat. (Maryknoll archives)

"I am on the side of the people who are being burned, cut to pieces, tortured, held as hostages, gassed, ruined, destroyed. They are the victims of both sides. To take sides with massive power is to take sides against the innocent. The side I take is then the side of the people who are sick of war and want peace in order to rebuild their country."

(Faith and Violence)

Sunday lecture, was truly a monk's answer, revealing the essence without wasting a word.

Merton described the rigorous formation of Buddhist monks in Vietnam and the fact that instruction in meditation doesn't begin early. "Before you can learn to meditate," he said, quoting Nhat Hanh, "you have to learn how to close the door." The monks laughed; they were used to the reverberation of slamming doors as latecomers raced to church.

In 1967 Dan Berrigan had suggested Merton go to Vietnam as a "hostage for peace," using his presence as a human shield, making the place where he was living less likely to be bombed. Merton had been haunted with the idea and was willing in principle to take part, though the project never materialized.

For fifteen years texts on Asian religions had been part of his reading, writing, and talks within the community. Now he had the chance to *be* in Asia. Always geared to imagine himself living elsewhere, he even wondered if Asia might not be the place to live—perhaps a hermitage in the Himalayas? Dom Flavian expressed openness to monks, while remaining part of the Gethsemani community, to live at a distance from the monastery.

At times Gethsemani, once so remote, no longer seemed to Merton far enough off the beaten path. Sometimes he felt he was living next to a highway intersection. In April, just two days after the murder of Martin Luther King Jr., a visitor describing herself as the Woman in Revelation (a "problematic apocalyptic woman," Merton noted in his journal) found her way to the abbey. There had been other unexpected and unknown people turning up. Merton had good reason to wonder, in an America in which so many people were armed and trigger-happy, whether the day might come when he was confronted by a visitor with a gun. It was partly to summon help that an intercom was installed linking the hermitage to the monastery.

He was also troubled about the problem of staying in the United States and thus, as he wrote his Belgian Benedictine friend, Jean Leclercq, "to some extent remaining identified with a society which I believe to be under the judgment of God and in some sense under a curse for the crimes of the Vietnam War." He wondered aloud again about the possibility of becoming part of a small monastic community in Nicaragua or Chile. Yet he didn't see how leaving his adopted country would be fully honest either, for "if this society is under judgment, I too should remain and sustain myself the judgment of everyone else, since I am after all not that much different from the others. The question of sin is a great one today—I mean collective guilt for crimes against humanity."[368]

Dom Flavian not only okayed the Asia trip but gave his permission for a preliminary journey within the United States. On May 6, Merton flew to the West Coast to visit the Trappist monastery of Our Lady of the Redwoods in Eureka, California. Besides giving several talks to the nuns, he explored the immediate area to see if there was a suitable place there for one or several hermitages. The most inviting spot was Bear Harbor, though Merton was alarmed by the number of cars in the area.[369] In San Francisco on May 15, he loaded up on avant-garde poetry at City Lights bookshop and had dinner with its poet-owner and friend by correspondence, Lawrence Ferlinghetti.

Next he visited Christ of the Desert Monastery in a remote desert canyon near Abiquiu, New Mexico. The community of three included one hermit. The monks gave him a Navajo rug for his hermitage chapel.

After only twelve days away from Gethsemani, Merton found himself homesick. He was back home May 21.

News arrived a few days later of the sentencing of

"I have been asked to attend two meetings in Asia, one of them a meeting of the Abbots of Catholic Monastic Orders in that area, the other an interfaith meeting with representatives of Asian religions. . . . The length of my stay in Asia is indeterminate. Needless to say, this is not anything unusual in the monastic life. I ask your prayers for the success of this undertaking: and of course, please do not believe anything that rumor may add to this simple scenario."

(Circular Letter to Friends, Fall 1968)

Merton with nuns at Our Lady of the Redwoods in California. (Photograph courtesy of the Thomas Merton Center)

Merton's friend Dan Berrigan, along with his brother Phil and seven others, for burning several boxes of draft records in Catonsville, Maryland. The judge ordered the nine imprisoned for six years. While incendiary methods of protest didn't attract Merton, his heart was with those protesting the war in Vietnam. Once again Merton considered what the war in Vietnam might yet require in his own life. "*Six years!* . . . how long will I myself be out of jail? I suppose I can say 'as long as I don't make a special effort to get in'—which is what they did. All I can say is that I haven't deliberately broken any laws. But one of these days I may find myself in a position where I will have to."[370]

America seemed to be a shooting gallery. Martin Luther King had been shot down on April 4. Louisville was among the cities ignited by racial riots. Farmworkers trying to organize a union were being jailed and beaten on the fields in California. On June 5 Robert F. Kennedy was killed in Los Angeles. The publication in July of *Faith and Violence*, a collection of Merton's essays on non-violence and peacemaking, was timely.[371]

On June 24, starting to prepare for the Asia trip,

Merton went to Louisville to get information for inoculations and visas. He continued to be amazed to have an abbot who shared his enthusiasms and was so willing to allow new freedoms. Dom Flavian suggested the possibility of Merton taking responsibility for setting up a small colony of hermits somewhere on the West Coast. "I get a real sense of openness, of going somewhere—at times it is almost incredible," Merton noted in his journal July 5. His prayer life was flourishing.

Increasingly his thoughts were Asia-centered. A few lines of poetry catch his mood: "O the mountains of Nepal, / And the tigers and the fevers. / And the escaped bandits from all the world. / And the escaped Trappists, lost, forgotten."[372]

Merton's passport photo, taken before his trip to Asia. (Photograph courtesy of the Thomas Merton Center)

Late in July an invitation arrived from an ecumenical group called the Temple of Understanding asking if Merton would speak at a conference in India. Two weeks later Archbishop Joseph Ryan in Anchorage, Alaska, wrote to ask Merton to lead a retreat for contemplative nuns. In both cases both Merton and his abbot were willing. In Alaska, Dom Flavian pointed out, he should take time to see if there might be suitable places for hermitages. In India, he could visit Tibetan Buddhists, perhaps even meet the Dalai Lama. On the way there he would make return visits to Christ of the Desert in New Mexico and Our Lady of the Redwoods in California, and a stop in Santa Barbara to see his friend W. H. Ferry and give a talk at the Center for the Study of Democratic Institutions.

As July ended, Merton felt he was saying goodbye to Gethsemani and perhaps even to America. "In eight weeks I am to leave here. And who knows—I may not come back. Not that I expect anything to go wrong." There was the possibility of finding a hermitage site in California or Alaska and staying there, or perhaps some isolated place in Asia. "Really I don't care one way or another if I never come back." He noted the problem of nearby traffic, guns, dogs barking in the woods, kids on

Merton with his secretary, Brother Patrick Hart, on the day of his departure for the Asian journey.
(Photograph by Brother Maurice Flood, courtesy of the Abbey of Gethsemani)

"Our real journey in life is interior; it is a matter of growth, deepening, and of an ever greater surrender to the creative action of love and grace in our hearts. Never was it more necessary for us to respond to that action."
(Circular Letter to Friends, September 1968)

the lake. "If I can find someplace to *disappear* to I will. And if I am to begin a relatively wandering life with no fixed abode, that's all right too."[373]

Getting ready to leave, in August he went shopping in Louisville with Frank O'Callaghan, buying luggage and a drip-dry suit.

As September began, though still unsure whether he could visit the Dalai Lama, details of the journey were fairly clear. With departure imminent, Merton's feeling about leaving Gethsemani were more ambiguous than they had been a month before. He experienced a renewed attachment to the monastery fields, felt nervous and insecure, had blisters, and suffered more than ever from allergies. He wrote a form letter to be sent to friends revealing that he was shortly leaving for Asia. It was a nonpolitical trip, he said, not linked to the war in Vietnam.

On September 9 his recently appointed secretary, Brother Patrick Hart, came up to the hermitage. He had recently returned from Rome with a gift from Pope Paul for the monk-author he much admired: a beautiful bronze cross. Brother Pat would live in the hermitage while Merton was away. Brother Maurice Flood and Phil Stark, a Jesuit scholastic who was helping with *Monks Pond*, came with him. The three celebrated Mass, had breakfast together, and said goodbye. Merton sent James Laughlin the draft of his long poem, *Geography of Lograire*, though it wasn't finished.

"I hope [in Asia]," he wrote in his journal, "to find something or someone who will help me advance in my own spiritual quest." He had no intention either to return or not return. "I remain a monk of Gethsemani. Whether or not I end my days here, I don't know—and perhaps it is not so important. The great thing is to respond perfectly to God's will in this providential opportunity, whatever it may bring."

The next morning Merton met briefly with Dom Flavian, promising he would behave himself and avoid the press. Dom Flavian gave him money for his travels and the old Bond Street wallet originally given to Merton on his eighteenth birthday by Tom Bennett. Ron Seitz, a Louisville poet who taught at Bellarmine, picked Merton up at 10 AM and helped with final errands in Louisville: the collection of allergy pills and the purchase of a pair of shoes. After showering at the O'Callaghan house, there was a dinner party. Merton spent the night at Saint Bonaventure's Friary on the Bellarmine campus.

In the morning Merton was away on an early flight to Albuquerque, the first stop on the way to Asia.

I am about to make my home
In the bell's summit
Set my mind a thousand feet high
On the ace of songs
In a mood of needless and random lights
To purify
The quick magnetic sodas of the skin . . .

I am about to build my nest
In the misdirected and unpaid express
As I walk away from this poem

Hiding the ace of freedoms
(Cables to the Ace)

Everything Is Compassion

Yin-yang palace of opposites in unity!

THOMAS MERTON
The Asian Journal

"Before I grasped Zen, the mountains were nothing but mountains and the rivers nothing but rivers. When I got into Zen, the mountains were no longer mountains and the rivers no longer rivers. But when I understood Zen, the mountains were only mountains and the rivers only rivers."

(Zen saying,
Zen and the Birds of Appetite)

Merton's stay in New Mexico centered on attending a two-day Indian celebration of the Feast of the Tabernacles. An event closed to the public, Merton had been invited to witness and even photograph the event because he was recognized as a holy man. He flew to Chicago September 16 to give a talk to the Poor Clares, then two days later went on to Alaska to lead a retreat for nuns at the Convent of the Precious Blood in Eagle River.[374]

The local bishop had arranged for Merton to be taken to possible hermitage sites. On September 27, traveling by bush plane, he reached Yakutat, a Tlingit village. The nearby Eyak Lake especially appealed to him. It was silent, surrounded by mountains and populated mainly by thousands of wild geese. Merton could imagine living in such a place, he wrote Dom Flavian, but realized that the key issue to be settled in his life wasn't the postal address. "The important thing for me," he wrote his abbot, "is not acquiring land or finding an ideal solitude but opening up the depths of my own heart. The rest is secondary."[375]

Waiting at the airport to meet Merton when he arrived in San Francisco October 2 was one of his youngest correspondents, Suzanne Butorovich, and her family. Merton had dinner with them, then stayed the night in a hotel, catching a morning flight to Santa Barbara where W. H. ("Ping") Ferry was waiting. A postcard to Dom Flavian sent a few days later showed a view of a bright pink room with king-sized bed at a local hotel: "No!" Merton wrote on the back, "I did NOT sleep here!"

Ping Ferry had arranged a talk and discussion at the Center for the Study of Democratic Institutions, a well-endowed establishment for dialogue and research that was slightly to the political left. In his exchange with the resident fellows, Merton was critical of the tendency of radical Christians to move toward a "revolutionary mystique," considering everything else irrelevant. His own commitment was to go further with the examination of tradition "because I happen to have an opening towards it, I happen to have the background to do it. . . . A man can only do one thing at a time, and this is the thing that I think I should do." He dismissed forms of renewal that were more concerned with improving breakfast than in "recovering the depths of purpose."[376]

After his several days in Santa Barbara, he drove up the coast with Ping Ferry. "How was Merton when you last saw him?" I asked Ping two months later. "He was like a kid going to the circus," he replied.

On October 9 Merton arrived at Our Lady of the Redwoods for three days of conferences. The second visit made him certain that this stretch of the California coast wasn't the right place for a hermitage—there was a land boom in progress and bulldozers everywhere.

Six days later Merton was over the Pacific writing in his journal, "May I not come back without having settled the great affair. And found also the great compassion, *mahakaruna*."[377]

After changing planes in Tokyo, Merton arrived in Bangkok October 16 for a two-day stay. He felt assaulted by the city's wild, filthy streets crowded with motorbikes and buses, though the people were "lovely, beautiful, gentle—except those who are learning too fast from the Americans."[378]

Away from the city's noisy center, he found his way to Phra Khantipalo, an English Buddhist monk, who

Merton at the Center for the Study of Democratic Institutions in Santa Barbara. (Photograph courtesy of the Thomas Merton Center)

proved helpful despite having "the look of a strict observer." They discussed the Satipatthana Sutra—the Buddha's Discourse on Mindfulness.[379] After saying Mass at the local cathedral, Merton got out into the countryside to visit one of the oldest Buddhist shrines, Phra Pathom Chedi.

On October 18 he arrived in Calcutta for the "Spiritual Summit Conference" of the Temple of Understanding, but the topic of interfaith dialogue was immediately driven from his thoughts by the proximity to absolute poverty: technically a monk vowed to poverty, here he was simply a rich American among the destitute, ashamed of the money in his pocket and the camera around his neck. He hardly dared open his mouth until he found Amiya Chakravarty, the scholar to whom Merton had dedicated *Zen and the Birds of Appetite*.[380] He also met an exiled Tibetan lama, Chogyam Trungpa Rimpoche, whose stories of escaping before the Chinese Red Army so impressed Merton that they were to become part of the lecture he gave just before his death.

Perhaps Calcutta, in which penitential life was normal for so many, made Merton regret having left the monastery without asking forgiveness from Dom James, now living as a hermit in a trailer. On October 20 Merton wrote to assure his old abbot that he had "never personally resented" any of his restrictive decisions "because I knew you were following your conscience and the policies that seemed necessary then."

Speaking at the Calcutta conference October 23, Merton defended all those who are intentionally irrelevant, including those offering monastic witness. He regretted that the current upheaval in Western Christian monasticism was resulting in "much that is of undying value . . . being thrown away irresponsibly" and hoped the situation in the East was better. "I will say as a brother from the West to Eastern monks, be a little careful. . . . Your fidelity to tradition will stand you in good stead. Do not be afraid of that fidelity."

With Amiya Chakravarty in Calcutta. (Photograph courtesy of the Thomas Merton Center)

In a conference bursting at the seams with talk of convergence and religious oneness, Merton stressed that unity will not be achieved at the level of intellectual discourse:

> The deepest level of communication is not communication, but communion. It is wordless. It is beyond words, and it is beyond speech, and it is beyond concept. Not that we discover a new unity. We discover an older unity. My dear brothers, we are already one. But we imagine that we are not. What we have to recover is our original unity. What we have to be is what we are.[381]

Communion is not a goal, Merton stressed, that can be attained by "interminable empty talk, the endlessly fruitless and trivial discussion of everything under the sun, the inexhaustible chatter with which modern man tries to convince himself that he is in touch with his fellow man and reality." Nor will minimizing differences be of any help. "There can be no question of a facile syncretism, a mishmash of semi-religious verbiage and pieties, a devotionalism that admits everything and therefore takes nothing with full seriousness." Rather "there must be a scrupulous respect for important differences."[382]

The next day brought a telegram with the news that Merton was invited to Dharamsala, the residence of the 14th Dalai Lama, the exiled leader of Tibetan Buddhism.

Arriving in New Delhi October 27, Merton was met by Harold Talbott, an American student of Buddhism with whom he corresponded. Talbott was under instruction with the Dalai Lama. They went together to look at Tibetan *tankas* (icons), then visited with a local Tibetan refugee community. Merton was delighted with Tibetan laughter. He was dazzled by the way they rallied every conceivable sound to make, as it seemed to him, clamorous icons of sound. "The deep sounds renew life, repel

"Thinking about my own life and future, it is still a very open question. I am beginning to appreciate the hermitage at Gethsemani more than I did last summer when things seemed so noisy and crowded."

(The Asian Journal)

the death-grin (i.e., ignorance). The sound is the sound of emptiness. It is profound and clean. We are washed in the millennial silent roar of a rock-eating glacier."[383]

With Talbott on the night train north to Pathankot October 31, Merton was reminded of his momentous train trip to Kentucky in 1941. The next day, winding their way into the Himalayas by jeep, they reached Talbott's cottage high up in Dharamsala. Ignoring the rain, Merton went off to explore the "beautiful silence" and came upon Tibetans praying with rosaries. The sound of a goatherd's flute floated up from a pasture in the valley a couple of thousand feet below. Yet here too the world of violence made its noises: he could hear the crack of shots from an Indian Army small-arms range in the distance, just as he could hear the cannons at Fort Knox at his hermitage at Gethsemani.

The next day one of the Tibetan lamas, Sonam Kazi, taught Merton the use of the *mandala* as a method of inner control while meditating and explained the Dzogchen Way (the Great Way of All-Inclusiveness). Merton was delighted to learn that *Trapas* (the closest sound to Trappist) was the Tibetan word for monk.

At Merton's first meeting with the Dalai Lama, November 4, they talked about illusions, misconceptions, metaphysics, and the ideal course of study for monks. Originally only one meeting had been planned, but at the end of their conversation the Dalai Lama suggested they come together again in two days. Merton was impressed with the Dalai Lama: "a most impressive person . . . strong and alert, bigger than I expected . . . very solid, energetic, generous, and warm . . . charismatic."[384]

There were two mild earthquakes the next day. Merton thought of the election under way in the United States. That night he dreamed he was back at Gethsemani, not in his Trappist robes but wearing a Zen habit enriched with Tibetan colors, the black joined by red and gold.[385] Another dream took him to the south of France, his original home.

Merton with the Dalai Lama on November 4, 1968. (Photograph courtesy of the Thomas Merton Center)

"The Dalai Lama is strong and alert, bigger than I expected . . . and very solid, energetic; generous and warm. . . . He is a very consecutive thinker and moves from step to step. His ideas on the interior life are built on very solid foundations."

(The Asian Journal)

At their meeting November 6, Merton and the Dalai Lama talked about theories of knowledge and compared methods of concentration. Merton said it was important for monks in the world "to be living examples of the freedom and transformation of consciousness which meditation can give." The lamas, he knew, opposed absolute solitude, stressing compassion. Solitude should provide a base for engagement. They talked about methods of concentration and the riddle of the mind concentrating on the mind, while at another level the mind is aware of mind concentrating on mind: "All three one mind." It was a lively conversation. The Dalai Lama "insists on detachment, on an 'unworldly life,' yet sees it as a way to complete understanding of, and participation in, the problems of life and the world." Merton was impressed with the Dalai Lama's step-by-step way of exploring a subject. They agreed to have one more meeting in two days.[386]

The next day Merton wrote in his journal that contemplative life should open the way to experiencing *temps vierge*—"virginal time": not time as simply a blank sheet to be filled or a territory to be conquered and dominated but time illuminated by compassion.[387] A conver-

"The unspoken or half-spoken message of the talk [with Chatral Rimpoche] was our complete understanding of each other as people who were somehow on the edge of great realization and knew it and were trying (somehow or other) to go out and get lost in it – and that it was a grace for us to meet one another. . . ."
(The Asian Journal)

sation later in the day with Chobgye Thicchen Rimpoche, a former prisoner of the Chinese, centered on love and compassion. The ideal model of holiness, he said, was not the king (who first of all saves himself) or the boatman (who ferries people to salvation, arriving with them) but the shepherd who goes behind the others, deferring salvation until those he serves have achieved it.

At their third meeting the Dalai Lama wanted to understand the place of vows in a monk's life and what methods Western monks used to free the mind from the rule of passions. He also wanted to know what the reason was for avoiding meat? Did monks ever drink alcohol? Or see movies? Merton asked a question about Marxism and monasticism, the subject he planned to discuss at the Bangkok meeting. Was there a connection between the Buddhist dialectic and the Marxist concept of alienation? What kind of dialogue was possible between a monk and a Marxist? The Dalai Lama said that dialogue would be possible between the believer and the Marxist only "if Marxism meant only the establishment of an equitable economic and social structure" and if religious leaders were not servants of secular structures. In actual practice militant atheists seemed unable to make any accommodations and simply struggled to "suppress all forms of religion, good and bad." Merton was impressed by the Dalai Lama's lack of bitterness toward Communists. "I have seldom met anyone with whom I clicked so well," Merton wrote Dom Flavian.[388]

There were meetings with other Tibetan monks as well, each with his own small house somewhere on the mountain. "What was for me on Friday a rugged, nondescript mountain with a lot of miscellaneous dwellings, rocks, woods, farms, flocks, gulfs, falls, and heights, is now spiritually ordered by permanent seated presences, burning with a lamp-like continuity and significance, centers of awareness and reminders of *dharma*. . . . The central presence is a fully awake, energetic, alert, non-dusty, non-dim, non-whispering Buddha."[389]

Following the days at Dharamsala, Merton and Talbott spent a weekend in New Delhi. After exploring an eighteenth-century observatory, Jantar Mantar, they met a Cambodian monk, then visited a Muslim college. Merton said Mass at a local Catholic hospital and worked on his impending Bangkok lecture. Money was running low. In a letter to Gethsemani, he confessed, "The cost of stamps is breaking me!"

When Merton returned to Calcutta, he had been in India long enough to see not only the destitution but the beauty. He was sensitive to a certain nobility in the city's squalor. He noticed ponds and lotuses, Communist slogans painted on walls, water buffalo and sacred cows, rickshaws and movie posters, but couldn't find his old friend Bramachari's ashram. The city seemed, if not colorful, more colorful than he had perceived the first time. The urban noise had become a kind of silence. "For the masses of Calcutta, you dimly begin to think, there is no judgment. Only their misery. And instead of being judged, they are a judgment on the rest of the world."[390]

On November 12 Merton and Talbott flew to Darjeeling, the tea district tucked between Nepal, Sikkim, and Bhutan in India's high country. Making the Windamere Hotel his home, he drank tea to soothe a cold he had acquired. The prices for Western medicine shocked him. Though not well, the next day he said Mass at the Loreto Convent, and the day after went looking for Tibetan refugees, finding them scratching out a living in carpet factories or local workshops, but still carrying on the vital religious life which had caused their exile.

On November 16 Merton met Chatral Rimpoche, a lama who looked like a solid old peasant and impressed Merton as the greatest *rimpoche* (spiritual master) he had met so far. They talked for two hours with complete understanding of each other as people "on the edge of great realization." Chatral Rimpoche, amazed to find himself so fully at home with a Christian, said Merton was a "natural Buddha." There was much laughter. "If I

One of the statues at the Buddhist shrine at Polonnaruwa, Sri Lanka, photographed by Merton. (Courtesy of the Thomas Merton Center)

were to settle down with a Tibetan guru," Merton noted, "I think Chatral would be the one I'd choose." Before parting they promised each other that they would try to attain complete realization in this life.[391]

For four days Merton rested in a quiet bungalow at the Mim Tea Estate. He wondered if he had yet found "the real Asia." A "well-behaved, nonviolent Himalayan bee" landed on him several times without stinging. Merton let the bee crawl on his head, collecting sweat "for some electric and gentle honeycomb." He was still struggling with the question of where he ought to settle down at the end of the pilgrimage. He had the feeling that he would end his days at Gethsemani.

In the distance was one of the great mountains of the Himalayas, Kanchenjunga, which at first struck Merton as a 28,000-foot postcard, but within a few days he realized the mountain had a side not seen in postcards, a hidden mountain that was "a yin-yang palace of opposites in unity." The hidden mountain cannot be photographed, though Merton tried. Its full beauty "is not seen until you consent to the impossible paradox" of knowing that the mountain both is and is not. "When nothing more needs to be said, the smoke of ideas clears, the mountain is SEEN."[392]

Back in Darjeeling on November 21, Merton said Mass at the Loreto Convent, then gave a talk voicing his reservations about the renewal going on in the West. "We need the religious genius of Asia and Asian culture to inject a fresh dimension of depth into our aimless thrashing about. I would almost say an element of heart, of *bhakti*, of love."[393]

He met Karlu Rimpoche, who lived at the hermit center at Sonada, the most soft-spoken lama Merton had yet encountered. They talked at length about the hermit life: who can live it, the spiritual life at its center, the appropriate methods and subjects of meditation, the schedule to be followed. The lama told Merton that he possessed the "true *Mahayana* spirit."[394] *Mahayana*—literally, Great

Vehicle—is the branch of Buddhism that gives particular stress to compassion and universal salvation.

Traveling back to Calcutta, Merton happened to meet a man named John Balfour, who years later still recalled the encounter. Balfour was impressed at Merton's halo-like, cleaner-than-clean, "washed" face, the kind of face that usually belongs to those in "some major mystic dimension."[395]

By the time Merton returned to Calcutta for a third visit, it had become "a city I love." There were still the disintegrating slums, yet Calcutta had become more colorful, graced with white cranes and green coconut palms. It was a very brief stay this time. Then Merton was off to Madras in the south of India.

On November 27 he visited the cathedral of his namesake, Saint Thomas, the apostle who came all the way to Asia and died there. Afterward he said the Mass of Saint Thomas at the Church of Our Lady of Expectation on Saint Thomas Mount, then visited a center for abandoned children next door. The next day he went to the coastal temple complex of Mahabalipuram, a Hindu shrine on the coast covered with handsome gods and shapely goddesses in bas-relief. He was impressed by a nearby *lingam* (a phallic symbol) of black stone standing in the ocean near the shore, endlessly washed by wave after wave, an image of the communion of man and woman. Merton had a sense of ancient India before the British Raj.

Arriving in Colombo, Ceylon, now Sri Lanka, on November 29, Merton found himself in the midst of strikes, with police and soldiers everywhere. After checking into the Hotel Karma, he went to the United States Information Agency, hoping to get assistance in making contact with local Buddhist scholars. The director turned out to be a great fan of Merton's, Victor Stier, who at the time was reading *Conjectures of a Guilty Bystander.*

Early the next day Merton was off by train to the center of Ceylon, riding second class on the Kandy Express in a compartment reserved for clergy, checking into a

"Heartrending routine of the beggars— the little girl who suddenly appeared at the window of the taxi, the utterly lovely smile with which she stretched out her hand and then the extinguishing of the light when she drew it back empty. (I had no Indian money yet.) She fell away from the taxi as if she were sinking in water and drowning and I wanted to die."

(The Asian Journal)

One of Merton's photos taken at Polonnaruwa of the colossal statue of the Sleeping Buddha. (Photograph courtesy of the Thomas Merton Center)

hotel in Kandy with a view of a church so English that, were it not for the coconut palms, it might have been in Sussex. He set off to find the *bhikkhu* (monk, from the Sanskrit word for beggar) Nyanaponika Thera at his monastery in the jungle not far from the city. The two walked to a nearby temple. What most impressed Merton was an old Buddha statue carved out of a rock rising out of the earth.

The climax of Merton's visit to Ceylon, and one of the significant moments in his life, came when he visited Polonnaruwa on December 3. Polonnaruwa, an ancient ruined city in the northeast of Ceylon, is a place of pilgrimage known mainly for its colossal figures of the Buddha carved out of huge stones. He had been able to wander among the huge figures alone while the Catholic priest who had driven him there, alarmed at such proximity to such pagan art, kept his distance. Most impressive was the vast sculpture of the sleeping/dying Buddha, a vast reclining figure with a seraphic face absolutely free of anxiety, enmity, and doubt, with his disciple Ananda standing with crossed arms nearby, like a child waiting to receive communion. Merton was so stunned by what he experienced in the presence of the carvings that it was three days before he attempted writing about it.

I am able to approach the Buddhas barefoot and undisturbed, my feet in wet grass, wet sand. Then the silence of the extraordinary faces. The great smiles, huge and yet subtle. Filled with every possibility, questioning nothing, knowing everything, rejecting nothing, the peace . . . that has seen through every question without trying to discredit anyone or anything—*without refutation*—without establishing some other argument. For the doctrinaire, the mind that needs well-established positions, such peace, such relief and thankfulness, can be frightening. I was knocked over with a rush of relief and thankfulness at the *obvious* clarity of the figures, the clarity and fluidity of shape and line, the design of the monumental bodies composed into the rock shape and landscape, figure, rock and tree. . . .

I was suddenly, almost forcibly, jerked clean out of the habitual, half-tied vision of things, and an inner cleanness, clarity, as if exploding from the rocks themselves, became evident, obvious. The queer *evidence* of the reclining figure, the smile, and the sad smile of Ananda, standing with arms folded (much more "imperative" than da Vinci's Mona Lisa because completely simple and straightforward). The thing about all this is that there is no puzzle, no problem, and really no "mystery." All problems are resolved and everything is clear, simply because what matters is clear. The rock, all matter, all life, is charged with *Dharmakaya* [the state of absolute awakeness, being fully in touch with reality and free of all illusion] . . . everything is emptiness and everything is compassion. I don't know when in my life I have ever had such a sense of beauty and spiritual validity running together in one aesthetic illumination.

Surely, with Mahabalipuram and Polonnaruwa, my Asian pilgrimage has come clear and purified itself—I mean I know and have seen what I was obscurely looking for. I don't know what else remains but I have now seen and have pierced through the surface and have got beyond the shadow and the disguise. This is Asia in its purity, not covered over with garbage (Asian or European or American) and it is clear, pure, complete. It says everything—it needs nothing. And because it needs nothing it can afford to be silent, unnoticed, undiscovered. It does not need to be discovered. It is we (Asians included) who need to discover it.[396]

Jonas Overshadowed

We can ask ourselves if we are planning for the next twenty years to be travel-ing with a train of yaks.

THOMAS MERTON
"Marxism and Monastic Perspectives," in *The Asian Journal*

"Abbot Lot came to Abbot Joseph and said: Father, according as I am able, I keep my little rule, and my little fast, my prayer, meditation and contemplative silence; and according as I am able to strive to cleanse my heart of thoughts: now what more should I do? The elder rose up in reply and stretched out his hands to heaven, and his fingers became like ten lamps of fire. He said: Why not be totally changed into fire?"

(The Wisdom of the Desert)

Merton stopped in Singapore December 4, stay-ing in comfort at the Raffles Hotel. He booked a flight to Djakarta, now Jarkarta, for December 15, his intended next stop after the conference of abbots and abbesses. He planned to spend Christmas at Rawa Seneng (Peaceful Swamp), a Trappist monastery on Java. From there he would proceed to Hong Kong to stay with the Trappists on Lantao Island.

Merton returned to Bangkok December 6. Just as Calcutta had changed each time he came back to it, Bangkok too was different; overwhelmed the first time by noise and dirt, now he was impressed by playing chil-dren and the plentitude of fruit, rice, meat, bottles, med-icines, shoes, machinery, lights, and trinkets. Merton went to the fabulous Temple of the Emerald Buddha, magnificent, bizarre, and slightly flattened by the feet and flashbulbs of so many tourists. "There are of course Disneyland tendencies in all these Thai wats," Merton noted. "And I suppose at times they go over the line."[397]

On December 8, the Feast of the Immaculate Conception, Merton made his last journal entry. He was off to say Mass at the Church of Saint Louis, whose name had become his in Trappist life, then to have lunch at the Apostolic Delegation before going to the Sawang Kaniwat (Red Cross) Conference Center.

The meeting place was at Samutprakan, 29 miles south of Bangkok. Merton arrived in the afternoon and

was housed on the ground floor of Cottage Two. The conference began the next day with a welcoming address from the Supreme Patriarch of Thai Buddhism. Events of the day included an evening discussion on marriage and celibacy.

Few of the monks got much sleep that night. A chorus of cats had come out to sing the night office on nearby roofs. Following crescendos of cat howling, those in adjacent rooms heard Merton's laughter.[398]

Merton's paper, "Marxism and Monastic Perspectives," so much on his mind for many weeks, was presented the next morning, December 10. Merton, under orders from his abbot to avoid the press, was made nervous by Dutch and Italian television crews which had turned up to film his lecture.

One of the crucial issues confronting the monk, Merton pointed out, is what his position is and how he identifies himself in a world of revolution. This wasn't simply a matter of how to survive an enemy who is intent on either destroying religion or converting those of religious convictions to atheism. Rather, it was a matter of understanding, beyond present models of Marxism and

Thomas Merton (center) sits among other participants in the Bangkok conference of Benedictine and Trappist abbots on the day of his death. Beside Merton (second from the left) is Jean Leclerq, O.S.B. (Photographed by Dom Cees Tholens, O.S.B., courtesy of Boston College, Burns Library)

Merton in Bangkok delivering his
talk on Marxism and Monastic
Perspectives, shortly before his death.
(Photograph courtesy of the Abbey of
Gethsemani)

*"This, I think, is what Buddhism is all
about, and what Christianity is about,
what monasticism is about—if you
understand it in terms of grace. . . . We
can no longer rely on being supported by
structures that may be destroyed at any
moment. . . . The Zen people have a
saying: . . . 'Where do you go from the
top of a thirty-foot pole?'"*

(From Merton's last talk,
The Asian Journal)

monasticism, the fundamental points of similarity and
difference.

He recognized significant similarities. The monk,
after all, "is essentially someone who takes up a critical
attitude toward the world and its structures . . . [saying]
that the claims of the world are fraudulent." In addition,
both monk and Marxist share the idea that each should
give according to his capacity and receive according to
his need. But while the Marxist gives primary emphasis
to the material and economic structures of life, seeing
religious approaches as empty mystification, the monk is
committed to bringing about a human transformation
that begins at the level of consciousness.

"Instead of starting with matter itself and then moving
up to a new structure, in which man will automatically
develop a new consciousness, the traditional religions
begin with the consciousness of the individual seeking to
transform and liberate the truth in each person, with the
idea that it will then communicate itself to others."

This is emphatically the vocation of the monk "who
seeks full realization . . . [and] has come to experience the
ground of his own being in such a way that he knows the
secret of liberation and can somehow or other communicate it to others." At the deepest level, the monk is teaching others how to live by love. For Christians, this is the
discovery of Christ dwelling in all others.

Only with such love, Merton went on, is it possible to
realize the economic ideal of each giving according to his
ability and receiving according to his need. But in actual-
ity many Christians, including those in monastic communities, have not reached this level of love and realization. They have burdened their lives with too many false
needs, and these have blocked the way to full realization,
the monk's only reason for being.

Merton told a story he had heard from Chogyam
Trungpa Rimpoche of a Buddhist abbot fleeing from his
Tibetan monastery before the advance of Chinese
Communist troops. He encountered another monk lead-

ing a train of twenty-five yaks loaded with the treasures of the monastery and "essential" provisions. The abbot chose not to stay with the treasure or the treasurer; traveling light, he managed to cross the border into India, destitute but alive. The yak-tending monk, chained to his treasure, was overtaken by the soldiers and was never heard of again.

"We can ask ourselves," Merton said, "if we are planning for the next twenty years to be traveling with a train of yaks." Monasticism, after all, is not architecture or clothing or even rules of life. It is "total inner transformation. Let the yaks take care of themselves." The monastic life thrives whenever there is a person "giving some kind of direction and instruction to a small group attempting to love God and reach union with him."

Authentic monasticism cannot be extinguished. "It is imperishable. It represents an instinct of the human heart, and it represents a charism given by God to man. It cannot be rooted out, because it does not depend on man. It does not depend on cultural factors, and it does not depend on sociological or psychological factors. It is something much deeper."[399]

Finishing the talk, Merton suggested putting off questions until the evening session. He concluded with the words, "So I will disappear," adding the suggestion that everyone have a Coke.

At about 3 PM, Father François de Grunne, who had a room near Merton's, heard a cry and what sounded like someone falling. He knocked on Merton's door but there was no response. Shortly before 4 o'clock Father de Grunne came down again to get the cottage key from Merton and to reassure himself that nothing was the matter. When there was no answer he looked through the louvers in the upper part of the door and saw Merton lying on the terrazzo floor. A standing fan had fallen on top of him. Father de Grunne tried to open the door but it was locked. With the help of others, the door was opened.

There was a smell of burned flesh. Merton, clearly

"The monk belongs to the world, but the world belongs to him, insofar as he has dedicated himself totally to liberation from it in order to liberate it. You can't just immerse yourself in the world and get carried away with it. That is no salvation. If you want to pull a drowning man out of the water, you have to have some support yourself."

(The Asian Journal)

237

After Merton's death, his body was dressed and laid out, and the abbots attending the conference maintained a constant vigil over him. (Photograph by Dom Cees Tholens, O.S.B., courtesy of Boston College, Burns Library)

"In death Father Louis' face was set in a great and deep peace, and it was obvious that he had found Him Whom he had searched for so diligently."
(Letter from the abbots attending the Bangkok conference to the Abbot of Gethsemani)

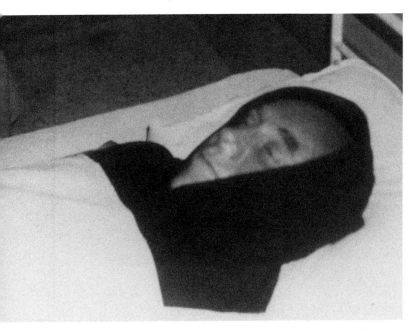

dead, was lying on his back with the five-foot fan diagonally across his body. Dom Odo Haas, abbot of Waekwan, tried to lift it and received an electric shock that jerked him sideways, holding him fast to the shaft of the fan until Father Celestine Say pulled the plug.

A long, raw third-degree burn about a hand's width ran along the right side of Merton's body almost to the groin. There were no marks on his hands. His face was bluish-red, eyes and mouth half open. There had been bleeding from the back of the head. The priests gave Merton absolution; then Dom Odo went to get the Abbot Primate of the Benedictines, Dom Rembert Weakland, who gave Merton extreme unction. A doctor arrived, Mother Edeltrud Weist, prioress of Taegu Convent in Korea. She checked for pulse and eye reaction to light.

A police test of the fan showed that a "defective electric cord was installed inside its stand. . . . The flow of electricity was strong enough to cause the death of a person if he touched the metal part."

After Merton's body was released to Dom Weakland, it was washed, then taken to the chapel. There was a prayer vigil throughout the night at the side of the body.

The next day Merton's body was taken to the United States Air Force Base in Bangkok and from there flown back to the United States in company with dead bodies of Americans killed in Vietnam. From Oakland, California, it continued by civilian carrier, at last reaching the Abbey of Gethsemani the afternoon of December 17.

The monks at the abbey had been informed of the death by Dom Flavian during their midday meal on December 10. In the days that followed, *The Seven Storey Mountain* was read aloud during meals in the refectory. "Some of us saw a considerable irony in fact that the refectory reader was Father Raymond Flanagan," recalls Father Patrick Reardon, then a member of the community, "who had been carrying on a running feud with Father Louis for about as long as any of us could remember."

One of the brothers drove a truck out to the hermitage of Dom James Fox to bring him back for the funeral. Dom James remarked that Merton "now knows more theology than any of us." The brother responded, "Well, Reverend Father, he always did."[400]

Dom Flavian and Father John Eudes Bamberger identified the body at the undertakers in New Haven, Kentucky, where the casket was briefly opened. "I readily identified the body though it was already bloated and swollen considerably," Father John Eudes wrote. "There was no doubt it was Father Louis."

The casket arrived at the monastery only a couple of hours before the afternoon funeral Mass and was placed in the abbey basilica. Father Timothy Kelly, later to succeed Dom Flavian as abbot, and Father Patrick Reardon prayed the psalms over the body for the hour or more prior to the funeral.

The funeral Mass was composed by Father Chrysogonus Waddell. On the cover of the liturgy booklet was a text from *The Sign of Jonas:* "I have always overshadowed Jonas with My Mercy. . . . Have you lost sight of me Jonas My Child? Mercy within mercy within mercy." Part of the Book of Jonah was read aloud. At the end of the Mass, there was a reading from *The Seven Storey Mountain*, concluding with the book's prophetic final sentence, "That you may become the brother of God and learn to know the Christ of the burnt men."

His brother monks buried Merton in their small cemetery next to the abbey church. Normally Trappists were

The funeral Mass for Thomas Merton was held in the renovated Abbey Chapel at Gethsemani. (Photograph courtesy of the Abbey of Gethsemani)

"The world knew him from his books: we knew him from his spoken word. Few, if any, know him in his secret prayer. Still, he had a secret prayer, and this is what gave the inner life to all he said and wrote. His secret was his secret to himself to a great extent, but he was a skillful reader of the secret of the souls that sought his help. It is because of this that although we laughed at him, and with him, as we would a younger brother, still we respected him as the spiritual father of our souls."

(Dom Flavian Burns, Abbot of Gethsemani, in a homily to the monastery community)

"I will give you what you desire. I will lead you into solitude. I will lead you by the way that you cannot possibly understand, because I want it to be the quickest way....

"Everything that touches you shall burn you, and you will draw your hand away in pain, until you have withdrawn yourself from all things. Then you will be all alone....

"Do not ask when it will be or where it will be or how it will be: On a mountain or in a prison, in a desert or in a concentration camp or in a hospital or at Gethsemani. It does not matter. So do not ask me, because I am not going to tell you. You will not know until you are in it.

"But you shall taste the true solitude of my anguish and my poverty and I shall lead you into the high places of my joy and you shall die in Me and find all things in My Mercy which has created you for this end....

"That you may become the brother of God and learn to know the Christ of the burnt men."

(The Seven Storey Mountain)

Icon, among the personal effects returned with Merton's body.
(Courtesy of the Abbey of Gethsemani)

buried without a casket. Merton was one of two exceptions. The other had been Dom Frederic Dunne, the abbot who had received Merton in 1941 and encouraged him to write. Dom Frederic had also died while traveling.

"A whole bunch of us grabbed shovels to fill in Father Louis's grave at the end of the service," Father Patrick recalled. "I remember Father Raymond going at it with the gusto he brought to every enterprise. Toward the end of the burial, it began to rain, so we were quite damp when we returned to the church."[401]

With the body came an official declaration of Merton's effects, appraised in dollars:

1 Timex Watch $10.00
1 Pair Dark Glasses in Tortoise Frames Nil
1 Cistercian Leather Bound Breviary Nil
1 Rosary (broken) Nil
1 Small Icon on Wood of Virgin and Child Nil[402]

There was also the memory of Merton's last words. Following the morning conference, Father de Grunne told Merton that a nun in the audience was annoyed that Merton had said nothing about converting people.

"What we are asked to do at present," Merton responded, "is not so much to speak of Christ as to let him live in us so that people may find him by feeling how he lives in us."

The icon Merton had with him contains its own last words, silent on one side, and on the back a brief extract from the *Philokalia*, written in Greek in Merton's hand:

If we wish to please the true God and to be friends with the most blessed of friendships, let us present our spirit naked to God. Let us not draw into it anything of this present world—no art, no thought, no reasoning, no self-justification—even though we should possess all the wisdom of this world.[403]

Afterword

In the decades since his death, far from fading from memory, Thomas Merton seems to have influenced even more people than he did while he was alive.

Not only do a great many of his books remain in print, but many new, posthumous collections have been published. These include his complete journals (seven volumes, plus an additional volume, *The Intimate Merton*, with journal highlights) and five substantial collections of letters, along with numerous exchanges of letters giving both sides of the correspondence—Bob Lax, Jean Leclercq, James Laughlin, Czeslaw Milosz, Rosemary Ruether, and others. Various series of conferences presented to young monks in his charge, originally circulated only in mimeographed form, are now available as books. What might please him most was the recent publication of two still-timely books that had once been banned by his Abbot General: *Peace in the Post-Christian Era* and *Cold War Letters*. Also now available is a book he wrote and rewrote many times, but never quite finished: *The Inner Experience*. (Yet even now not everything he wrote for publication has appeared in print, including *Art and Worship*.)

Patricia Burton, now preparing a new Merton bibliography, tells me that, since 1948, the average number of Merton editions, re-issues, and new publications per annum worldwide has been fifteen.

A good many of Merton's books are available not only in English but in twenty-nine other languages, including Dutch, French, German, Italian, Japanese, Korean, Polish, Portuguese, Russian, Spanish, and Swedish.

Besides his writings, many of Merton's works of art and photographs have also become much better known. The Thomas Merton Center has created a collection of Merton's photos that has traveled as far from Louisville as Avila, Spain, and Vienna, Austria.

Apart from Merton's own books, which in our house fill more than three shelves, there are many books by other authors that are either about Merton or refer to him in a substantial way. In our case, with a collection far from complete, these currently take up another two shelves.

Many claim Merton's writings had a truly life-changing role in their lives. My mother was one such person. Raised in a devout Methodist home, she became estranged from Christianity as a college student and for many years described herself, somewhat sadly, as an atheist. In her fifties, she borrowed my copy of *The Seven Storey Mountain*. Reading it was all she needed to toss her atheism in the trashcan and return to the local Methodist church, which remained at the center of her life until she died several decades later. (When I told Merton about the impact of *The Seven Storey Mountain* on my mother, he was delighted that his far-from-ecumenically-minded autobiography had restored at least one reader to Protestant Christianity.)

Yet Merton is not without his critics.

In 2005, Bishop Donald Wuerl of Pittsburgh, chairman of a committee responsible for a new American Catholic Catechism aimed especially at young adults, decided that a profile of Merton should be struck from the draft text. The catechism was to include a profile in every chapter of an exemplary American Catholic, each entry giving an idea of the unexpected paths faith can open in one's life. (In the book as published, the section on prayer is the only chapter missing a profile.) One of the reasons given by the bishop for the removal of the Merton profile from the text was that "the generation we were speaking to had no idea who he was." Another factor, he said, was that "we don't know all the details of the searching at the end of his life."

Perhaps Bishop Wuerl is one of those who has the impression that Merton's interest in other religions was evidence of his being disenchanted with Catholicism. "It's obvious," one bitter ex-Catholic told me, "that Merton was beginning to realize that the Catholic Church— indeed Christianity in all its forms—is a dead-end street. If only he had lived a little longer, he would certainly have become a Buddhist and probably remained in Asia." Merton-the-almost-Buddhist remains a popular myth.

There are still others who dismiss him as a pseudo-monk whose books reveal his longing not to disappear into the monastic shadows but rather to stand in the spotlight. "A real monk," one person wrote me, "doesn't want his name on a book. With his lust for fame, Merton should have gone to Hollywood and become a star. I like his autobiography, but everything after that was another step down."

Yet Merton's grateful readers far outnumber those who avoid his books. In my own experience, they range from scholars to bartenders, from nuns to taxicab drivers, from artists to house painters. They include people one might easily imagine would carefully avoid books by a monastic author. In that latter category, it comes as a surprise to many people to discover that one of the main figures of the "Beat Generation," Jack Kerouac, not only read Merton but made contact with him. Kerouac dedicated two poems to Merton; both were published in the small literary journal Merton edited late in his life, *Monks Pond*.

Equally surprising is the discovery that Merton's readers included at least three popes: John XXIII, Paul VI, and John Paul II. Meeting with Pope John Paul in 1980, I gave him a copy of my first biography of Merton (a much thinner book that had just been issued by Paulist Press). After looking through the photos, John Paul told me how important Merton's writings had been to him. He took pride in the fact that his own publisher, a personal friend, was also the publisher of Polish translations of Merton's books.

Thousands of people inspired by his writings have come as pilgrims to the Abbey of Gethsemani, some for just a few hours, many for longer periods. The most dramatic such visit was made by the Dalai Lama in 1994, when he arrived at the monastery by helicopter and then sat in silent meditation at Merton's grave. He has commented, "Whenever someone speaks to me about Jesus Christ, I think of Thomas Merton." Asked on another occasion if he believed in God, a question many Buddhists find problematic, the Dalai Lama replied, "It depends on what you mean by 'God.' If you mean by 'God' what Thomas Merton means, then yes, I do."

Visitors to Louisville who may never have heard of Thomas Merton sometimes become aware of him thanks to a memorial plaque installed in 1998 at the downtown intersection where Merton had his famous "Epiphany at Fourth and Walnut." (Walnut has since been renamed Muhammad Ali Boulevard.) Following a presentation by Paul Pearson, director of the Merton Center, Louisville's Planning and Zoning Committee recently gave unanimous support to a proposal to rename the intersection "Thomas Merton Square." Additionally, Louisville's Metro Council declared 2008 "The Year of the Epiphany" in honor of Merton's experience while waiting for the stoplight to turn green fifty years earlier.

One resident of Louisville, Tom Williams, was inspired by the Merton plaque to propose to the U.S. Park Service the creation of a Martin Luther King Jr. marker in Washington, DC. As a result, visitors to the Lincoln Memorial today find an inscription carved into stone at the exact spot where Dr. King was standing when he gave his "I have a dream" speech. "Recently I learned that Dr. King was planning a retreat with Merton," Williams wrote me while I was writing this afterword. "Sadly, it never took place because of King's assassination."

Many Merton societies are active—about forty in the United States plus national associations in fifteen countries. Most of the national groups organize occasional conferences. For an address list, see www.merton.org/ITMS/chapters.htm.

Linking all the national societies is the International Thomas Merton Society, based at the Merton Center in Louisville. Since its founding in 1987, it has arranged major conferences every two years, while the Merton Society of Canada has organized not only many conferences but a number of Merton pilgrimages to France, Italy, Alaska, Cuba, New York, the Abbey of Gethsemani and Rome.

Scholars from all over the world have made extensive use of the books, journals, letters, photographs, drawings, recordings, and manuscripts in the care of the Thomas Merton Center at Bellarmine University in Louisville. There are also substantial Merton collections at Columbia, Harvard, St. Bonaventure University, Boston College, Boston University, the University of Kentucky, Syracuse University, Georgetown University, and the University at Buffalo.

In addition to *The Merton Seasonal*, published quarterly by the Merton Center and the International Thomas Merton Society, a number of other Merton journals appear from time to time thanks to the efforts of national Merton groups. For many years, there has also been a book-sized *Merton Annual* issued in the United States. As I write, the twentieth volume is ready to go to press.

Among the several films made about his life, no doubt the most widely seen is *Merton: A Film Biography*, by Paul Wilkes, now available on DVD. It manages not only to condense Merton's life into a one-hour film but also includes interviews with some of the people who knew him best.

Compact disk recordings and cassette tapes of many talks he gave at the monastery, either to novices or to anyone in the community who cared to attend, have been produced by Credence Communications. As a consequence, those who knew him only via the printed page are now able to hear Merton's voice and experience his way of teaching. Merton's informality and sense of humor often come as a surprise; readers sometimes imagine him in quite a different way. Nancy, my wife, reminds me that listening to recordings of Merton while ironing has been for her a happy combination.

Several friends have told me that the mere fact that Merton died in 1968 hasn't prevented him from acting as a kind of spiritual guide. As Donald Grayston, currently president of the International Thomas Merton Society, put it in a recent letter, "One dimension of the Merton phenomenon that only became clear to me about ten years ago was his role as spiritual director (staretz, yes!) in absentia. I found myself shaping my own Christian life in response to the dynamics of Merton's—contemplation and struggle, as Brother Roger of Taizé so often said. Rooted in his own Christian faith, engaging the faith of members of other traditions, bringing together the spiritual and the political, mining the centuries of tradition for treasure—it's all there!"

Not long ago, Maurizio Renzini, the founder of the Italian Thomas Merton Society, sent me a letter about Merton's role in his life in recent years: "Five years ago, in my mid-fifties, I had a conversation with a friend who was interested in monastic life. Our discussion made me decide to deeply explore Merton's works and this in turn led me to make contact with Paul Pearson at the Merton Center in Louisville. I also studied carefully several Merton books—*The Sign of Jonas, The Waters of Siloe, Conjectures of a Guilty Bystander,* and *The Silent Life*. These gave me a fascination with silence. I started to look at the world from a new perspective. Merton stimulated me both spiritually and intellectually. His writing gave me an answer to many problems of life and woke up my faith in Christ. It was truly a new world for me because my training is entirely in the world of science—I'm a biologist specializing in clinical analysis and nutritional science."

Jeannette Cantrell, who manages a mail-order bookshop specializing in Merton books, wrote to me from Bardstown, Kentucky: "When I began to sell Merton books in 1980 at the request of the Abbey of Gethsemani, little did I know how many times I would hear visitors say, 'Merton changed my life.' Their stories have all been quite touching. Most of the time it was such an epiphany in their lives that they remember the exact book, how it came into their possession, etc. I remember one man, a recovering alcoholic, who told me, 'My life took a turn for the better thanks to *New Seeds of Contemplation,* page 58!' One gentleman told me he read *The New Man* when his wife was dying. He was so moved by it that he bought a dozen copies to give to other people."

What is it about Merton that still speaks to so many people? How can we account for his enormous popularity, even if measured only in the rough arithmetic of book sales?

Perhaps part of what draws so many of us to Merton is how this astonishingly gifted writer opens a door to a deeper spiritual life without pretending he is far ahead of us on the ladder to heaven. We recognize in him someone whose struggles with various demons (success, fame, sensual pleasures, the quest for greener pastures) are not hugely different from our own. Any reader of his journals and letters will quickly realize that Merton was no stranger to insecurity, nor was he ever tempted to send himself any fan letters. Like us, he was a product of the modern world with all its attractions and distractions. But in the end, by an amazing working of grace, he was able to maintain his search for true wisdom. He attracts us because he is more than a gifted theologian and brilliant writer. He is a brother in Christ who was—and through his writings still is—able to show us the way.

A small collection of Merton sources and web links

The Thomas Merton Center: www.merton.org

The International Thomas Merton Society: www.merton.org/ITMS/

A listing of Merton-related websites: www.merton.org/links.htm

Thomas Merton Books: www.thomasmertonbooks.com

Helpful web sites in searching for out-of-print books:

www.abebooks.com
www.alibris.com

The Merton Institute for Contemplative Living: www.mertoninstitute.org

The Thomas Merton Society of Great Britain and Ireland: www.thomasmertonsociety.org

Notes

1   Thomas Merton, *The Seven Storey Mountain* (New York: Harcourt Brace, 1948), 3. Hereafter referred to as SSM.

2   SSM, 7.

3   SSM, 3.

4   SSM, 5.

5   SSM, 11.

6   Entry of January 2, 1950, Thomas Merton, *The Sign of Jonas* (New York: Harcourt Brace, 1953), 262. Hereafter referred to as SJ. In a journal entry dated November 4, 1961, recording a visit to the monastery by his Aunt Kit, he recalled a visit to Long Island by Kit and his paternal grandmother when he was four. "I remember [Granny] very well. The reason: her affection. Kit and Granny and my mother didn't get along. Mother said Granny was being too indulgent with me and that I ought to be made to obey. I remember Mother as strict, stoical and determined. Granny believed children ought to be brought up on love."

7   SSM, 8.

8   SSM, 9.

9   SSM, 14.

10   Evelyn Scott, letter to Lola Ridge, January 15, 1926. Reprinted in Michael Mott, *The Seven Mountains of Thomas Merton* (Boston: Houghton Mifflin, 1984), 26. Hereafter referred to as Mott.

11   SSM, 18.

12   SSM, 23.

13   SSM, 36.

14   SSM, 36.

15   SSM, 37.

16   SSM, 56.

17   Mott, 37-38.

18   SSM, 51.

19   Mott, 37.

20   SSM, 51-52.

21   SSM, 54.

22   SSM, 54.

23   SSM, 60.

24   SSM, 61.

25   SSM, 62.

26   SSM, 64-65.

27   SSM, 67.

28   SSM, 73-74.

29   SSM, 79.

30   SSM, 80.

31   Thomas Merton, "A Tribute to Gandhi," in *Seeds of Destruction* (New York: Farrar, Straus & Giroux, 1964), 222; idem, *The Nonviolent Alternative,* ed. Gordon C. Zahan (New York: Farrar, Straus, Giroux, 1980), 178.

32   Mott, 60.

33   SSM, 82-83.

34   SSM, 83.

35   SSM, 83.

36   SSM, 85.

37   SSM, 88.

38   SSM, 93.

39   SSM, 103.

40   Thomas Merton, *My Argument with the Gestapo* (New York: Doubleday, 1969), 5. Hereafter referred to as MAG.

41   SSM, 108.

42   SSM, 108.

43   SSM, 109.

44   Letters to June Yungblut, June 22, 1967, and March 29, 1968; in Thomas Merton, *The Hidden Ground of Love: The Letters of Thomas Merton on Religious and Social Concerns*, ed. William H. Shannon (New York: Farrar, Straus, Giroux, 1985), 637, 642-43. Hereafter referred to as HGL. For further attention to this aspect of Merton, see Donna Kristoff, "Light That Is Not Light: A Consideration of Thomas Merton and the Icon," *The Merton Annual*, 2 (New York: AMS Press, 1989): 84-117; and Dom John Eudes Bamberger, "Thomas Merton and the Christian East," in *One Yet Two: Monastic Tradition East and West* (Kalamazoo, MI: Cistercian Publications, 1976), 440-51.

45   SSM, 110.

46   SSM, 111.

47   SSM, 111.

48   SSM, 113.

49   SSM, 175-77.

50   SSM, 122.

51   Thomas Merton, *Faith and Violence*: *Christian Teaching and Christian Practice* (Notre Dame, IN: University of Notre Dame Press, 1968), 228. Hereafter referred to as FAV.

52   SSM, 120.

53   SSM, 122.

54   See Mott, 77.

55   Page 162 of the typesetting draft of *The Seven Storey Mountain*, now part of the Merton Archive at Boston College.

56   SSM, 128.

57   Mott, 78.

58   Mott, 79.

59   Mott, 79.

60   MAG, 138.

61   Thomas Merton, *Collected Poems* (New York: New Directions, 1977), 104.

62   SSM, 124.

63   Letter to Jim Forest, undated.

64   SSM, 121.

65   SSM, 124.

66   Restricted Journal, January 30, 1965; Mott, 77.

67   Merton's will on taking simple vows at the Abbey of Gethsemani, Abbey Archives; also see Mott, 90.

68   SSM, 124-25.

69   There was some very occasional correspondence. It wasn't until 1945, four years after coming to Gethsemani, that Merton wrote the Bennetts to let them know he was now a monk. In 1957, Iris Bennett, now a widow, wrote Merton to say, in part, how distressed she and her husband had been by the passages in *The Seven Storey Mountain* (published in England as *Eternal Silence*) concerning the Bennett household. Friends had urged her, she said, to take legal action. Extracts from Iris Bennett's letter are included in *The Road to Joy: The Letters of Thomas Merton to New and Old Friends*, ed. Robert E. Daggy (San Diego: Harcourt Brace Jovanovich, 1993), 76-77. Hereafter referred to as TRTJ.

70   Journal entry January 30, 1965; Thomas Merton, *Dancing in the Water of Life: The Journals of Thomas Merton, 1963-1965*, ed. Robert E. Daggy (San Francisco: HarperCollins, 1997), 198. Hereafter referred to as DIN-TWL. Also included in Thomas Merton, *A Vow of Conversation: Journals, 1964-1965*, ed. Naomi Burton Stone (New York: Farrar, Straus, Giroux, 1988), 140. Hereafter referred to as AVOC.

71   SSM, 123.

72   SSM, 126.

73   SSM, 127.

74   SSM, 128.

75   MAG, 149.

76   SSM, 133.

77   SSM, 134.

78   SSM, 133.

79   SSM, 137.

80   SSM, 139.

81   SSM, 147.

82   SSM, 147-48.

83   SSM, 148.

84   SSM, 145-46.

85   SSM, 149.

86   SSM, 149.

87   SSM, 153.

88   SSM, 153.

89   Almost every issue contained Merton cartoons. On his "Declaration of Intention" from 1938, Merton put his occupation as "cartoonist and writer." In this "subscribed and sworn" statement, Merton also said he had "no children."

90   For a study of the Lax-Merton friendship, see *Merton & Friends: A Joint Biography of Thomas Merton, Robert Lax, and Edward Rice,* by James Harford (New York: Continuum, 2006). Also see *When Prophecy Still Had a Voice: The Letters of Thomas Merton and Robert Lax*, ed. by Arthur Biddle (Lexington: University of Kentucky Press, 2001).

91   SSM, 181.

92   Bob Lax, "A Poet's Journey," *Columbia Forum* 12:4 (Winter 1969): 12-13.

93   *The Jester* (September 1936).

94   SSM, 159.

95   SSM, 171.

96   SSM, 174.

97   SJ, 362.

98   SSM, 175.

99   May 18, 1941, Saint Bonaventure Journal, in *Run to the Mountain: The Journals of Thomas Merton, 1939-1941,* ed. Patrick Hart (San Francisco: Harper San Francisco, 1995). Hereafter referred to as RTTM.

100 SSM, 185.

101 William Blake, "Poems from the Notebook 1800-1803," in *Complete Writings* (Oxford: Oxford University Press, 1969), 418.

102 SSM, 190.

103 William Blake, preface to "Milton: A Poem in 2 Books," in *Complete Writings*, 480.

104 SSM, 203; William Blake, "Augeries of Innocence," in *Complete Writings*, 431-34.

105 SSM, 189, 191.

106 Mona Wilson, *The Life of William Blake* (London: Peter Davies Limited, 1932), 346.

107 SSM, 196.

108 SSM, 196.

109 SSM, 198.

110 SSM, 201.

111 SSM, 200. Pat Hickman was his girlfriend at the time.

112 Published posthumously in Thomas Merton, *The Literary Essays of Thomas Merton,* ed. Patrick Hart (New York: New Directions, 1981), 387-453.

113 SSM, 204.

114 SSM, 206.

115 SSM, 207.

116 SSM, 210-11.

117 SSM, 205.

118 SSM, 214.

119 SSM, 214.

120 SSM, 215-16.

121 SSM, 216.

122 Mott, 120-21.

123 SSM, 224-25.

124 SSM, 235.

125 SSM, 236.

126 SSM, 237-38.

127 SSM, 241.

128 Journal entry, dated October 6, 1939; RTTM, 41-42.

129 SSM, 248.

130 SSM, 250.

131 SSM, 220.

132 RTTM, 58; entry dated October 16, 1939.

133 SSM, 259.

134 SSM, 264.

135 SSM, 255.

136 SSM, 279.

137 Thomas Merton, *The Secular Journal of Thomas Merton* (New York: Farrar, Straus & Cudahy, 1958), 75-78. Hereafter referred to as SJTM. This is an expurgated text. The unexpurgated text was later published in the first volume of Merton's collected journals, RTTM.

138 SSM, 284-85.

139 SSM, 292-93.

140 SSM, 296.

141 SSM, 298.

142 SSM, 301.

143 SSM, 305-6.

144 SSM, 306.

145 SSM, 301. There is a specific reference in a journal entry dated January 30, 1965; see DINTWL, 198. Also see Mott, 162.

146 RTTM, 246; entry dated November 2, 1940.

147 RTTM, 264; entry dated November 28, 1940.

148 SJTM, 110; RTTM, 231; entry dated June 10, 1940.

149 MAG, 21.

150 MAG, 26-28.

151 MAG, 76-77.

152 MAG, 160-61.

153 March 4, 1941: Saint Bonaventure Journal; RTTM.

154 SSM, 311-12.

155 SJTM, 267; RTTM, 454; entry dated November 25, 1941.

156 SJTM, 183; RTTM, 333; entry dated April 7, 1941.

157 SJTM, 203.

158 For details about Catherine Doherty's life, see www.madonnahouse.org.

159 RTTM, 382; entry dated August 4, 1941.

160 SSM, 345.

161 SSM, 345.

162 SSM, 348.

163 RTTM, 464-65; entry dated November 30, 1941.

164 Letter to Mark Van Doren, November 28, 1941; TRTJ, 13.

165 RTTM, 452; entry dated November 24, 1941.

166 SJTM, 269.

167 HGL, 10.

168 This was the journal published first in expurgated form as SJTM and then unexpurgated in RTTM.

169 Letter to Bob Lax, December 6, 1941; TRTJ, 163.

170 Quoted in Edward Rice, *The Man in the Sycamore Tree: The Good Times and Hard Life of Thomas Merton* (New York: Doubleday, 1970), 71.

171 TRTJ, 15.

172 TRTJ, 164-67.

173 SSM, 398.

174 SSM, 404.

175 SJ, 18.

176 SSM, 410.

177 Thomas Merton, *New Selected Poems of Thomas Merton*, ed. Lynn R. Szabo (New York: New Directions, 2005).

178 Letter to James Laughlin, March 1, 1945; see Mott, 226.

179 Chrysogonus Waddell, *The Merton Annual*, 2 (1989): 69.

180 See Mott, 227.

181 Robert Giroux, in *Merton, by Those Who Knew Him Best*, ed. Paul Wilkes (New York: Harper & Row, 1984), 20.

182 SJ, 110.

183 Giroux, in *Merton by Those Who Knew Him Best*, 20.

184 Journal entry, dated July 11, 1948; Thomas Merton, *Entering the Silence: Becoming a Monk and Writer,* ed. Jonathan Montalolo (San Francisco: Harper SanFrancisco, 1995), 217-18.

185 SJ, 165.

186 SJ, 14.

187 SJ, 72.

188 SJ, 59.

189 SJ, 41.

190 SJ, 154.

191 SJ, 89.

192 SJ, 22.

193 SJ, 28.

194 SJ, 60.

195 SJ, 95, 97.

196 Letter to Naomi Burton, dated December 24, 1957.

197 Journal entry, dated September 2, 1962.

198 SJ, 113.

199 SJ, 120.

200 SJ, 157.

201 SJ, 125.

202 Thomas Merton, *The Ascent to Truth* (New York: Harcourt Brace, 1951).

203 Merton *Ascent to Truth*, 179.

204 Merton *Ascent to Truth*, 317.

205 SJ, 151-52.

206 SJ, 170.

207 SJ, 186.

208 TRTJ, 193.

209 TRTJ, 23.

210 SJ, 193.

211 SJ, 207.

212 SJ, 269.

213 SJ, 251-52.

214 SJ, 273.

215 Thomas Merton, "Prologue to Cassian," in *Cassian and the Fathers: Initiation into the Monastic Traditions*, ed. Patrick R. O'Connell (Kalamazoo, MI: Cistercian Publications, 2005), 5.

216 Conversation with Jim Forest.

217 SJ, 328. Nonetheless it is striking the Merton seems never to have considered writing a new autobiography or revising the first. The closest he came to updating his best-selling book was to write an introduction to the Japanese translation in 1963. Asked in 1967 by one of his correspondents what, looking back, he would cut out of *The Seven Storey Mountain*, he responded, "I'd cut a lot of the sermons . . . including the sales pitch for Catholic schools."

218 SJ, 322.

219 SJ, 334.

220 SJ, 337.

221 SJ, 338-39.

222 SJ, 340-41.

223 SJ, 11.

224 Thomas Merton, *The Silent Life* (New York: Farrar, Straus & Cudahy, 1957), 153-54.

225 Journal, October 10, 1952.

226 Journal, October 22, 1952.

227 Thomas Merton, *Bread in the Wilderness* (New York: New Directions, 1954), 53.

228 Thomas Merton, *The Last of the Fathers: Saint Bernard of Clairvaux and the Encyclical Letter, Doctor Mellifluus* (New York: Harcourt Brace, 1954), 43.

229 Thomas Merton, "From Pilgrimage to Crusade," in *Mystics and Zen Masters* (New York: Farrar, Straus & Giroux, 1967), 107.

230 Journal, December 20, 1959.

231 For a more detailed account of the Merton-Zilboorg meeting and its aftermath, see Mott, 290-99.

232 Mott, 298.

233 Mott, 298. Michael Mott notes that "[Robert] Giroux sensed there was a good deal of the rival writer in Zilboorg's attitude. There may also have been another kind of rivalry: both men were Catholic culture heroes in the eyes of others, if not in their own. . . . . There is plenty of evidence that Gregory Zilboorg was in no state of objectivity when he went to St. John's."

234 Thomas Merton, *Conjectures of a Guilty Bystander* (New York: Doubleday, 1966), 12. For the original journal entry, see Thomas Merton, *A Search for Solitude: Pursuing the Monk's True Life,* ed. Lawrence S. Cunningham (San Francisco: HarperSanFrancisco, 1996), entry for April 28, 1957, 87. Hereafter referred to as ASFS. Also see Mott, 306.

235 Boris Pasternak and Thomas Merton, *Six Letters,* intro. Lydia Pasternak Slater (Lexington, KY: King Library Press, 1973). The Merton side of the correspondence is included in Thomas Merton, *The Courage for Truth: Letters to Writers*, ed. Christine M Cochen (New York: Farrar, Straus, Giroux, 1993), 87-93. Also see "The Pasternak Affair," in Thomas Merton, *Disputed Questions* (New York: Farrar, Straus & Cudahy, 1960); and *Literary Essays.*

236 Pasternak and Merton, *Six Letters,* October 23, 1958; Merton, *The Courage for Truth*, 89-90.

237 Merton, *Conjectures of a Guilty Bystander*, 140-42. For the complete original, see ASFS, 181-82.

238 ASFS, 183.

239 The comment was made in conversation with Jim Forest. See also William H. Shannon, *Thomas Merton's Dark Path: The Inner Experience of a Comtemplative* (New York: Penguin, 1982).

240 HGL, 136-37, letter, dated July 9, 1959.

241 Thomas Merton, *No Man Is an Island* (New York: Harcourt Brace, 1955), 138.

242 Journal, December 17, 1959.

243 Mott, 340-41.

244   Thomas Merton, *The New Man* (New York: Farrar, Straus & Cudahy, 1961), 91.

245   Journal, May 8, 1960.

246   HGL, 483-84; letter to Pope John, dated November 10, 1958.

247   HGL, 484-85.

248   Thomas Merton, *The Wisdom of the Desert: Sayings from the Desert Fathers of the Fourth Century* (New York: New Directions, 1970).

249   Letter from Merton to John XXIII, dated April 11, 1960; HGL, 485-86.

250   See Mott, 350, quoting journal entry, April 24, 1960.

251   Journal entry, October 3, 1960.

252   Mott, 616 n.1, misquoting Merton; original text in Latin.

253   Thomas Merton, *Turning Toward the World: The Pivotal Years*, ed. Victor A. Kramer (San Francisco: Harper Collins, 1996), 79-80.

254   Undated letter to Sister Madeleva, included in Merton, *Seeds of Destruction*, 274-75. For Julian of Norwich's writing, see *Showings* (Ramsey, NJ: Paulist Press, 1978).

255   Journal entry, dated April 25, 1957; ASFS, 85-86.

256   Journal, March 4, 1958.

257   Journal, March 19, 1958.

258   Letter to Victor Hammer, dated May 14, 1959.

259   Journal, July 2, 1960.

260   Journal, October 29, 1960.

261   "The Nature Who makes nature" or nature naturing. See Saint Thomas Aquinas, *Summa*, I.2, 85 n. 6. Also see Merton's comment on *natura naturans* in a journal entry dated January 26, 1961.

262   The text of *Hagia Sophia* was published in Thomas Merton, *Emblems of a Season of Fury* (New York: New Directions, 1963), 61-69; later it was included in the revised *Thomas Merton Reader*, ed. Thomas P. McDonnell (Garden City, NJ: Image Books, 1974) and in *Collected Poems*, 363-71.

263   Thomas Merton, *The Behavior of Titans* (New York: New Directions, 1961), 65-71.

264   Originally published in *The Catholic Worker*; included in *Collected Poems*, 345-49.

265   Thomas Merton, *Original Child Bomb* (New York: New Directions, 1962), and included in *Collected Poems*, 293.

266   Thomas Merton, *Emblems of a Season of Fury* , 70-89.

267   Thomas Merton, "Grace's House," in *Collected Poems*, 330.

268   Thomas Merton, "The General Dance," in *The Thomas Merton Reader,* 500-505.

269   Letter to Dorothy Day, July 23, 1961; HGL, 139.

270   Letter to Dorothy Day, August 23, 1961; HGL, 139-40.

271   Thomas Merton, "The Root of War Is Fear," *The Catholic Worker*, October 1961.

272   Journal, October 23, 1961.

273   Letter to Pope John, November 11, 1961; HGL 486.

274   Interview with William Shannon by Jim Forest.

275   Though a man of very different convictions about the political order and a fervent French patriot, Dom Gabriel Sortais had lived a life as remarkable as Merton's. While an architectural student in Paris, he had been active with L'Action Française, a monarchist counter-revolutionary movement, and took part in street battles with left-wing students and also republicans of the center. His political activities had resulted in arrest. While serving as a chaplain in the French Army during World War II, he had been captured and imprisoned by the Germans.

276   Letter to Jim Forest, January 5, 1962; HGL, 261. Portions of this letter as published here were not included in HGL.

277   *Breakthrough to Peace,* introduction by Thomas Merton (New York: New Directions, 1962).

278   Thomas Merton, *Cold War Letters*, ed. Christine M. Bochen and William H. Shannon (Maryknoll, NY: Orbis Books, 2006).

279   Letter to Jim Forest, April 29, 1962; HGL, 266-68.

280   Letter to Jim Forest; HGL, 266-68.

281   Letter to Jim Forest, June 14, 1962; HGL, 268-69.

282   See Mott, 379, and 623 n. 228.

283   Thomas Merton, *Peace in the Post-Christian Era,* ed. Patricia A. Burton (Maryknoll, NY: Orbis Books, 2004).

284   Interview with Bob Grip, television journalist, NBC, Mobile, Alabama.

285   Letter to poet and printer John Beecher, July 9, 1963.

286   For a detailed summary of *Art and Worship*, see Kristoff, "Light That Is Not Light."

287   Letter to Jim Forest, July 7, 1962; HGL, 269.

288   Merton, *Seeds of Destruction*, 7.

289   Pope John XXIII, *Pacem in Terris*, sec. 51.

290   Letter to Jim Forest, April 26, 1963; HGL, 274.

291   Journal, May 10, 1963; Mott, 386.

292   Thomas Merton, "In Acceptance of the Pax Medal, 1963," in *The Nonviolent Alternative*, 257-58.

293   The introduction to the Japanese edition of *The Seven Storey Mountain* is included in *Honorable Reader:*

Reflections on My Work, ed. Robert E. Daggy (New York: Crossroad, 1989), 63-67.

294 Letter to Dorothy Day, June 16, 1962; HGL, 145.

295 Merton, *Seeds of Destruction*, 129.

296 Letter to Jim Forest, January 17, 1963; HGL, 273.

297 Thomas Merton, *Seasons of Celebration* (New York: Farrar, Straus & Giroux, 1965), 18.

298 Letter to Jim Forest, January 29, 1962; HGL, 261-63.

299 Letter to Jim Forest, January 29, 1962; HGL, 262.

300 Letter to Dorothy Day, December 20, 1961; HGL, 140-43.

301 Letter to Jim Forest, February 6, 1962; HGL, 263-64.

302 Letter to Jim Forest, December 8, 1962; HGL, 272.

303 Letter to Jim Forest, January 29, 1962; HGL, 262.

304 Letter to Jim Forest, February 21, 1966; HGL, 294-97.

305 Thomas Merton, *Gandhi on Non-Violence* (New York: New Directions, 1965), 20.

306 Thomas Merton, *Raids on the Unspeakable* (New York: New Directions, 1966), 45-53.

307 For more about Merton's interest in Shakers with a selection of his Shakertown photos, see Thomas Merton, *Seeking Paradise: The Spirit of the Shakers*, ed. Paul Pearson (Maryknoll, NY: Orbis Books, 2003). Also see *Geography of Holiness: The Photography of Thomas Merton*, ed. Prasad Patnik (New York: Pilgrim Press, 1980), and *A Hidden Wholeness: The Visual World of Thomas Merton* (Boston: Houghton Mifflin, 1970).

308 Merton, *Seeking Paradise*, 44.

309 AVOC, 32-33.

310 AVOC, 101.

311 Merton, *Raids on the Unspeakable*, 9-23.

312 A paper by Merton on the retreat theme is included in *The Nonviolent Alternative*, 259-60. Also see Mott, 406-7. In October 2007, Jägerstätter was declared Blessed by the Catholic Church. Many anticipate his full canonization.

313 DINTWL, 180.

314 AVOC, 140.

315 AVOC, 144-45.

316 AVOC, 193-94.

317 Letter to Jim Forest; HGL, 285.

318 Thomas Merton, cassette tape, *Life and Solitude*, side B, "Hermit's Legacy: Life without Care" (Electronic Paperbacks).

319 Letter to Bob Lax, October 16, 1965; published in Bob Lax and Thomas Merton, *A Catch of Anti-Letters* (Mission, KS: Sheed, Andrews & McMeel, 1978), 61.

320 Letter to Jim Forest, November 11, 1965; HGL, 285-86.

321 Letter to Jim Forest, November 19, 1965; HGL, 287-88. For a more detailed account of this event in Merton's life see Jim Forest, "Thomas Merton's Struggle with Peacemaking," in *Thomas Merton: Prophet in the Belly of a Paradox,* ed. Gerald Twomey (New York: Paulist Press, 1978), 15-54; and Mott, 427-30.

322 Letter to John Heidbrink, Church Work Secretary of the Fellowship of Reconciliation, December 4, 1965; HGL, 424-26.

323 FAV, 27.

324 Letter to Marco Pallis, December 5, 1965; HGL, 473-74.

325 Journal entry, dated March 23, 1966; Thomas Merton, *Learning to Love: Exploring Solitude and Freedom*, ed. Christine M. Bochen (San Francisco: HarperSanFrancisco, 1997), 23.

326 Letter to Abdul Aziz, January 2, 1966; HGL, 62-64.

327 Letter to John Harris dated June 22, 1959; HGL, 392.

328 Merton, *Learning to Love,* 22-23; journal entry, dated March 2, 1966.

329 To preserve her privacy, I refer to her only as Margie.

330 For a detailed account of this period of Merton's life, see Mott, 435-54 and 461-62, and John Howard Griffin, *Follow the Ecstasy: Thomas Merton, the Hermitage Years, 1965-1968* (Fort Worth, TX: Latitudes Press, 1983), 77-131. Unless otherwise noted, all the quotations used in this chapter are from these two sources.

331 SJ, 201; journal entry, dated June 27, 1949.

332 Journal entry, dated April 10, 1966; Merton, *Learning to Love*, 38.

333 Journal entry, dated April 19, 1966; Merton, *Learning to Love*, 41-42.

334 Journal entry, dated April 22, 1966; Merton, *Learning to Love*, 43.

335 Journal entry, dated April 27, 1966, Merton, *Learning to Love*, 46.

336 Journal entry, dated April 28, 1966, Merton, *Learning to Love*, 48.

337 Thomas Merton, "Louisville Airport," in *Eighteen Poems* (New York: New Directions, 1985).

338 Journal entry, dated May 19, 1966; Merton, *Learning to Love*, 66.

339 Thomas Merton, "Certain Proverbs Arise Out of Dreams," in *Eighteen Poems*.

340 "Never Call a Babysitter in a Thunderstorm," in *Eighteen Poems*.

341   Thomas Merton, "Cherokee Park," in *Eighteen Poems*.

342   Thomas Merton, *Love and Living* ed. Naomi Burton Stone and Patrick Hart (New York: Farrar, Straus & Giroux, 1979), 112-19.

343   Merton, *Love and Living*, 31. "Love and Need" was first published in *Ave Maria* in December 1966. The typescript on file at the Thomas Merton Center, dated September 1966, has extensive handwritten corrections. An earlier draft, "Notes on love and need," was dated April 1966.

344   TRTJ, 97.

345   Journal entry dated January 15, 1966; Merton, *Learning to Love*, 7.

346   Thomas Merton, *At Home in the World: The Letters of Thomas Merton and Rosemary Radford Ruether* (Maryknoll, NY: Orbis Books, 1995), 20.

347   Merton, *At Home in the World*, 23-24.

348   Journal entry, May 1, 1967.

349   Letter to Bob Lax, January 26, 1967; published in *A Catch of Anti-Letters*, 110.

350   The graphs are among the papers held at the Thomas Merton Center in Louisville.

351   Journal entry, dated June 1, 1968. Baker's study, *Thomas Merton: Social Critic*, was published in 1971 by the University of Kentucky Press.

352   Guy Davenport, "The Anthropology of Table Manners," in *The Geography of the Imagination* (San Francisco: North Point Press, 1981), 348.

353   Griffin, *Follow the Ecstasy*, 139-40.

354   These are among pieces collected in *Literary Essays*. Regarding Simone Weil, in reading an account of her life Merton discovered an unexpected personal connection: her doctor in the last phase of her life had been Merton's childhood godfather and guardian, Tom Bennett, who found Weil his most difficult patient. "Funny that she and I have this in common," Merton noted in his journal. "We were both problems to this good man."

355   Thomas Merton, *Ishi Means Man* (Greensboro, NC: Unicorn Press, 1976).

356   Some of Merton's essays on these themes are collected in *Contemplation in a World of Action* (New York: Doubleday, 1971) and *The Monastic Journey* (Mission, KS: Sheed, Andrews & McMeel, 1977).

357   Merton's prefaces for foreign editions of his books are collected in *Honorable Reader*.

358   The four issues of *Monks Pond* were published in book form by the University of Kentucky Press in 1989.

359   Many of Merton's taped lectures are available on cassette tape, one series produced by Electronic Paperbacks, another by Credence Cassettes. Merton's lecture on the Cargo Cults was transcribed and published in edited form in *Love and Living*, 80-94. Transcriptions of the Sufi lectures are included in *Merton & Sufism: The Untold Story, a Complete Compendium,* ed. Rob Baker and Gray Henry (Louisville: Fons Vitae, 1999), 130-62.

360   TRTJ, 308-13.

361   Letter to Jim Forest, June 17, 1967; HGL, 303.

362   December 17, 1967; Griffin, *Follow the Ecstasy*, 175.

363   Mott, 504.

364   Letter to June Yungblut, November 19, 1967; HGL, 638.

365   Merton's letters to Dom Flavian are included in Thomas Merton, *The School of Charity: The Letters of Thomas Merton on Religious Renewal and Spiritual Direction*, ed. Patrick Hart (New York: Farrar, Straus, Giroux, 1990).

366   Letter to D. T. Suzuki, March 12, 1959; *Encounter: Thomas Merton and D. T. Suzuki,* ed. Robert E. Daggy (Lexington, KY: Larkspur Press, 1988), 5-6.

367   For Merton's description of the meeting with Suzuki, see *Encounter*, 84-86.

368   Letter to Jean Leclercq, March 9, 1968; Merton, *School of Charity,* 369-70.

369   Thomas Merton, *Woods, Shore, Desert: A Notebook, May 1968* (Santa Fe: Museum of New Mexico Press, 1982), the journal of Merton's trip to California and New Mexico. Photos from the trip appear in this book as well as in Merton, *A Hidden Wholeness* and *Geography of Holiness*.

370   Journal, May 28, 1968.

371   FAV. More recently there has been another anthology of Merton social essays: *Passion for Peace,* ed. William H. Shannon (New York: Crossroad, 1995).

372   Journal, July 19, 1968; Mott, 529.

373   Journal, July 29, 1968; Mott, 532.

374   The seven talks he gave at the retreat were later transcribed and are included in *Thomas Merton in Alaska: Prelude to the Asian Journal: The Alaskan Conferences, Journals, and Letters* (New York: New Directions, 1989), 69-162.

375   Letter to Dom Flavian Burns, October 9, 1968; Merton, *School of Charity,* 402. For details of Merton's Alaska visit, see *Thomas Merton in Alaska*.

376   Walter H. Capps, ed., *Thomas Merton: Preview of the Asian Journey* (New York: Crossroad, 1989) , includes the transcript of the formal dialogue with Merton at the center.

377   Thomas Merton, *The Asian Journal of Thomas*

Merton, ed. Naomi Burton, Patrick Hart, and James Laughlin (New York: New Directions, 1973), 4-5. Hereafter referred to as AJ.

378   AJ, 13-14.

379   An essay on mindfulness by Bhikkhu Khantipalo is included in AJ, 297-304.

380   Thomas Merton, *Zen and the Birds of Appetite* (New York: New Directions, 1968).

381   AJ, 307-8; also see 315-17.

382   AJ, 316.

383   AJ, 68-69.

384   AJ, 100-102.

385   AJ, 107.

386   AJ, 112-13.

387   AJ, 117.

388   AJ, 178-79.

389   AJ, 106.

390   AJ, 132.

391   AJ, 142-45.

392   AJ, 156-57.

393   From a tape transcribed by Patrick Hart.

394   AJ, 163-66.

395   Letter of John Balfour to Brother Patrick Hart, February 11, 1976; Mott, 555.

396   AJ, 233-35. For details about Polonnaruwa, see this website: www.lakpura.com/articles/polonnaruwa-sri-lanka.html.

397   AJ, 250.

398   Among various accounts of Merton's last days, the most thorough that I know of is by Michael Mott; see Mott, 561-68.

399   Thomas Merton, "Marxism and Monastic Perspectives," in AJ, 326-43.

400   Story included in an e-mail from Father Patrick Reardon, dated September 25, 2007.

401   According to the memory of Brother Patrick Hart, the rain turned to sleet. He recalls the way it was hitting and bouncing off the coffin.

402   The list of personal effects did not include Merton's journals, camera, or the eight relics of saints that he had carried with him throughout his final journey. The PanAm docket for the later return of other personal effects, chiefly books, accounted for four packages weighing 36 kilos.

403   The quotation is from the *Philokalia*, a collection of writings on the spiritual life, especially Prayer of the Heart, widely read in the Orthodox Church. An English translation is published in several volumes by Faber & Faber.

Index

Abdeslam, Sidi (Islamic scholar), 207

Adler, Mortimer, 35

Ahern, Father Barnabas (Merton friend, biblical scholar), 122

Arendt, Hannah, 178

Armstrong, Louis, 96

Art and Scholasticism (Jacques Maritain), 54

Art and Worship, 161, 241

Ascent to Truth, The, xxii, 106, 114, 206

Augustine, 54, 65, 97

Aziz, Abdul (Muslim Sufi scholar), 190

Baez, Joan (singer and peace activist), 197, 207

Baker, James, dissertation on Merton, 207

Balfour, John, 231

Bamberger, Father John Eudes, 116, 127, 239

Barbato, Lorenzo (friend of John XXIII), 141

Basil the Great, 113

Beatles (rock group), 210

Ben, Uncle, 17

Benedict, Saint, 86, 113

Bennett, Dr. Thomas (Merton's godfather and guardian), xx, 20, 21, 24, 36, 37, 38, 221

Berchmans, Mother, 98

Berdyaev, Nikolai (Russian philosopher), 129

Bernard of Clairvaux, Saint, 124

Berrigan, Father Daniel, S.J., 172 (photo), 182, 205, 208, 215, 216
    sentencing of, 218

Berrigan, Philip, 182, 205
    sentencing of, 218

"Biography, The," (Merton poem), 34

Blake, William (poet and mystic), xxi, 23, 52, 53, 84, 96, 214
    and Catholicism, 53

"Blessed Are the Meek" (Merton essay on nonviolence), 188

Bonaventure, Saint, 65

Bourne, Father Paul: and suspension of censorship, 207

Bramachari (Hindu monk and friend of Merton), 53 (photo), 54, 213, 229

Bread in the Wilderness, xxii, 114, 115, 124, 206

Breakthrough to Peace, 156

Brother John Spaniard (imagined name of Thomas Merton), 69

Brynner, Yul, xii

Bulgakov, Sergei (Orthodox theologian), 129, 144, 146

Bullough, Edward (professor at Cambridge), 37

Burns, Dom Flavian (Trappist abbot), xxv, 212, 216, 217, 219, 221, 222, 228, 239
    as hermit, 211, 212

Burton, Jinny (friend of Merton), 64, 70

Burton, Patricia, 241

Butorovich, Suzanne (correspondent), 210, 222

Cables to the Ace, xxv

Campbell, Will, 208

Camus, Albert, 209

Canterbury Tales, 18

Cantrell, Jeannette, 245

Canzoniere (Dante), 84

Capovilla, Monsignor (secretary to John XXIII), 155

Cardenal, Ernesto (poet), 137, 138, 140, 186

Catholic Worker, The (newspaper), x, 136, 151, 154, 160, 162

"Certain Proverbs Arise Out of Dreams" (Merton poem), 197

Chagall, Marc, 96

Chakravarty, Amiya, 224

Chamberlain, Neville, 57

"Chant to Be Used around a Site with Furnaces" (Merton poem), x, 148

Chaplin, Charlie, xi, 44, 96

Chatral Rimpoche, 229, 230

Chaucer, Geoffrey, 18

Chobgye Thicchen Rimpoche, 228

Chogyam Trungpa Rimpoche, 224, 236

Chuang Tzu (Chinese philosopher), 214, 215

Clément, Oliver (Orthodox theologian), 129

Cold War Letters (Merton letters), xxiv, 156, 241

Collected Poems (Merton), 94

Columbia Review, The (Columbia publication), 46

Communist Manifesto, 24

Confessions (Augustine), 54, 97

Conjectures of a Guilty Bystander, xxv, 128, 133, 207, 231, 244

Conrad of Palestine, Saint (Cistercian saint), 125

Coomaraswamy, A. K., 213

Cooper, Jackie (actor), 45

Dalai Lama, xxv, 219, 220, 225, 226, 227, 228
   at Abbey of Gethsemani, 243
   meetings with Merton, 226, 227 (photo), 228

Dante, 37, 84

Davenport, Guy, 208

Day, Dorothy, 135 (photo), 136 (photo), 137, 150, 151, 167, 169, 170
   correspondence with Merton, ix-x

Delmas, Monsieur (teacher of Merton), 15

"Devout Meditation in Memory of Adolf Eichmann, A" (Merton essay), 178

Diadochus of Photike, 113

Dickens, Ray (friend of Merton at Cambridge), 32

Disputed Questions (Merton essays), xxiii, 139, 206

Divine Comedy (Dante), 37, 84

Doctor Zhivago (Pasternak), 129-30

Duncan, David (photographer), xi

Dunne, Dom Frederic (Trappist abbot), 1, 85, 92, 94 (photo), 95, 104, 240
   death of, 105

Duns Scotus, 65

Dylan, Bob, 210

Edmund, Father (Franciscan), 66, 70

Eichmann, Adolf, x, 178

Elected Silence, 97. See also *Seven Storey Mountain*

Ellington, Duke, 96

Emblems of a Season of Fury, xxiv, 148, 207

Ends and Means (Aldous Huxley), 51

Evdokimov, Paul (Orthodox theologian), 129

Exile Ends in Glory (Merton biography of Mother Berchmans), 98, 99, 206

Ezekiel (prophet), 149

Fadiman, Clifton, 96

Faith and Violence, xxv, 188, 218

Family of Man, The (photo collection), 135

Faulkner, William, 209

Faye, Alice (actress), 45

Ferlinghetti, Lawrence, 217

Ferry, W. H. ("Ping"), 219, 222, 223

Figures for an Apocalypse (Merton poems), 98, 99

Firmian, Saint (Cistercian saint), 125

Flanagan, Father Raymond (Trappist author), xii, 92, 239, 240

Flood, Brother Maurice, 211, 221

Ford, Father (pastor at Corpus Christ church), 59

Fox, Dom James (Trappist abbot), xi, xii, xxii, xxiii, xxiv, xxv, 94, 97, 107, 108 (photo), 111, 115, 117, 122, 123, 126, 127, 137, 138 (photo), 142, 143, 156, 177, 180, 190, 207, 209, 214, 224, 239
   as hermit, 211
   meeting with Merton and Zilboorg, 127
   and monastery commercial life, 121
   reaction to Merton's relationship with Margie, 199, 200, 201

Francis of Assisi, 66, 74, 76, 96, 136

Francis, Father, xi

Frater Maria Ludovicus (Brother Mary Louis, monastic name of Thomas Merton), xxii, 85

Freedgood, Helen, 53

Freedgood, Sy, 53, 59, 69, 110, 208, 209

Freud, Sigmund, 35

Frisbee, Marco J. (pseudonym of Thomas Merton), 162

Fry, Roger (art critic), 13

Galan, Saint (Cistercian saint), 125

Gandhi on Non-Violence, xxiv, 177, 178

Gandhi, Mahatma, x, 21 (photo), 51, 96, 110, 128, 136, 169, 177, 178, 213
   and John XXIII, 178

"General Dance, The," (Merton article), 150

Geography of Lograire (Merton poem), 221

Gerdy, Bob, 59

Gibney, Bob (Merton friend), 69, 70

Gillet, Dom Ignace (Trappist Abbot General), xxiv, 164, 177
   relaxation of restrictions on Merton, 177

Gilson, Etienne, 49, 50, 55, 65

Giroux, Robert (editor and friend of Merton), 46, 95, 98, 110
Goss-Mayr, Hildegard and Jean, 163
"Grace's House" (Merton poem), 149, 150
Grayston, Donald, 244
Greene, Graham, 96
Gregory of Nyssa, 113
Griffin, John Howard, 208
Grip, Bob, 160
Grunne, Father François de, 237, 240

Haas, Dom Odo (abbot of Waekwan), 238
Hagia Sophia (Merton prose poem), 147, 148
Hammer, Carolyn, 214
Hammer, Victor (painter), 146, 148, 214
Harris, John, 130
Hart, Brother Patrick (Merton secretary), 220 (photo), 221
Haughton, Rosemary, 208
Herscher, Father Irenaeus (librarian at St. Bonaventure), 79
Heschel, Abraham, 215
Hidden Ground of Love, The (Merton letters), 135
Hitler, Adolf, 38, 44, 57, 64, 75, 78, 148
Holloway, James, 208
Hopkins, Gerard Manley (English poet), 58, 66, 59 (portrait), 97
Horrigan, Monsignor Alfred, 202
Hueck, Catherine de (Doherty), 79, 80 (photo)
Huxley, Aldous, 51

Imitation of Christ, The, 54, 84
Inner Experience, The, 241
Intimate Merton, The, 241
Ishi, 209

Jäggerstätter, Franz, 182
Jenkins, Martha (Merton's maternal grandmother), xix, xx, xxi, 6, 10, 11, 26, 30
death of, 48
Jenkins, Ruth (Merton's mother), xix, 6, 7, 8, 9 (photo)
association with Quakers, 7
death of, 8, 10
Jenkins, Sam (Merton's maternal grandfather), xix, xx, xxi, 6, 10, 11, 18, 19, 20, 26, 30, 37, 48 (photo)
death of, 48
at Grosset & Dunlap, 11
Jester, The (Columbia publication), 46
Merton as art editor of, xxi
John Cassian, 113

John of the Cross, Father (Merton friend and confessor), 177
John of the Cross, Saint, 144
spirituality of, 106
John of the Ladder, 113
John Paul II, 243
John XXIII, xxiii, 3, 141 (photo), 155, 243
interest in Thomas Merton's retreats with Protestants, 142
and Mahatma Gandhi, 178
and Vatican Council II, 162
Jonas (prophet), 120
Jubilee (magazine), xiv
Julian of Norwich, 144
Jung, Carl, 35

Kafka, Franz, 94, 95
Karlu Rimpoche, 230
Kaye, Bob (*Catholic Worker* staff member), xi, xii
Kazi, Sonam, 226
Kelly, Father Timothy, 239
Kennedy, John F. (U.S. president), xiv, 154, 176
Kennedy, Robert F., assassination of, 218
Kerouac, Jack, 242, 243
Khantipalo, Phra (Buddhist monk), 223, 224
King, Martin Luther, Jr., 128, 210, 216, 218, 243
assassination of, 218
Kit, Aunt, 3 (photo), 153 (photo)

Labré, Saint Benedict Joseph, 103
"Labyrinth, The" (autobiographical novel of Thomas Merton), 33, 67
LaPorte, Roger, self-immolation of, 186, 187, 188
Larraona, Cardinal, 137
Last of the Fathers, The (Merton biography of Bernard of Clairvaux), 124, 206
Laughlin, James (publisher), 94, 95, 110, 195, 241
and Merton's poems for Margie, 202
Lawrence, D. H., 20, 28, 96
Lax, Robert (Bob) (poet and friend of Merton), xiv, 35, 46, 47 (photo), 51, 54, 59, 62 (photo), 70, 84, 89, 110, 185, 206, 208, 241
influence on Thomas Merton, 62
at *Jester*, 46, 47
with Rice and Mertin at Olean, 63, 64, 69
Leahy, G. F. (biographer of Hopkins), 58
Leclercq, Jean, 217, 241
Lentfoehr, Sister Therese, 109
"Letter to Pablo Antonia Cuadra concerning Giants, A," 149
"Letters to a White Liberal," 161

Life and Holiness, 206
Living Bread, The, xxiii
Loftus, Father John, 202
Lossky, Vladimir (Orthodox theologian), 129
Louis, Father (Thomas Merton name in Trappist community), xii
Louis, King, 85
"Love and Need" (Merton essay), 203
Lowell, Robert, 215
Lutagarde, Saint, 98

Man in the Divided Sea, A (collection of Merton poems), 94
Margie: relationship with Thomas Merton, 193-203
Maritain, Jacques (Catholic philosopher), 54, 55, 65, 207
Marsh, Reginald (artist), 31
Mary Louis, Brother. *See* Frater Maria Ludovicus
Marx Brothers, 44, 162
Marx, Harpo, 44, 96
"Marxism and Monastic Perspectives" (Merton paper at Bangkok conference), 235, 236, 237
McNair, Carol Denise, 176
Meatyard, Ralph Eugene (photographer), 208
Merton, John Paul (Merton's brother), xix, xx, xxii, 8, 10, 11 (photo), 12, 13, 20, 26, 44, 48, 69, 90 (photo)
    baptism of, 89
    death of, 90, 91
    in Royal Canadian Air Force, 89
Merton, Owen (Merton's father), xix, xx, 6, 10, 16 (photo)
    as artist, 6, 13, 17, 22
    illness and death of, 18, 20, 21, 22
    religious faith of, 16, 22
Merton, Thomas
    as abbey forester, 117-19
    as abbot-maker, 212
    on Adolf Eichmann, 178
    and agricultural pollution at monastery, 121, 122
    appeal to Vatican to enter another order, 126
    art editor at *The Jester*, 47
    Asian travels of, 222-37
    attempt to join Camaldolese, 122, 123
    attitudes of friends on monastic life, 70
    autobiography, 33
    awarded medal by Pax, 164
    at Bangkok conference of abbots and abbesses, 234, 235
    baptism of, 59
    birth, 5, 6
    as book reviewer, 67
    and Buddhism, 51, 223-33

    at Calcutta Spiritual Summit Conference, 224, 225
    "calligraphs" of, 179
    at Cambridge, 32-37
    and capitalism, 41
    and Catherine de Hueck, 80, 81, 83, 84
    and Catholic Peace Fellowship, 187, 188
    and censorship, 49, 50, 103, 104, 122, 156, 157, 161
    childhood of, 4 (photo), 7 (photo), 8, 10, 11, 12
    and Christ of Byzantine icons, 26, 27, 28, 29, 30
    at Columbia University, 41-47
    and commercialism at monastery, 121, 122
    communication with John XXIII, 141, 142, 155
    as Communist, 24, 40, 41, 42, 43, 44
    as conscientious objector, 76, 77
    conversion to Catholicism, 56-60
    correspondence with Boris Pasternak, 130, 131, 132
    correspondence with Dorothy Day, ix, x
    correspondence with Rosemary Radford Ruether on monastic life, 205
    critics of, 242
    on the Crusades, 124, 125
    and D. T. Suzuki, 213, 214, 215
    and the Dalai Lama, 226, 227 (photo), 228
    on Daniel Berrigan, 173
    death of, 237, 238
    on detachment, 173, 174, 175
    disposal of possessions, 84
    and Dr. Gregory Zilboorg, 127
    as editor of *The Oakhamian*, 24
    education in England, 18, 22, 23, 26
    in England, 17-24
    entrance into Abbey of Gethsemani, 1, 2, 3, 78, 79, 84, 85
    epiphany of, 133, 134, 146
    exclusion from Franciscan monastery, 70, 71
    and feminine dimension of creation, 180, 181
    on Franz Jäggerstätter, 182
    as fraternity brother, 45
    and Friendship House, 80, 81, 84
    in Harlem, 80, 81
    health of, 25, 26, 104, 114, 176, 186, 193, 207
    as hermit, xiv, 125, 126, 184-92, 201
    hermitage of, 142, 143
    in Hitler Germany, 25
    as hostage for peace, 216
    on identity and mission of the church, 158
    influence of Aldous Huxley, 51
    influence of Etienne Gilson, 50
    interest in Asian religions, 213-21
    interest in biblical sapiential books, 144
    interest in early Christian sources, 114

interest in Orthodox theologians, 129, 142
interest in psychoanalysis, 126, 127
interest in Russian literature, 128, 129, 130
and jazz, 64
and Jesus Prayer, 191, 192
and John of the Cross, 106
as Jonas, 120
and journalism at Columbia, 46
and just war, 167
with Lax and Rice at Olean, 63, 64, 69
as letter writer, 210
life as Trappist, 85-90, 100, 102, 105
and Mahatma Gandhi, 21, 177, 178
Margie, relationship with, 193-203
and Mark Van Doren, 42
and Mary (mother of Jesus), 106
as master of novices, 126
as master of scholastics, 117
    as member of Franciscan Third Order, 73
method of meditation, 191
on monastic life as protest, 165, 166
and Mount Olivet Retreat Center, 142, 143
move to U.S., 6
mystical experience of, 68, 69
on nonviolence, 171, 188, 189
ordination as Father Louis, 101 (photo), 107, 108, 109
    (photo), 110
as pacifist, 70
parents, radical convictions of, 7
paternity of, 36
perpetual vows of, 103, 104
photography of, 178, 179, 209
poem on death of brother, 91
political writings of, 148-54, 155, 156, 157, 158, 161
with Privat family, 14
and progressive Catholics, 204-6
and Proverb, 131, 144, 146, 147, 181, 183, 193
on the Psalms, 124
psychoanalysis with Dr. James Wygal, 139
on purity, 202, 203
and quest for solitude, 100, 102, 104, 122, 123, 125,
    126, 140
on racism, 161
reflections on relations with women, 183
relation with Dom James Fox, 111, 112
religious awakening of, 26, 28, 29
religious life of, 61, 62, 63, 65, 66, 67, 68, 69
and respect for conscience in the church, 138
return to France, 13, 14, 15
role in peace movement, 169, 170, 171, 172, 173, 181,
    182, 187

in Rome, 26, 27, 28, 29, 30
search for hermitages in Alaska, 222
self-evaluation as writer, 206, 207
sexual experience of, 35, 36
silencing of, 157, 158, 159, 160, 161
"stigmata" of, 34
Sunday lectures of, 210
and suspension of censorship, 207
and Sylvia, 36
teacher at Columbia, 67
teacher at St. Bonaventure, 72-77
teacher in Trappist monastery, 112, 113, 114
and Thich Nhat Hanh, 215, 216
transformation of idea of monastic vocation, 133, 134,
    135
and Trappist censors, 103, 104, 122, 156, 157, 161
and travel, 209, 222-37
as traveling hermit, 213, 214, 217, 218, 219, 220
and U.S. citizenship, 116, 117
on war, 151, 152, 153, 154
and William Blake, 52, 53, 54, 61
on World War II in Europe, 73, 74, 75, 76
as writer, xiii, 15, 17, 61, 62, 63, 64, 67, 92, 94-99, 106,
    107, 110, 209
Merton: A Film Biography, 244
Merton Annual, 244
Merton Seasonal, The, 244
Meyendorff, John (Orthodox theologian), 129
Michelangelo, 29
Midsummer Diary, A, 200
Miller, Arthur, 215
Milosz, Czeslaw, 241
Monk, Benedict (pseudonym of Thomas Merton), 162
Monks Pond (Merton's literary journal), xxv, 210, 221,
    243
Montini, Cardinal (Pope Paul VI), 126
Mott, Michael, 34, 212
Mussolini, Benito, 38
Muste, A. J., 182
My Argument with the Gestapo, 34, 39, 74, 75, 76
Mystics and Zen Masters, xxv, 206

"Nature and Art in William Blake" (Merton thesis), 54
New Man, The, 139, 206, 209, 245
New Seeds of Contemplation, xxiii, 151, 206, 245
New Selected Poems of Thomas Merton, 94
Nhat Hanh, Thich (Vietnamese Buddhist monk and Zen
    master), xxv, 215, 216
1937 Yearbook (Columbia University), Merton editor of,
    xxi
No Man Is an Island, xxii, 124, 137, 206

Nogues, Dom Dominique (Trappist Abbot General), 104

Nonviolent Alternative, The, 188

O'Callaghan, Frank, 204, 210, 220, 221
O'Callaghan, Tommie, 204, 221
Okamura, Miss, 214
Original Child Bomb (Merton poetry), 148, 149
Other Side of the Mountain, The: The Journals of Thomas Merton, 1967-68, xii

Pacem in Terris (Peace on Earth), 3, 155, 163, 164
Pallis, Marco, 189, 190
Palmer, Samuel (painter), 53
Parker, Charlie (jazz musician), 97
Parra, Nicanor (Chilean poet), 195
Pasternak, Boris, 129, 130, 139, 156
    correspondence with Merton, xxiii, 146
Paul VI, xiv, 184, 186, 220, 221, 243
Peace in the Post-Christian Era, xxiv, 157, 160, 161, 163, 241
Pearce, Maud Grierson (Merton's aunt), xx, 17, 18
    death of, 35
Pearson, Paul, 243, 244
Percy, Walker, 208
Philippe, Cardinal Paul, 186
Philotheus, Father (Franciscan friar), 83
Picasso, Pablo, xi, 96
Pickford, Mary (actress), 96
Privat family, 14

Raids on the Unspeakable, xxv, 207
Rancé, Abbé Armand-Jean de (founder of Cistercians), 1
Reardon, Father Patrick, 239, 240
Reinhardt, Ad (artist, friend of Merton), xiv, 70
Reinhardt, Joan, 70
Renzini, Maurizio, 244
Rice, Ed (editor/friend/godfather of Merton), xiv, 46, 59, 110
    with Lax and Merton at Olean, 63, 64, 69
Riley, Dr. Lester (pastor of Zion Church), 31, 50
Rise and Fall of the Third Reich, The (Shirer), 148
Roger of Taizé, Brother, 244
"Root of War Is Fear, The" (Merton article), xxiii, 151, 155
Ruether, Rosemary Radford, 241
    on monastic life, 205
Run to the Mountains: The Journals of Thomas Merton, 1938-1941, 32
Ryan Archbishop Joseph, 219

Say, Father Celestine, 238
Schmemann, Alexander (Orthodox theologian), 129
Scott, Cyril Kay, 10
Scott, Evelyn (novelist), xix, 10, 13
Seasons of Celebration, xxiv, 169, 206
Seeds of Contemplation (Merton meditations), xxii, 98, 99, 151, 207
Seeds of Destruction, xxiv, 177, 207
Seitz, Ron (Louisville poet), 208, 221
Seven Storey Mountain, The, ix, xi, xxii, 15, 33, 37, 41, 46, 68, 113, 116, 121, 154, 161, 164 (Japanese edition), 200, 207, 239, 242
Shannon, Monsignor William (editor of Merton letters), 135, 155
Shirer, William, 148
Sign of Jonas, The, xxii, 120, 122, 124, 207, 239, 244
"Signed Confession of Crimes against the State, A," (Merton essay), 148
Silent Life, The, xxiii, 122, 207, 244
Sortais, Dom Gabriel (Trappist Abbot General), xxiv, 122, 156, 160, 163, 164
    death of, 164
Spaeth, Eloise (art critic and historian), 161
Spectator, The (Columbia publication), 46
Spirit of Medieval Christianity, The (Etienne Gilson), 49
Spiritual Direction and Meditation, 206
Stalin, Joseph, 127
Stark, Phil, 221
Stier, Victor, 231
Stone, Naomi Burton (friend and literary agent of Merton), 33, 34, 67, 95, 104, 128, 208
Story of a Soul, The (Thérèse of Lisieux), 79
Strange Islands, 206
Styron, William, 209
Suzuki, D. T. (Zen Buddhist scholar), xxiv, 213, 214 (photo), 215
Swanson, Gloria (actress), 11
Swift, Frank (pseudonym of Thomas Merton), 43
Swift, Jonathan, 43
Sylvia: and Thomas Merton, 36, 183

Talbott, Harold, 225, 226, 229
Tardini, Cardinal (Vatican Secretary of State), 142
Tears of the Blind Lions (Merton poems), 98, 207
Thera, Nyanaponika, 231
Thérèse of Lisieux, Saint, 79 (photo), 83
Thirty Poems (collection of Merton poems), 94, 207
Thomas Aquinas, 65, 96
Thoughts in Solitude, xxiii, 207
Truman, Harry, 110

Ulysses (James Joyce), 33

Valeri, Cardinal, 137
Van Doren, Mark (professor at Columbia and Merton friend), 42 (photo), 61, 83, 84, 88, 109
Vita Nuova (Dante), 84
Vow of Conversation, A, 209

Waddell, Father Chrysogonus, 239
Walsh, Daniel (professor at Columbia), 64, 65 (photo), 66, 70, 110
   ordination of, 210
Washington Catholic Standard: critique of Merton, 156
Waters of Siloe, The (Merton history of Trappists), 98, 99, 112, 207, 244
Waugh, Evelyn, 96, 97, 107
Way of Chuang Tzu, The, xxiv, 207, 214
Weakland, Dom Rembert (Benedictine Abbot Primate), 238
Weil, Simone, 209
Weist, Mother Edeltrud (prioress of Taegu Convent, Korea), 238

What Are These Wounds? (Merton biography of Saint Lutagarde), 98, 206
Wilkes, Paul, 244
Willett, Thompson and Virginia: friendship with Merton, 204
Williams, Jonathan, 208
Williams, Tom, 243
Winser, Andrew (friend of Merton at Cambridge), 32
Winser, Anne, 183
Wisdom of the Desert, The, xxiii, 141, 142, 207
"With the World in My Blood Stream" (Merton poem for Maggie), 195
Wu, John, 214
Wuerl, Bishop Donald, as Merton critic, 242
Wygal, Dr. James (psychologist), 127, 139, 198

Yungblut, June, 210

Zen and the Birds of Appetite, xxv, 210, 224
Zilboorg, Dr. Gregory, 127, 128, 139